BTEC First

Hospitality

Frances Ovenden • Sue Holmes

Sarah Horne • Paul Wilson

www.heinemann.co.uk

✓ Free online support
✓ Useful weblinks
✓ 24 hour online ordering

01865 888118

Heinemann

Heinemann is an imprint of Pearson Education Limited, a company incorporated in England and Wales, having its registered office at Edinburgh Gate, Harlow, Essex, CM20 2JE.
Registered company number: 872828

www.heinemann.co.uk

Heinemann is a registered trademark of Pearson Education Limited

Text © Pearson Education Limited 2008

First published 2008

12 11 10 09 08
10 9 8 7 6 5 4 3 2 1

British Library Cataloguing in Publication Data is available from the British Library on request.

ISBN 978 0 435 465 28 5

Typeset by Saxon Graphics Ltd, Derby
Illustrated by Saxon Graphics Ltd, Derby
Cover design by Wooden Ark
Cover photo/illustration © Ariel Skelley/Photographers's Choice/ Getty Images
Printed in the UK by Scotprint Ltd

Every effort has been made to contact copyright holders of material reproduced in this book. Any omissions will be rectified in subsequent printings if notice is given to the publishers.

There are links to relevant web sites in this book. In order to ensure that links are up-to-date, that the links work, and that the sites are not inadvertantly linked to sites that could be considered offensive, we have made the links available on our website at www.heinemann.co.uk/hotlinks. When you access the site, the express code is 5285P.

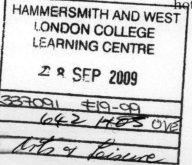

Contents

337091

Acknowledgements

The authors and publisher would like to thank the following organisations for their kind permission to reproduce material:

Sodexo, a food and facilities management services company (p6); The Compass Group (p6); Aramark – www.aramark.co.uk (p6); The Dorchester (p10); Frankie & Benny's (p10); The Food Standards Agency (p162); Thomas Cook (p178); Airtours (p178); Brittany Ferries (p178); totaljobs.com (p188).

The authors and publishers would like to thank the following individuals and organizations for permission to reproduce photographs:

© Courtesy of The Ritz Hotel (p1, p5, p13); © istockphoto/Robert Weber (p15 upper); © istockphoto/heiko etzrodt (p15 lower); © Courtesy of The Dorchester (p16); © Jupiter Images/Thinkstock (p32, p175); © Corbis/Eric K. K. Yu (p34, p38); © Alamy/Robert Stainforth (p40); © Courtesy of The Hilton Group (p47, p52, p60, p61, p79 upper); © Courtesy of Bellagio Hotel (p79 lower); © fotolia/Irwin Ps (p90); © Rex Features Ltd/SIPA (p104); © Photolibrary/Corbis (p107, p130); © Alamy/ Image Source Black (p122); © Pa Photos/Empics/Paul Faith (p124); © Arnos Design Ltd (p127); © istockphoto/Lars Christensen (p141, p151); © Rex Features Ltd/Geoff Moore (p146); © istockphoto/Myles Dumas (p150 upper left); © istockphoto/Arne Trautmann (p150 upper right); © istockphoto/Shane Kato (lower); © Courtesy of Marks and Spencers (p151); © Pa Photos/ ABACA/Gregorio Binuya (p155); © Pearson Education/Ben Nicholson (p159); © Courtesy of Debenhams (p177 left); © www.arnosdesign.co.uk (p177 right); © Fotolia/Yuri Arcurs (p206 right); © istockphoto/Justin Horrocks (p206 left); © Photolibrary.com (p214 upper); © Getty Images/ photonica (p214 lower); © Pearson Education/Ben Nicholson (p219 upper); © Pearson Education/Ben Nicholson (p219 lower); © www. arnosdesign.co.uk (p221); © Pearson Education/Ben Nicholson (p227 both); © Corbis/Tim Pannell (p228); © Pearson Education/Ben Nicholson (p230, p233, p234 both, p235, p236 upper); © Photolibrary/Foodpix/ Burke/ Triolo Productions (p236 lower); © Pearson Education/Ben Nicholson (p237, p239, p240 all); © Alamy/Oso Media (p241); © Courtesy of The Hilton Group (p242); © Photolibrary/Fresh Food Images (p246, p260); © Courtesy of The Hilton Group (p249); © Corbis/FusionPix (p254 upper); © www. arnosdesign.co.uk (p254 lower); © www. arnosdesign. co.uk (p255); © Corbis/Brigitte Sporrer/zefa (p257 upper); © Punchstock/ Uppercut Images (p257 lower); © Photolibrary/Foodpix (p259); © Alamy/ Gary Roebuck (p259 lower); © Fresh Food Images/Robert Lawson (p262 right); © www. arnosdesign.co.uk (p262 left); © Fresh Food Images/John Carey (p263); © Ian Trower/Alamy (p264); © Fresh Food Images/John Carey (p265 left); © Alamy/Simon Holdcroft (p265 right); © Pearson Education/Ben Nicholson (p266, p267); © Courtesy of The Hilton Group

About this book

Hospitality is an exciting and diverse industry offering opportunities for work in different situations all over the world. It provides food, drink and accommodation to travellers when away from home whether they are working or on holiday. We have all had the opportunity to make use of hospitality when eating out for a celebration, taking a day trip or holiday, or eating in a local café. There are a variety of skills to learn, such as cooking a meal, looking after the customer, planning and running an event, and many more. These skills can be used when working in international hotels, cruise ships and restaurants and can give you great job satisfaction, an interesting life and the chance to travel.

What's in this textbook?

The *BTEC First Certificate and Diploma in Hospitality* is certificated by Edexcel, one of the country's leading awarding bodies for vocational qualifications. This textbook covers all of the core and specialist (optional) units you will need to study to complete your course and achieve your qualification.

In summary
This sums up the main points throughout each unit section.

Talking point
Questions for you to discuss in your group.

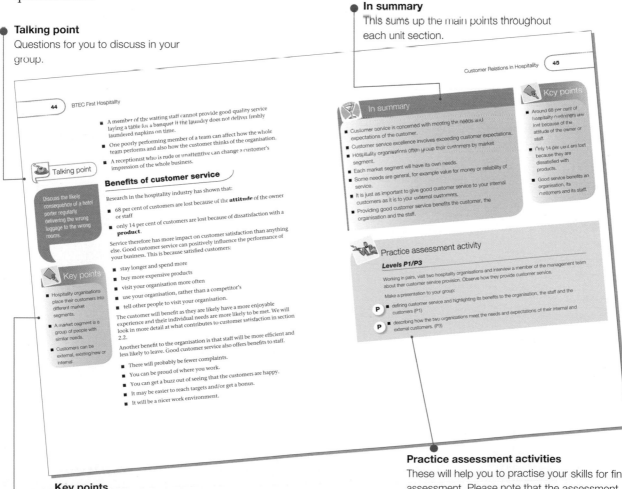

Practice assessment activities
These will help you to practise your skills for final assessment. Please note that the assessment activities are designed to contribute towards practice for the candidates' assessment.

Key points
Summarise the key topics or important points raised.

Assessment

You will be assessed by a series of assignment. You will need to demonstrate your understanding of a number of learning outcomes.

Each unit may be assessed by one or a series of small assignments. These will cover the grading criteria published by Edexcel and will be available for you to check your progress against.

Each unit has a Pass, Merit and Distinction grade. You will need to provide evidence for:

- each of the criteria at Pass grade to obtain a pass
- all of the Pass grade and the Merit grade criteria to obtain a Merit grade
- all of the Pass, Merit and Distinction grades to obtain a distinction.

Reading this book and completing any exercises will give you some ideas of how to explore the industry and find out as much about it as you can. There has been a lot of publicity recently in the media over our food and diet. Professional chefs also give advice about how to cook through TV programmes and magazines, turning cooking into an art form. As a customer there is a lot you can do to research the industry yourself, such as getting hold of hotel brochures and menus. When you visit an establishment look around as a discriminating customer and observe different aspects of the business. All of this will help you to understand the hospitality industry and enable you to get good grades on your course.

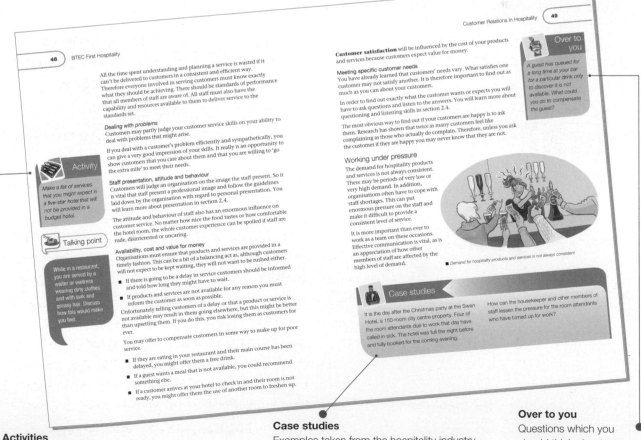

Activities
Guide you towards further research.

Case studies
Examples taken from the hospitality industry to help you understand the theories.

Over to you
Questions which you should think about or discuss.

1 Exploring the Hospitality Industry

Introduction

Most people have experienced the hospitality industry, whether by staying in a five-star hotel or in a bed and breakfast, by enjoying a meal in a Michelin-star restaurant or enjoying a meal in McDonald's; we will all have had our own experiences of the hospitality industry. The hospitality industry is vast, on both a national and international scale.

- In the UK alone there are 182,343 hospitality and leisure establishments. One third of these are pubs, bars and clubs; another third are restaurants.
- The industry employs 2 million people.
- The restaurant industry is the largest in terms of jobs, employing over half a million people.
- The industry employs a young workforce – just over a third of the staff are under 25.

This unit will develop your knowledge and understanding of this extremely exciting and fast-moving industry. It first considers the hospitality industry on a national and local level. It looks at the commercial and catering services sectors along with the different types of businesses in these categories. It then examines the industries which support the hospitality businesses and the products and services offered in different hospitality settings. The unit ends with an exploration of the different types of jobs found within the hospitality industry, along with the expected requirements of each job.

How you will be assessed

Unit 1 is assessed internally so the Centre delivering the qualification will assess you against the criteria. On completion of this unit you should:

1.1 know the hospitality industry and its settings

1.2 know the products and services offered in different hospitality settings

1.3 understand support given by other industries to hospitality businesses

1.4 know about staffing in the hospitality industry, the jobs and their requirements.

Assessment grades

The Edexcel Assessment Grid for Unit 1 details the criteria to be met. In general, to gain a Pass (P) you are asked to identify, describe and define; to gain a Merit (M) you are also asked to explain, review and compare; to gain a Distinction (D) you are also asked to analyse.

1.1 Know the hospitality industry and its settings

This section covers:

- the hospitality industry
- types of settings.

The hospitality industry

From the introduction to this unit you can see just how big the hospitality industry is. The industry can be looked at on a national and local level.

National

There are many companies which have chains of hospitality outlets around the UK. A few well-known examples are given below:

Burger King
Pizza Hut
Yates's
Starbucks
Nando's
Travel Inn.

One of the advantages of visiting a chain outlet is that you know what you will be getting. All the outlets look the same, with the same style of furnishing, menus and pricing.

Local

There are also many hospitality businesses that are unique to a particular town or local area. These are independent businesses. They are owned by individuals or partners and are not part of a national chain.

Although the experience for the customer is less predictable than with a national chain, local hospitality outlets can offer a wide variety of specialised and interesting menus, accommodation and prices.

Types of settings

There are 14 different types of businesses which make up the hospitality sector, operating at both national and local level. These are listed below:

1 Hotels
2 Restaurants
3 Pubs
4 Nightclubs

Talking point

In pairs add to this list other hospitality businesses that can be found all over Britain. Once completed combine all the lists to produce one list.

From this exercise you will have put together a long list of businesses that can be found up and down the country.

Over to you

Make a list of all the independent businesses in your local area. You will probably find that your list is quite long.

5 Contract food service provision
6 Membership clubs
7 Travel services
8 Tourist information services
9 Events
10 Gambling
11 Visitor attractions
12 Hostels
13 Holiday centres
14 Self-catering accommodation.

Another way of grouping these industries is to divide them into the **commercial sector** and the **catering services sector**.

Commercial sector

The commercial sector includes any businesses where the sale of food and drink or accommodation is the main source of income. Businesses such as hotels, restaurants, pubs, clubs and fast-food outlets fall into this category. The ones you will learn about are hotels, restaurants, pubs and clubs.

Hotels
The hotel industry is large.

- There are over 22,000 hotels in Great Britain.

- The hotel industry employs nearly a quarter of a million people.

Hotels can be grouped under the following categories:

- budget hotels, for example Travel Inn, Holiday Inn Express

- bed and breakfast (B&B) accommodation

- one-star to five-star hotels.

What they all have in common is that they offer rooms for sale in exchange for payment. All hotels offer bedrooms and bathrooms. Larger hotels often also offer more public spaces such as large foyers for business meetings, private meeting rooms, conference rooms and function rooms.

Pricing
Room prices vary widely. You can expect to pay over £300 per night for a bedroom in a five-star hotel and as little as £30 per night in a bed and breakfast hotel. The Ritz in London charges £5,000 for its Royal Suite for one night!

Hotels are classified (grouped) into differing ratings. One common system is known as the **star rating**. A hotel with a one-star rating will offer basic facilities, whereas a hotel with a five-star rating, such as the Ritz, will offer every facility you could wish for. Often the price you pay for a room will give an indication of the the hotel's star rating.

Budget hotels and **bed and breakfasts** are not categorised in the same way as hotels, but, like hotels, often the price you pay reflects the

Over to you

Take a visit to your local town and make a list of the different businesses that fall within the hotel sector. Note down how many one- to five-star hotels and different categories of hotels you have.

standard of the accommodation and facilities provided.

Depending on where you live you will find that the four- and five-star hotels are more commonly found in the larger towns and cities. Bed and breakfasts are more common in small towns, villages and the country.

Restaurants

The restaurant industry is the largest in terms of the number of people employed and the number of outlets. In 2004 in Great Britain there were approximately:

- 64,560 restaurants generating £19 billion

- 513,740 people employed.

Like the hotel industry, the restaurant industry can be broken down into a number of different types of outlet.

■ *The Royal Suite at the Ritz Hotel, London*

- Fast-food establishments – these include international chains such as McDonald's, Burger King and KFC, but also local fish and chip shops and sandwich bars.

- Cafes and coffee shops – again these include big chains such as Starbucks, Costa Coffee, Café Nero and also small local cafes and teashops.

- Chain restaurants such as Café Uno, Pizza Hut and Nando's.

- Fine dining – these are restaurants offering high-quality food at expensive prices. An example would be Gordon Ramsay's restaurant at Claridge's Hotel in London. In this restaurant you can expect to pay £65 per person for a three-course lunch.

Restaurants can also be classified by their national cuisine, for example Chinese, Indian, Italian and European.

You will not be surprised to learn that McDonald's is the UK's largest restaurant chain, with over 1,000 outlets.

Pubs, bars and clubs

There are over 100,000 pubs, bars and nightclubs in Great Britain, making this a very large part of the hospitality industry.

Pubs and bars

Pubs and bars provide alcoholic and non-alcoholic drinks and some also provide food. Pubs can be broken down into the following types.

- Managed houses – these are owned by a brewery which employs managers and staff who work in the outlet.
- Tenanted or leased pubs – these are owned by a brewery but occupied by a licensee who holds the licence for the pub and serves the brewery's own beer.
- Freehouses – these are owned and managed by the licensee, who is free to serve drinks from his choice of supplier.

Clubs

Clubs are establishments whose main service is to provide music to dance to, and where food and drink can also be consumed. Clubs charge an entrance fee. Some large hotels have clubs within them.

Catering services sector

The catering services sector provides food and drink services within other organisations whose main focus is not hospitality. This sector includes catering in schools, hospitals, prisons and **contract catering**.

Figures show that in 2004 there were over 20,000 catering service operations in the UK, employing just under 180,000 people.

In many schools, colleges, universities, hospitals, prisons, residential and nursing homes and large private companies across Great Britain you will find that the catering will be managed by a contract catering company. Examples of contract catering companies are Aramark, The Compass Group and Sodexo, all of whom manage the catering in many different types of organisation.

Using a college as an example, the main catering provision of the refectory or restaurant will be run and managed by a separate company. This company will be responsible for providing food and drink to people on the premises, in this case students, lecturers and visitors.

Contract catering companies are often invited to tender (bid) for the contract to run the catering services within an organisation such as a school or college. Usually there will be some competition so each contract caterer must try to offer the best quality at the best possible price. The winner of the contract will then run the catering provision for that business for a fixed period of time.

Unlike hotels, restaurants, pubs and clubs, which expect employees to work evenings and weekends, if you work for a contract catering company you are less likely to be required regularly to work weekends or evenings.

Over to you

Find out if your school or college has a contract caterer and, if so, the name of the caterer. How big is the contract company?

■ *Examples of logos for some well-known contract caterers*

In summary

- The hospitality industry can be split into two groups: the commercial sector and the catering services sector.
- The commercial sector includes hotels, restaurants, pubs and clubs.
- Some companies such as Pizza Hut and McDonald's operate at a national level.
- Contract catering companies are found in schools, colleges, hospitals, prisons and many other types of businesses.

Practice assessment activity

Level P1

P Draw up two posters, one that clearly explains the commercial sector of the hospitality industry and the other the catering services sector. For each poster describe the types of setting each sector operates in. (P1)

1.2 Know the products and services offered in different hospitality settings

This section covers:

- products
- drink
- accommodation
- levels and types of services.

Products

In section 1.1 you learned about the different hospitality settings that make up the commercial sector and the catering service sector. In this section we will look at the different products and services provided in these different settings.

The three main products that are offered across hotels, restaurants, pubs, clubs and contract catering are:

- food
- drink
- accommodation.

Food

The type, quality and pricing of the food on offer varies enormously depending on the type of setting and the type of outlet. Some outlets pride themselves on offering a very wide choice of foods, even if their main business is in offering drinks.

Let us look, for example, at Starbucks. The food products they sell fall into the categories shown below:

- biscuits/cookies
- cakes/muffins
- fruit salad
- pastries/scones
- sandwiches – many different types using various types of bread
- Paninis – several different lunch Paninis
- salads
- hot breakfasts – including three different breakfast Paninis.

Other outlets may offer a more limited menu because they have worked out exactly what appeals to their customers. For example, a transport cafe may offer a short menu of all day breakfast food with large portions at reasonable prices.

Fine dining restaurants and others may change their menu frequently to offer food that is in season, or specialities. Prices will be higher because ingredients are more expensive and the dishes can only be made by very highly trained chefs.

Contract catering businesses provide a wide range of foods to different clients. For example a school canteen will require a small number of popular dishes which are rotated regularly. Prices need to be kept quite low. At the other end of the scale, the directors' dining room in a City banking firm will need a varied menu of high-quality food. The prices would be much higher.

Activity

In pairs select a hospitality setting from the list below. Draw up a list of all the different food products sold in that business, together with the price for each item. As a whole group you must ensure every setting on the list is covered.

- *hotels – different categories, for example, bed and breakfast, two-star hotels, four-star hotels and so forth*
- *restaurants*
- *pubs*
- *clubs*
- *contract caterers.*

Having completed the activity, draw up one single list covering all the settings.

Compare the food products on offer in the settings and their prices. What might this tell you about the standard of the setting?

The Dorchester

Main Courses

Pan Fried Line Caught Sea Bass with red wine pearl barley and cockles	£30.00
Red Mullet with chicken liver, cepes and oysters	£26.00
Pan Fried John Dory with smoked foie gras mousse and red cabbage	£26.00
Grilled Dover Sole with bearnaise sauce	£42.00
Stuffed Loin of Lamb with celeriac boulangere, artichokes and walnuts	£27.00
Squab Pigeon with pickled cabbage and sweet garlic butter sauce	£26.00
Fillet of Veal with lobster, Jabugo ham and apple	£34.00
Aubergine Macaroni with stuffed sweet peppers and honey roast aubergine	£19.50
Roasted Hare with autumn vegetables and hare hot-pot	£28.00

Pizza

Pizza. Possibly the best get together food ever. As you can see, we've got all kinds and every one is freshly baked to order. Our mozzarella cheese is made only with milk from British cows and our tomato bases are made with vine-ripened tomatoes. So enjoy sharing your pizza with whoever you're with. Unless you want it all to yourself, which we quite understand.

Bases

Pan™	Unique to Pizza Hut, our classic thick and fluffy pan baked pizza is loved the world over.	Cheesy Bites™	A ring of 28 doughy bites filled with melted cheese. Large only, add £1.75.
The Italian™	A traditional-style pizza that's deliciously thin and crispy.	NEW LARGER Stuffed Crust™	A ring of melted cheese baked into the crust. Large only, add £1.75 .

Pepperoni Stuffed Crust pizza — If you like happy endings, you'll love our new, larger Pepperoni Stuffed Crust pizza. After all, the crust is filled with delicious melted cheese at the end of every slice plus that crust is packed with tasty pepperoni too. Superb! Available in large only. Limited time only. Add £2

If you can't make up your mind don't worry – we can make up a pizza with half of one combination of toppings and half of another. And if you'd like a lighter pizza, simply ask and we'll make it with half the cheese.

Speciality
Large £13.49   Medium £11.49   Individual £6.49

Super Supreme™ A selection of spicy pork*, pepperoni, spicy beef*, red onions, whole black olives*, ham slices*, mushrooms and green peppers.

Mountain Fantastico ⊙ Goats' cheese, cherry tomatoes, whole black olives* and red onions, garnished with fresh rocket.

Barbecue Deluxe Barbecue sauce, smoky bacon, hand torn chicken breast, cherry tomatoes and red onions.

Mediterranean Meats Deluxe Pepperoni, Spanish-inspired chorizo, smoky bacon and ham slices*.

Favourites
Large £12.99   Medium £10.99   Individual £5.99

Supreme™ An appetising combination of pepperoni, spicy beef*, mushrooms, green peppers and red onions.

Chicken Supreme™ Hand torn chicken breast, mushrooms, green peppers and red onions.

Vegetable Supreme™ ⊙ A delectable mixture of sliced mushrooms, green peppers, red onions and tomato chunks.

Meat Feast A flavoursome blend of spicy pork*, ham slices*, pepperoni and spicy beef*.

Pepperoni Feast Double pepperoni and extra British mozzarella cheese.

Vegetarian Hot One ⊙ ✓ Double green chillies, green peppers, red onions and tomato chunks.

Seafood Lovers Juicy prawns with crayfish tails and cherry tomatoes, garnished with fresh rocket and a drizzle of lemon infused oil.

Classic
Large £10.99   Medium £8.99   Individual £4.99

Hot 'n' Spicy ⁄⁄ Spanish-inspired chorizo and hot jalapeño peppers, served with Tabasco® sauce on the side.

Hawaiian Ham slices* and juicy pineapple.

Farmhouse Ham slices* and mushrooms.

Margherita ⊙ Large £8.99   Medium £7.99   Individual £3.99

Create your own

Add 2 toppings to a Margherita	Large £10.99	Medium £8.99	Individual £4.99
Add 5 toppings to a Margherita	Large £12.99	Medium £10.99	Individual £5.99

Toppings On Large £1.00 On Medium 80p On Individual 50p

Veggie Green peppers/ red onions/ tomato chunks/ pineapple/ mushrooms/ sweetcorn/ whole black olives*.

Meat Pepperoni/ ham slices*/ spicy beef*/ spicy pork*/ hand torn chicken breast.

Fish Tuna/ anchovies.

Cheese Add extra mozzarella.

Premium On Large £1.25 On Medium £1.05 On Individual 75p
Goats' cheese/ cherry tomatoes/ smoky bacon/ Spanish-inspired chorizo/ prawns & crayfish.

Dips ⊙ 35p each or 3 for 99p

Above are two examples of a selection of main courses, along with their prices, taken from The Grill Restaurant in the Dorchester Hotel, London and an extract from the pizza menu at Pizza Hut.

The two menus shown in the picture illustrate how prices differ across the different settings

The Dorchester is a five-star hotel. Here the restaurant is quite formal; guests are expected to dress smartly and behave appropriately. The prices are quite high – around £30 for a main course.

Alternatively customers choosing to dine at a Pizza Hut restaurant would expect a relaxed, informal atmosphere and lower prices – around £9 to £12 for a main course.

For hospitality businesses offering food the opening hours also vary depending on the type of outlet.

- Some pubs now serve food all day from 11 a.m. (sometimes earlier for breakfast) through to 9.30 p.m.

- Most coffee shops and cafes are open during the day, so their opening hours could be from 8 a.m. to 5 p.m.

- Restaurants tend to serve food from around noon to 2.30 p.m. and then re-open from 7 p.m. to 10 p.m.

- Many hotels will serve breakfast from 7 a.m. to 10 a.m., lunch from noon to 2.30 p.m. and dinner from 7 p.m. to 10 p.m. Room service may be available 24 hours a day.

Drink

Hotels, restaurants, pubs, clubs and catering services all provide drinks to their customers. Drinks can be broken down into three main categories:

- soft drinks – such as lemonade, orange juice, cola and other mixers (for example, tonic water)
- alcoholic drinks – beer, lager, wine, spirits, liqueurs
- hot drinks – tea, coffee, hot chocolate.

Soft drinks and alcoholic drinks

Any hospitality business may sell soft drinks and hot drinks, but only businesses that have been granted an alcohol licence can sell alcohol.

In November 2005 the licensing laws made under the Licensing Act 2003 for the UK were changed. These changes modernised the drinking laws and gave licensees more flexible opening hours. Before November 2005 if people wanted to go for a drink in their local pub they had to drink up by 11 p.m. Under the new laws persons selling alcohol, for example in a pub, can now apply to their local authority for an extension to their usual opening hours.

Pricing

Prices for alcohol vary considerably. You are likely to pay more for a drink in a pub, club or restaurant in London than in a smaller town. The drinks and prices listed below are taken from 2007 price lists.

- The average price for a glass of wine in a restaurant in London is £7; in Colchester it is £3.50.
- For a pint of lager in London the average you would pay is £5; in Colchester you would pay £3.

Prices will differ even in the same town; often pubs will charge a little less than restaurants, and clubs will charge more.

In pubs, clubs and restaurants drinks are likely to be served in the bar and restaurant areas. In hotels drinks will be consumed in a number of different areas. For example, guests will drink in public areas such as the restaurant, bar and lounge areas, and they can also drink in their bedrooms.

Hot drinks

There has been a boom in the number of coffee shops appearing in the UK's high streets. Branded shops such as Starbucks, Costa Coffee and independent coffee shops serve a host of different coffees, teas and hot chocolate. When visiting a coffee shop it is often difficult to choose the type of coffee or tea that you want due to the huge choice. Below is an example of some of the different coffees on the Starbucks menu. Some you may recognise, some you may not.

- Espresso
- Caffè Americano
- Caffè Latte
- Cappuccino

- Caffè Mocha
- Caramel Macchiato
- Fresh Brewed Filter Coffee.

If you were to enjoy Afternoon Tea at The Ritz you would be presented with a menu totally dedicated to a wide selection of teas. There are 17 in total, including:

- Ritz Royal English
- Darjeeling First Flush
- Assam Leaf (Tippy Orthodox)
- Ceylon Orange Pekoe

- Russian Caravan
- Earl Grey
- Lapsang Souchong Imperiale.

There may be one or two teas that you recognise but probably the majority you will not.

Accommodation

Hospitality settings offering accommodation include hotels, guesthouses, bed and breakfasts and hostels. We shall concentrate here on hotels. Hotel accommodation can be divided into the bedrooms and the public areas.

Bedrooms

The more luxurious hotels will have a number of features in their bedrooms that you would not expect to see in a bed and breakfast or tourist (budget) hotel. These might include:

- trouser press
- minibar
- satellite TV
- DVD player
- CD player

- alarm clock
- Internet points
- private bathroom and shower (**en suite**).

Generally speaking the more facilities provided the more expensive the room.

Prices
Hotels often have different rates for their rooms; these are described below.

- Rack rate – this is the rate that is displayed in the hotel reception.

Over to you

Next time you visit a restaurant, hotel, cafe or coffee shop note down the range of drinks on offer. You will find that in most places there will be plenty of choice whether they are soft drinks, hot drinks or alcoholic drinks (licence holders only).

- Business rate – this is often a special rate for business users only.
- Internet rate – this is often cheaper than the rack rate but available only to those booking online.

Hotels will also have different prices for different room types. For example, the Internet rates for different types of bedrooms in a Holiday Inn hotel are:

- single £121.50
- double £121.50
- executive queen £148.50.

Rates also depend on how busy the hotel is. If a hotel is half empty it is likely the room rate will be reduced to attract more customers. If it is fully booked the hotel will be able to charge the full rack rate.

Often hotels have a lower rate at the weekend than the week rates. There may be many business people staying on weeknights who can afford higher prices. At the weekend most of the guests will be leisure guests or tourists with less money to spend.

Public areas

Most of the larger three- to five-star hotels will have public areas, where customers can come and enjoy these areas of the business without having to stay in the hotel. Hotels such as The Ritz and The Dorchester have public areas where they serve Afternoon Tea. Afternoon Tea is available to members of the public who wish to visit these beautiful luxurious hotels but do not wish to stay at the hotels. Below is the menu for Afternoon Tea at The Ritz, at £36 per person.

Afternoon Tea sandwiches

Smoked salmon
Egg mayonnaise with cress
Ham
Chicken and mayonnaise
Cucumber with cream cheese
Freshly baked raisin and apple scones with Devonshire clotted cream and organic strawberry preserve
Assortment of Afternoon Tea pastries with English cream
Fruits of the Forest compote with English cream
Ritz selected teas or Ritz blend filter coffee

Key points

Hotel room prices can depend on a number of factors, including:

- how busy the hotel is
- location
- season
- day of week.

■ *The magnificent Palm Court room at The Ritz*

As you can see, to have Afternoon Tea costs a lot of money, but you are paying not only for the food but for the overall experience of The Ritz Hotel. The room where Afternoon Tea is served is pretty spectacular!

Levels and types of services

Wherever you go to eat and or drink you can expect the service to differ. Often the level of service you can expect reflects the price that you pay for products. For instance, if you were going to pay £36 for Afternoon Tea at The Ritz, you would expect exceptional service, firstly due to the price you were paying and secondly because you were sampling the products of The Ritz Hotel. However, if you were going to have a cup of tea in your local cafe you would not be expecting a high level of service and you would not expect to pay a high price.

Levels of service also differ across the different styles of service. You will learn in more detail about styles of food and drink service in *Unit 8: Serving Food and Drink*.

All of these services provide a different experience to the customer. Traditionally **silver service** was and still is most often seen in high-class restaurants. However, fewer restaurants now use this style of service, instead opting for the more familiar **plated** style of service.

The level of service you would expect to find in the catering service sector will also differ. Taking contract catering in a prison for example, the food provided will be of a good quality but the choices offered will be fairly limited. Prisoners will not be given a menu like the ones you would expect in a restaurant. The type of service would be **counter service** as it is in schools and colleges.

There are, however, contract catering services that operate within very wealthy institutions such as banks. In this case the quality of the food would be of a very high standard, with many choices offered. It is also likely that the style of service would be counter for employees, and plated for higher level managers and directors who would dine in a restaurant within the building.

Business services

Four- and five-star hotels will provide a range of business services for their guests. Such services include:

- direct-dial phone
- fax
- secretarial
- computer and Internet access
- telephone messaging
- photocopying
- stationery (paper and pens)
- posting.

These services could be included in the room rate or provided at an additional cost to the guest.

Key points

Catering services can be:

- silver service
- plated
- self-service
- counter service.

Such services are often essential to business people staying in hotels. Many business people stay in hotels for several nights at a time. At times the hotel can become the guest's 'office', so the guest will expect the same business services that would normally be provided by a secretary or other support staff.

Vending

You will probably be familiar with the vending machines dotted around your school or college. In hotels and some workplaces they give access to food and drink 24 hours a day. Vending machines can provide:

- food – sweets, biscuits, crisps, sandwiches and other snacks
- drinks – hot and cold drinks, cans or bottles of cold drinks
- items a hotel guest may have forgotten, for example toothpaste, tights, hairbrush, razor. These types of machines can often be found in budget hotels.

An outside company usually owns the vending machines. A representative will come regularly to the premises to fill up the machines and empty the money.

■ Vending machines may be accessible at all times

Conferences

Another service that is provided, mainly in hotels, is conference facilities. Large hotels tend to have the best conference facilities, although some restaurants may also provide a conference service.

■ A typical hotel conference room

Business and leisure customers use conference rooms. Many larger hotels will have a number of conference rooms. Each room will hold a different number of people and will be used for different purposes.

■ Meetings – some businesses will hire a room at a local hotel or restaurant. Facilities they would expect to be provided with include stationery, overhead projector and screen, Internet access, TV and DVD, refreshments.

■ Company promotions – some businesses will use conference facilities to promote their company. Promotions could include recruitment and careers fairs or the launch of a new product.

■ Seminars – businesses hire rooms to conduct seminars (discussions or training sessions). There may be a need for a large room and several smaller ones.

Conferences are a service that can provide a lot of income and profit to a hospitality business. A hotel with good conference facilities is likely to attract additional customers.

Functions

Functions are another service that different hospitality settings can provide. Private function rooms are offered to guests who wish to have a celebration, such as a wedding. Hotels and restaurants around Great Britain have function rooms which vary in size from large rooms that can hold many people to smaller settings. The Dorchester Hotel, for example, has many function rooms, the largest of which is called The Ballroom.

■ The Ballroom at the Dorchester can hold up to 1,000 people

The facilities that would be provided at a function are:

■ tables and chairs
■ food and drink

■ music
■ decorations.

Over to you

Celebrities will pay hundreds of thousands of pounds for their weddings, wanting everything they can possibly have to make their day perfect. Working in groups, imagine that you are organising a celebrity wedding. Create a list of the products and services that the couple would expect to be offered in a hotel.

In summary

- Hospitality settings offer such services and facilities as food, drink and accommodation to their customers.
- All the services vary considerably in price, depending on the type of establishment and its location.
- Many larger hotels will offer business services to its guests, including fax, photocopying and Internet access.
- Hotels and restaurants provide facilities for events such as meetings, seminars, conferences, weddings and other functions.

Practice assessment activity

Levels P2/M1/D1

Identify and explain all the products and services available in the following three hospitality settings:

- a five-star hotel in London

- a restaurant in a local village

P **M** ■ a contract caterer in a primary school. (P2/M1)

Analyse the difference between the products and services offered in the commercial sector, for example hotels and restaurants, and the products and services offered in the catering services sector, for example the contract catering in a school. Your analysis should explain the difference across the two sectors. (D1)

D

1.3 Understand support given by other industries to hospitality businesses

This section covers:

- other industries
- support given.

Other industries and support given

In order for hospitality businesses to function properly and offer customers the products and services they expect, they need the support of other industries. These industries include:

- banks
- phone companies
- insurance companies
- suppliers
- staffing agencies
- transport companies
- additional services such as hairdressers and souvenir shops.

Banks

Why would a hospitality business need the support of a bank? Banks provide various financial services to the hospitality industry much as they do for individuals. Banks will open business accounts for hospitality businesses where:

- the business can pay money in, for example the **takings**
- and take money out to pay staff wages and suppliers.

You may have seen security vans such as Securicor pulling up outside businesses. They are collecting money from the business to pay into the bank. Small businesses will have a nominated (named) person to take cash and cheques to the bank. Usually this would be a manager.

Hospitality businesses often want to expand by opening new sites, or enlarging existing ones. In this case a business can go to a bank and request a loan. The bank is likely to loan the money as long as it believes that the money will be paid back in an agreed time.

If you are thinking of starting up a business banks can give good advice about business plans.

Phone companies

How could a hospitality business operate without phones or other communication services? The answer is it could not. Communication systems for hotels include:

■ Telephones in rooms which can be used to dial within the hotel and outside the hotel.

■ Internal telephones to different departments.

■ Reservations systems where customers can phone to make bookings.

■ Internet facilities where guests wish to dial up and use the Internet.

■ Business services such as fax, which requires a telephone line.

■ Customer services where customers will ring up and ask questions about the business, for example location and opening times.

To not have communication systems would be disastrous for almost all businesses. Phone companies which can provide such services include BT, TalkTalk and Virgin Media. All these companies are in competition with one another, so all try to offer the best package to businesses.

One of the more modern services particularly expected of the four- and five star hotels is Wi-Fi (wireless fidelity) access. Wi-Fi enables guests to connect to the Internet without wires or cables in different locations of the hotel, for example meeting rooms, lounge areas and bedrooms.

Insurance companies

In *Unit 3: Safety in Hospitality* you will learn about the various security threats that can occur in the hospitality industry. Due to this and in order to protect employees' personal possessions, hospitality businesses have to take out certain types of insurance.

One example of insurance that a business will purchase is building and contents insurance. This means that if there is any damage to the property, for example broken windows, the insurance company will pay to have the damage fixed. On a more serious level, if there is damage caused by fire or flood, most insurers will also cover the damage.

Contents insurance insures all the contents of the business premises. If there was a burglary and any contents were stolen, the insurance company would pay to replace the stolen items.

Suppliers

Suppliers are companies that supply hospitality businesses with the products they need in order to provide a good level of service.

Key points

Businesses need their suppliers to be reliable and to provide them with a good service. It is therefore worthwhile to all parties to build good working relationships.

Activity

Working in groups, choose one of the following departments of a hospitality business and make a list of all the different supplies that the departments would need in order to function. Make sure all departments are covered.

- *contract caterer in a school or college*
- *restaurant*
- *kitchen*
- *housekeeping*
- *bar*
- *bed and breakfast hotel.*

The departments cannot function without these supplies. Some supplies are delivered daily, for example fresh produce in a kitchen; some weekly such as drinks for the bar and linen for housekeeping. Other supplies may be delivered on a monthly basis, for example wine. When goods are delivered there has to be someone available to check them in.

Staffing agencies

There will be times when hospitality businesses have a shortage of staff. This may be because:

- they have a large function and need more staff or more skilled staff
- employees are off sick
- staff vacancies have not yet been filled.

For all these situations there is a back-up that can be used. This support comes from staffing or recruitment agencies. These agencies have skilled people that they can call upon at short notice who are willing to work in different businesses. Staff from the agencies are then 'loaned out' to the hospitality business for an agreed time and cost. Getting staff in this way has advantages and disadvantages.

Advantages

- Businesses can get staff as and when they need them.
- Staff are trained in specific skills.

Disadvantages

- It can be quite costly, as the business will have to pay both the agency fees and the staff salaries.
- Staff may not know how the business is run in terms of working practices.

Key points

- Many hospitality businesses have to use staffing agencies, but only when it is absolutely essential.
- Staffing agencies have both advantages and disadvantages.

- It may be difficult to build a good team as not all the staff will know each other.

Transport

Hospitality businesses need the support of local transport companies. For example, guests going out for the evening may ask for taxis to be ordered as a means of getting back to the hotel. Many businesses have a nominated taxi company that they will use to provide this service.

Many visitors also like to have details on local transport companies, which they can then use throughout their stay. The Ritz Hotel has a chauffeur-driven car service and The Dorchester Hotel has its own fleet of cars, which are used to transport guests around London.

Hotels in particular should also hold information on train times. This is a source of information guests may need particularly if they are visiting different parts of the country.

Airport information should also be accessible so that guests can easily check departure and arrival times and confirm flight bookings.

Additional services

Some hospitality businesses also offer other products and services. These include:

- hairdressers
- beauty treatment
- souvenir shops
- ticket agencies
- other retail outlets.

In most luxury hotels guests will expect these additional services as standard. Employees of the hotel may provide these services, but it is also likely that the hotel will turn to other industries to provide these services. For example, the five-star Ritz Hotel offers the following services:

- 24-hour currency exchange
- doctor on call and medical services
- babysitting
- hairdressers
- massage and beauty treatments
- gym/fitness room
- personal trainer
- fine jewellery retail store.

The Ritz also has a service where tickets can be booked for London shows and tourist attractions.

In summary

- The hospitality industry relies on many other industries in order to function and provide products and services to guests.
- These other industries include banks, phone companies, suppliers and transport providers.
- Additional services such as hairdressers, retail shops and ticket agencies are expected of luxury hotels.
- Support given to hospitality businesses includes financial services, communication systems, delivery of goods, hairdressing and ticket booking.

Practice assessment activity

Levels P3/M2/D2

P Prepare a short presentation to your tutor describing three examples of support other industries provide for the hospitality industry. (P3)

Working in groups, select and discuss two different hospitality industries. After discussion in your group review how these industries are supported by other industries. Choose from the following list:

    hotel

    contract caterer

    pub

M   restaurant. (M2)

D Using the two examples above analyse how the support received could be improved. Present your analysis in a short report. (D2)

1.4 Know about staffing in the hospitality industry, the jobs and their requirements

This section covers:

■ staffing

■ jobs

■ job requirements.

Staffing and jobs

There are many different types of jobs in the hospitality industry. All the different jobs require staff. Smaller businesses will naturally have fewer staff. For example a country pub serving food and drink may have eight staff; a busy McDonald's may have 20 staff. The five-star Bellagio Hotel in Las Vegas has over 9000 staff. Contract caterers could have three or 30 staff depending on the size of the unit they are operating.

The types of staffing and jobs which are found in the hospitality industry are as follows.

Manager

Managers are the people in charge of running and managing the outlet or business or a major part of the business.

In many hospitality businesses there will be a general manager who has overall responsibility for the business. Below them may be a number of different department managers. Examples of these are restaurant manager, housekeeping or accommodation services manager, head chef and **front of house** manager.

Some of the responsibilities at manager level are to:

■ prepare staff **schedules** (rotas)

■ carry out staff training

■ help set budgets and monitor spending

■ ensure wages are paid

■ ensure all **procedures** are followed

■ make sure all the relevant **legislation** is followed

■ ensure the supervisors are doing their jobs

■ ensure all goods are ordered

■ set and monitor **standards**.

Supervisor

The level below a manager is known as a **supervisor**. Supervisors report to their department managers, who will tell the supervisors what work needs to be done. Supervisors are found in hotels, restaurants and contract catering.

Some of the responsibilities of a supervisor are to:

- ensure staff are dressed appropriately
- ensure customer needs are being met
- process customers' bills
- receive orders/deliveries
- ensure that work procedures are being followed
- supervise **craft** and **operative** staff
- deal with customer complaints
- pass on orders from managers.

Craft staff

Staff working at craft level are likely to have specific practical skills and may have trained for a number of years. For example, chefs are craft staff as they have specialist skills.

Operative staff

Operative (or operational) staff are those whose main responsibility is to carry out the day-to-day tasks needed for the business to run smoothly. It is the operational staff who will have most contact with the guests. Operational staff include:

- bar staff – serving drinks to guests
- waiting staff – serving food to guests
- housekeeping staff – cleaning guests' rooms
- reception staff – welcoming guests.

You can see that an organisation chart of a hotel is quite big. There are lots of different levels to the organisation. Generally the higher up you are in the organisation chart the more you get paid and the more responsibilities you have.

It is important to remember that whatever level you are in an organisation you will be contributing to the running and the success of a business.

- How could a hotel do without the housekeeping staff to clean the guests' rooms?
- How could a hotel do without the kitchen porters who clean the pots and pans?

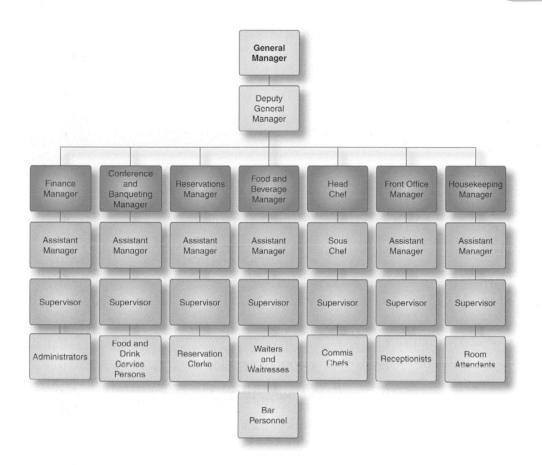

■ *The staff on this organisation chart all have certain responsibilities*

■ How would the restaurant manager cope without waiting and bar staff
  to serve the guests food and drink?

The answer to all these questions is that the hotel could not run without
these crucial operational staff.

Activity

*In groups list all the responsibilities that operative staff such as waiting
staff, room service attendants and reception staff would have in a hotel.
The points on your lists should show that although operation staff are fairly
low on the organisation chart, they still have many jobs and responsibilities
to carry out.*

Working relationships

Relationships among staff in the hospitality industry have to be good in
order for the business to run smoothly. Relationships need to be built
both across the organisation chart and up and down the organisation
chart.

The staff in different departments rely on each other to do their jobs effectively. If the staff across the different departments cannot work well together and support each other the result will be a poorly run business.

Activity

From the two lists below join up the staff that you think support each other the most.

Reception staff	*Chefs*
Restaurant staff	*Room service attendants*
Conferencing and banqueting manager	*Head housekeeper*
Front of house manager	*Head chef*

Working hours

Hotels are open 24 hours a day, seven days a week. Hospitality catering is a seven-day-a-week job and the job roles must be covered. For this reason staff in the hospitality industry tend to work in 9-hour shifts. **Full-time** staff will usually be at work for five days a week.

Typical working hours for various jobs might be:

- restaurant chef – 10 a.m. to 2 p.m. (lunch); 5 p.m. to 10 p.m. (dinner)
- contract catering chef – 6.30 a.m. to 3.30 p.m.
- hotel reception team shift – 6 a.m. to 3 p.m. or 1 p.m. to 10 p.m.
- room attendant – 7 a.m. to 4 p.m. five days a week
- waiting staff – 6 a.m. to 10 a.m. (breakfast); 6 p.m. to 11 p.m. (dinner).

Work routines

Work routines are planned for operative level staff but vary depending on the areas that you work in. Work routines may have a card to show how tasks should be carried out and in what order. Below are two examples of work routines.

Bar staff

Task 1 – stock the bar area with all the necessary drinks.
Task 2 – prepare lemons and oranges to put in drinks.
Task 3 – ensure all glasses are clean and in the correct place.
Task 4 – fill ice buckets.
Task 5 – ensure the **float** is in the till with sufficient change.
Task 6 – open the bar area and serve drinks to guests.
Task 7 – clear away and wash empty glasses.
Task 8 – close the bar, count the takings and store them correctly.
Task 9 – ensure all glasses are cleaned and stored correctly.
Task 10 – replace drinks so that the bar is fully stocked for the next day.

Room attendant

Task 1– ensure the housekeeping trolley is stocked.

Task 2 – check guest's room is empty by knocking on door.

Task 3 – clean the room.

Task 4 – ensure the room has sufficient supplies such as soap, minibar items.

Task 5 – close and lock the room and inform the head housekeeper that the room is ready.

This is just a general insight into the types of task staff in the hospitality industry do. They will differ slightly in different establishments.

Job contracts

In the section above you learned about the different job roles of chefs, waiting staff, bar staff, receptionists and room service attendants. All the staff in these different jobs may have different job **contracts**.

When you begin work your employer will give you a contract, which has to be signed by you and the employer when you start. Typical contracts will include:

- hours of work
- duties expected
- uniform to be worn
- salary or hourly rate
- holiday allowance
- sick pay
- period of notice – this is the time you have to give to the company if you wish to leave. It is common that staff have to give one month's notice before they can leave a company.

There are many different types of contracts that are given to employees in the hospitality industry. These are:

- **Part-time** – this type of contract is drawn up for people who only want to work on a part-time basis, for example three days a week. Part-time contracts will differ depending on the number of days worked.

- **Full-time** – a full-time contract is for people who work five or more days a week.

- **Temporary** – these contracts are issued when a job role will only exist for a fixed period of time. A common example of a temporary contract would be for maternity cover, which means the job is only available while the person in that job has their baby.

- **Seasonal** – the hospitality industry employs a lot of seasonal staff. The best example of seasonal staff is students who work in their Christmas, Easter and summer holidays.

- **Live-in** – this type of contract is common in large hotels that provide accommodation for their staff. There will be rules regarding deductions from pay for the accommodation, how it is to be looked after and other house rules.

- **Permanent** – permanent contracts are those given to job roles which are taken on a permanent basis, that is all the time. These contracts would be the same for most full- and part-time contracts.

- **Freelance** – freelance contracts are for people who are **self-employed**. This means that the person works for themselves. An example of this is when an employer uses a freelance person to carry out staff training. Such a contract will include the rate of pay, how long the work is expected to take, the number of employees to be trained and the location of the training.

- **Agency staff** – In section 1.3 you learned about agencies that provide staff to businesses that need them (see page 20). Agency staff might only work in a restaurant for one or two nights, so their contract is drawn up with the staffing agency and not the employer. The agency would have to sign a contract with the employer agreeing to supply the employer with professionally trained staff. They would state the fee to be paid to the agent and the hourly rate for the agency staff member.

The job and type of contract you choose will undoubtedly have an effect on your lifestyle. As you get older your lifestyle will change: you may get married, have children, buy a house.

Take a look at the case studies below to see how different lifestyles can affect our choice of job and equally how our choice of job can affect our lifestyles:

Case studies

Michael and Jill

1 Michael is 20, single and a full-time student studying management at Leeds University. When he is not at university he lives with his parents in his home town of Lincoln. Michael needs to earn money in the holidays to take back to university. When Michael is home he works in a local restaurant and is happy to work evenings and weekends. In fact Michael is willing to work as many hours as possible. Most of his friends live in Leeds, so if Michael was not working he would be bored just sitting at home.

- In what ways does Michael's holiday job affect his lifestyle?

- Why is such a job the right one for Michael?

- What type of contract would Michael have?

2 Jill is 35 and married with two children, one a newborn. Jill needs to work in order to help support her family. Jill's husband is a nightclub manager. He starts work at 6 p.m. and finishes at 3 a.m. Jill has applied for a part-time job as a housekeeper at the Travel Inn, which is only 15 minutes' walk away. The hours of work are 7 a.m.–3 p.m.

- How would this job give Jill a suitable lifestyle?

- What type of contract would Jill have?

These two different case studies clearly show how one person's lifestyle would not suit another and how different jobs suit different lifestyles. You must decide when you are ready to work what will be the right job for you, which job will give you the lifestyle that you would like to have.

Job requirements

For all the different jobs in the hospitality industry – both in the commercial and catering service sectors – there are certain requirements needed from the staff.

Qualities

Unit 6: Developing Employability Skills for Hospitality and Related Industries covers the type of qualities that are required of staff working in the hospitality and related industries (see pages 175–209). These include:

Punctuality

Whatever time you are expected to be at work you must be on time. If you are late then you will be letting yourself down and those who work with you. Imagine you are the only breakfast chef in a hospital; if you are late who would prepare and cook the patients' breakfasts?

Honesty

In any job staff must always be honest. It is very difficult to work with dishonest people, as you never know if they are telling the truth. Some staff find it hard to be honest if they have made a mistake. Often it seems easier to tell a lie to cover up a mistake, but nine times out of ten you will be found out, so it is always better to be honest.

Personality

You will find that people working in the hospitality industry have similar personalities. The main factor in common is that they like to work with people. You tend not to get shy people working in the industry, as you really need to be outgoing and confident when dealing with the public.

Efficiency

Most of the jobs in the hospitality industry require staff to be able to work quickly and under pressure. A contract caterer may have to serve 500 lunches in two hours. In The Ballroom in the Dorchester Hotel you could be serving drinks to 1,000 people. You have to be efficient; you have to be able to work to deadlines. To do this you need to be organised.

Skills

There are also many skills that staff must have when working in the hospitality industry. Many of these are looked at in Unit 6. Below are some of the skills that apply to all the different hospitality settings in both the commercial and the catering services sectors.

Key points

In order to work well in hospitality you must be:

- punctual
- honest
- confident and outgoing
- efficient.

Initiative

This is the ability to act independently. Basically to have initiative means that you are able to think for yourself, so that when faced with a situation you have not experienced before you can use your initiative to work through the situation without having to ask another member of staff.

An example of when a member of staff uses their initiative is when a chef runs out of a product such as salmon. A hotel chef unable to use their initiative would simply tell the waiting staff that they had run out and offer no alternative. A chef who uses their initiative would try to source some salmon from, for example, a local shop or restaurant. If this was not possible the chef would substitute the salmon with an alternative fish dish.

Staff's ability to use their initiative will grow as more experience is gained. Due to the nature of the hospitality business, where unexpected situations and problems arise on a daily basis, staff will soon become very good at using their initiative.

Taking responsibility

Experienced staff generally train new members of staff. This training is usually quite brief. The new member of staff is then expected to carry out their job role.

If you are starting work in your local pub, on your first day you will be shown how to work the till, the location of the different drinks and glasses, how to pour drinks and how to work the glass-washing machine. This will all be covered in a matter of hours. When the bar opens to the public you will then be expected to start serving drinks.

Taking responsibility starts right here. You are now responsible for serving the right drinks in the right glasses. You are also responsible for taking the customers' money and giving the correct change.

Following instructions

When you first start work you will be given instructions that apply to the department that you work in. Typical instructions a receptionist may be given might be how to:

- take or cancel bookings
- welcome guests
- answer the telephone
- deal with complaints
- deal with departures, including the paying of bills
- contact the correct taxi companies
- direct guests to local attractions.

Every department of a hospitality business will have a list of instructions that new staff have to follow.

It is very important that staff follow instructions. The instructions are for a purpose and if they are not followed someone or the business may be at risk. If a new chef does not cook food properly they may cause food poisoning and make the guests very ill.

Observing health, safety and security requirements

Health, safety and security are discussed in detail in *Unit 3: Safety in Hospitality*. There are many different rules that staff must follow concerning health, safety and security. These rules are there to protect staff and customers. When a new member of staff joins a company they will always be trained in health, safety and security and told the rules and procedures that must be followed.

These are rules that must not be broken. Failure to observe health, safety and security rules could result in a member of staff being asked to leave the job.

Teamwork

In the section under *staffing and jobs* you learned about the importance of good working relationships and teamwork. Most jobs in the different hospitality settings require teamwork:

- one chef cannot cook all the lunches
- one room attendant cannot clean all the rooms
- one waiting staff cannot serve all the guests
- one bar tender cannot serve all the drinks in a busy pub or club.

Teamwork is essential within departments and also across different departments.

- Reception staff need the housekeeping staff to tell them when rooms are ready.
- Housekeeping staff need the reception team to let them know of any early arrivals.
- Waiting staff need the chefs to cook the food.
- Chefs need the waiting staff to serve their food.

Look back at the organisation chart earlier in this unit (see page 25). You have to view the chart as people working in one team. All the people in the team have the same goal, which is to provide the best service to the guests.

Personal presentation

Most jobs in the hospitality industry require staff to wear a uniform. It is important that staff wear uniforms because:

- staff look smart if they are all dressed to the same standard
- guests can identify staff by their uniform
- uniforms can protect staff from harm, for example chefs' long apron and trousers can protect their legs from spillages and burns

■ *Typical uniforms for hotel room attendants*

■ staff who look smart give a good impression of the business.

It is not enough just to wear a clean uniform. Staff must also ensure that:

■ their bodies are clean

■ their hair is tidy

■ they do not show body piercings

■ they do not wear jewellery (except a wedding band)

■ they do not wear nail varnish or too much make-up.

Employers should provide their staff with the correct uniform. Some employers also arrange for the uniforms to be cleaned.

If you went for Afternoon Tea at the Ritz Hotel you would not expect to be served by waiting staff in ripped jeans and messy hair! At the Ritz all staff would be immaculately dressed in the same uniform. In restaurants such as Pizza Hut you will also see staff in the same uniform. Often bar staff will wear the same shirts or T-shirts.

Uniforms can set the standard of a business. A member of staff who does not wear the correct uniform will stand out and will soon be asked to change.

In summary

■ *The main types of staffing in the hospitality industry are managers, supervisors, craft and operative staff.*

■ *An organisation chart shows all the people who work in the organisation. Usually the person above you in the chart is the person you report to.*

■ *The most common types of job roles in the hospitality industry are chefs, waiting staff, bar staff, receptionists and room attendants.*

■ *It is important when looking for a job that you get the right contract and choose a job that suits your lifestyle.*

■ *Different types of contract include full-time and part-time, temporary and live-in.*

■ *Jobs require staff to be honest, punctual and efficient.*

■ *Staff must be able to follow instructions and take responsibility in their different job roles.*

Practice assessment activity

Levels P4/M3

P In pairs, visit one business which falls within the commercial sector and one business which falls within the catering services sector (you may be able to use the contract caterer at your school/college). The purpose of the visit is to speak to two members of staff in each sector to find out about their job roles in terms of the tasks they are required to do. Record your answers and share them with the group when you are next in class. (P4)

M In addition to the above, compare the different jobs in each of the sectors, explaining the differences and similarities. For example, how could a **commis** (junior, trainee) chef's job role in a five-star hotel differ from a commis chef's job role in a school? (M3)

Test your knowledge

1 Explain the difference between the commercial sector and catering services sector.

2 Give examples of two settings in the commercial sector and two settings in the catering services sector.

3 What types of products are sold across both sectors?

4 What different services are offered across both sectors?

5 List three other industries that support the hospitality industry.

6 What services do these three industries provide to the hospitality industry?

7 What types of staff would you have in a hotel?

8 What are some of the job roles these staff might have?

9 List three qualities that people need to have when working in the hospitality industry.

10 Explain why teamwork is important in the hospitality industry.

2 Customer Relations in Hospitality

Introduction

Hospitality is about people, all of whom have customer service needs. If you work in hospitality you will almost certainly be involved in making sure the needs of customers are met. You should have a passion for people and a desire to provide customer service excellence.

This unit aims to develop and broaden your understanding of customer service in hospitality businesses. You will identify different types of internal and external customers and the needs that each may have. You will also explore how hospitality staff deliver service that meets the needs and expectations of the business's customers through the range of products and services that it offers.

You will have the opportunity to develop your own customer service skills so that you can develop your understanding of the importance of delivering consistent and reliable customer service.

You will also look at how hospitality businesses monitor and evaluate their level of customer service by obtaining feedback from customers and how this enables them to make improvements to the services provided.

How you will be assessed

Unit 2 is assessed internally so that the Centre delivering the qualifications will assess you against the criteria. On completion of the unit you should:

2.1 understand customer service and its benefits

2.2 know how consistent and reliable customer service contributes to customer satisfaction

2.3 know how hospitality organisations monitor and evaluate customer service

2.4 be able to demonstrate appropriate customer service skills.

Assessment grades

The Edexcel Assessment Grid for Unit 2 details the criteria to be met. In general, to gain a Pass (P) you are asked to define, describe, identify, demonstrate and review; to gain a Merit (M) you are also asked to compare, analyse and deal independently and confidently with customers; and to gain a Distinction (D) you are also asked to evaluate and make recommendations.

2.1 Understand customer service and its benefits

This section covers:

- customer service
- customer needs
- customers
- benefits of customer service.

Customer service

The Institute of Customer Service defines customer service as:

'The sum total of what an organisation does to meet customer expectations and produce customer satisfaction.'

Good customer service means putting the needs of the customer first. It requires you, as a member of staff, to put yourself in the position of your customers. You should be aware of how you would like to be treated if you were a customer and deal with your customers accordingly.

Aims

Customer service is often at the heart of a successful business. For example, if you went to a local fast food outlet for a burger and you queued for ages only to be served by rude staff, would you go back? It's highly likely the answer to that question is 'no'. You are much more likely to find somewhere else to go.

If they have a choice, customers tend not to return to an organisation where they are not satisfied with the service. Therefore, one of the main aims of customer service is to satisfy the customer so that they will return to an organisation.

As people become more used to eating, drinking and sleeping away from home, customers' expectations are higher. This is especially true in the hospitality industry which is very competitive. Satisfying their needs is not always enough to make customers return to your organisation. Therefore, another aim of customer service is to exceed the customers' expectations and provide 'customer service excellence'. If there is a lot of choice, customers are more likely to choose your organisation over a competitor if they have received excellent service.

Finally, if a high standard of customer service encourages customers to return, it is highly likely that they will spend more money and tell their friends about your organisation. This means that the organisation is far more likely to meet its targets. Therefore, the final aim of customer service is to enable the organisation to meet its targets for growth and also for quality.

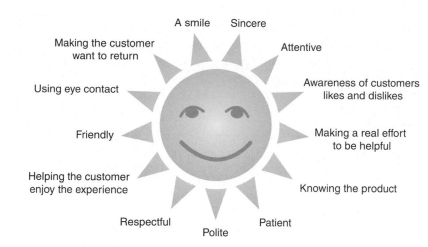

A smile   Sincere

Making the customer want to return

Attentive

Using eye contact

Awareness of customers likes and dislikes

Friendly

Making a real effort to be helpful

Helping the customer enjoy the experience

Knowing the product

Respectful

Polite

Patient

■ *Examples of good customer behaviour*

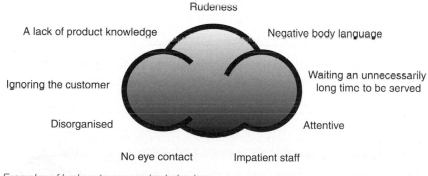

Rudeness

A lack of product knowledge

Negative body language

Ignoring the customer

Waiting an unnecessarily long time to be served

Disorganised

Attentive

No eye contact   Impatient staff

■ *Examples of bad customer service behaviour*

Over to you

Think of a time when the customer service that you received was good. In groups of two or three, share your experiences and make a list of words and phrases that make customer service good.

Now think of a bad customer service experience and list as many words and phrases as you can to describe it.

Customer needs

In this section you will learn about the general needs of customers. You will also learn about particular or special services that some customers may need.

Value for money

Everybody expects value for money, even in the most luxurious settings. This does not mean that customers will expect things to be cheap, but they must feel that the price they are paying for your goods and services are fair. If, for example, some of your bedrooms are more expensive than others, you will need to inform customers of the increase in benefits and services that go with the higher price.

Accuracy and reliability

Customers will expect you to deliver the service that was promised. It should be consistent, accurate and dependable.

■ If a response is promised in a certain time, does it happen?

■ Are menu items correctly described?

■ Are customer accounts free of error?

■ Is the service performed right the first time?

■ Are levels of service the same at all times of day and for all members of staff?

Information, advice and help

Many people working in hospitality spend a lot of time giving customers information and advice. This could include:

■ information and advice on your products and services to help them decide what to buy

■ recommending a suitable wine to go with a customer's meal

■ giving information about the local area

■ advising leisure customers on how they could spend their day.

Because customer service is all about understanding the needs of the customer, sometimes they will expect you to offer advice and help before they have even asked for it. It is wise to observe customers' behaviour. If they look hesitant and unsure ask them how you can help them.

Problems and complaints

Despite all your efforts and care, customers will sometimes encounter problems when visiting your organisation. It is important that any problems are dealt with immediately and that the customer is satisfied with your action.

■ *Customers will want information on your products and services*

Some problems may be beyond your control, for example:

- a customer has lost their wallet or handbag
- a customer has been taken ill
- a customer has had some bad news from home.

Unfortunately the problem is sometimes caused by your organisation. For example the customer:

- had booked a family room at your hotel and has arrived to find they have been allocated a twin
- finds the food they have been served in the restaurant is inedible
- finds a member of staff has been rude to them.

Whatever the problem, the customer needs to be assured that you are taking them seriously. The problem must be dealt with promptly and in a sensitive manner. (See also section 2.4 for dealing with complaints.)

Health, safety and security

When customers are on your premises you have a duty of care towards them.

In *Unit 3: Safety in Hospitality* you will learn in more detail about The Health and Safety at Work Act 1974 (see pages 84–85). This requires all employers and employees to make sure that the premises are healthy, safe and secure for the public and the staff.

Customers

In this section you will learn about the different types of customers dealt with in hospitality organisations, their individual needs and the benefits of providing service excellence.

Customers can be categorised as:

- **external** – those who purchase and use the products and services provided by an organisation. They are obviously very important to the organisation.
- **existing** or new – those who have used your business before or are using it for the first time.
- **internal** – those who work for the same organisation as you.

External customers

Delivering consistently great customer service is difficult because each customer has their own idea of what great customer service is. To ensure that all your customers are happy you must meet their individual needs.

To do this you need to understand what those needs are. For this reason hospitality organisations place their customers into different **market segments.** A market segment is a group of people with similar needs.

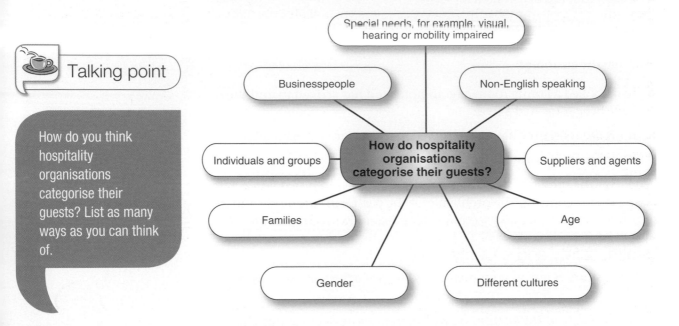

Talking point

How do you think hospitality organisations categorise their guests? List as many ways as you can think of.

Diagram: How do hospitality organisations categorise their guests?
- Special needs, for example, visual, hearing or mobility impaired
- Businesspeople
- Non-English speaking
- Individuals and groups
- Suppliers and agents
- Families
- Age
- Gender
- Different cultures

Individuals and groups

Members of organised groups will often have a tour guide and group leader with them who can help you to look after them. This can be very useful, especially if the organiser knows the group members well.

However, you must remember that each guest will have their own individual needs and expectations and it is your responsibility to make sure that these are identified and met.

■ *Members of a group will still have individual needs*

Business people

Business people will expect service to be speedy and efficient. If they use your hotel regularly they may expect you to recognise them and to anticipate their needs, for example, their favourite room or the newspaper they order. They will probably want home comforts and office facilities to allow them to get their work done. Their needs could include:

- TV/DVD
- phone/fax
- Internet access – increasingly wireless (Wi-Fi).

Non-English speaking customers

Non-English speaking customers will expect you to be able to communicate with them without too much difficulty. This may be tricky if no one in your organisation speaks their language, but there are some things you can do to help you to communicate.

- Use pictures and hand signs.
- Speak slowly and clearly.
- Use the Internet to look up useful phrases.

Making an effort to speak to non-English speaking guests in their own language will create a good impression.

Different ages

The age of your customers may affect their needs and expectations. The older generation may prefer a more formal approach to service, whereas younger customers may find this a bit daunting.

It is wrong to make assumptions based on age. For example, do not assume that older guests are necessarily slow or frail, and do not make the mistake of thinking that teenage customers do not expect to be treated respectfully.

Different cultures

It is important to respect other people's cultures so that you can understand their customer service needs and avoid causing offence. A customer's culture may influence:

- religious practices – days of worship, significance of particular festivals
- social customs – how people are greeted
- dress – the need to cover up
- food and drink – foods that are forbidden, whether alcohol is permitted
- gender – the position of women in society.

Gender

Whether your guests are male or female may influence their needs but, as with age, you must be careful not to make assumptions.

Find out how to say the following phrases in French, Chinese and Spanish:

'Good morning/ afternoon/evening'

'Welcome to our hotel'

'How may I help you?'.

Practise using these phrases with your classmates

■ *It is wrong to make assumptions based on age*

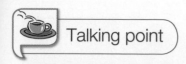

Many hospitality organisations will adapt their products and services to suit the needs of female or male customers. For example, a cafe that attracts males doing a manual job may offer food that is filling and offers good value for money.

Some hotels advertise the fact that they take special care of female guests. They will, for example, make sure that they do not allocate females travelling alone a room on the ground floor which backs onto the car park.

Families

Customers with children will want to feel that you welcome the children to your organisation and that they are not seen as 'a bit of a nuisance'. Facilities such as kids' clubs and play areas will entertain the children and provide a welcome relief for parents.

Although it is the adults who are paying for your products and services, the children may well be the ones that influence the purchase so they are worth looking after. Extra touches that give the impression that you have thought about the needs of the children will impress. These might include:

■ highchairs or booster seats

■ children's menus or smaller portions

■ activity packs

■ books or games.

Special needs

Some customers have special needs beyond those of most customers. This may be because they:

■ have a physical disability such as being unable to walk or having a hearing or sight impairment

■ have special dietary needs or preferences

■ are travelling with a baby or a small child on their own

■ have learning difficulties.

Careful consideration must be given to how to treat customers with special needs so that you look after their needs without causing offence or appearing to patronise them, make them feel inferior or not worth your time. Below are some examples of caring for people with special needs.

■ If a customer has impaired hearing you must speak clearly and slowly. Make sure you do not turn your back on them. They may only be able to understand you by lip reading.

■ People in wheelchairs need to know about access, lifts and disabled facilities and may need help moving around.

■ If a customer has a speech impediment, such as a stammer, it is important to listen carefully to their request. Repeat it back to them to be sure you have understood what they want.

Suppliers and agents

Suppliers and agents are also customers of your organisation and need to be treated accordingly. They will expect to be treated with courtesy and respect. If they are not treated well they may think that you treat all your customers the way you have treated them and advise their friends, family and other clients not to use you.

Existing and new customers (external customers)

Many organisations monitor and keep a record of the number of existing or returning customers they get. These customers are referred to as **repeat business**. They are monitored because they are very good customers to have, bringing a regular supply of business.

Consider the following points.

■ If customers are returning to an organisation, they are usually happy with what is being provided.

■ Once customers are known to an organisation it is easier to meet their needs.

■ The more repeat business an organisation has the less advertising it will have to do to attract new customers.

■ 'Word of mouth' is a very effective means of advertising. If customers use an organisation often their friends and family might use it too.

This does not mean that organisations are not interested in attracting new customers – of course they are important too. When new customers use your organisation it is an opportunity to create a good impression. The aim should always be to convert new customers to regular customers.

It is good practice to keep a database of customers' details. The Data Protection Act 1998 requires all organisations that hold data about individuals on computerised systems to register with the Data Protection Registrar. The Act also gives customers certain rights. These include to:

■ be informed of where the data is being processed

■ a description of the details being held

■ know why the data is being held

■ know who has access to it.

Internal customers

All staff – porters, room attendants, waiting staff, administrators or chefs – have a role to play in providing customer service. They must work as a team and communicate effectively to ensure that the needs of the customer are met. See *Unit 1: Exploring the Hospitality Industry* for more on teamwork, page 31.

The quality of service to customers will only be consistently achieved by quality service being provided internally.

Over to you

Make a list of the kind of information that could be included on a customer database in a four-star country house hotel.

What can the hotel do with the information it has gathered about its customers?

- A member of the waiting staff cannot provide good-quality service laying a table for a banquet if the laundry does not deliver freshly laundered napkins on time.

- One poorly performing member of a team can affect how the whole team performs and also how the customer thinks of the organisation.

- A receptionist who is rude or unattentive can change a customer's impression of the whole business.

Benefits of customer service

Research in the hospitality industry has shown that:

- 68 per cent of customers are lost because of the **attitude** of the owner or staff

- only 14 per cent of customers are lost because of dissatisfaction with a **product**.

Service therefore has more impact on customer satisfaction than anything else. Good customer service can positively influence the performance of your business. This is because satisfied customers:

- stay longer and spend more
- buy more expensive products
- visit your organisation more often
- use your organisation, rather than a competitor's
- tell other people to visit your organisation.

The customer will benefit as they are likely have a more enjoyable experience and their individual needs are more likely to be met. We will look in more detail at what contributes to customer satisfaction in section 2.2.

Another benefit to the organisation is that staff will be more efficient and less likely to leave. Good customer service also offers benefits to staff.

- There will probably be fewer complaints.
- You can be proud of where you work.
- You can get a buzz out of seeing that the customers are happy.
- It may be easier to reach targets and/or get a bonus.
- It will be a nicer work environment.

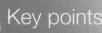

Talking point

Discuss the likely consequence of a hotel porter regularly delivering the wrong luggage to the wrong rooms.

Key points

- Hospitality organisations place their customers into different market segments.

- A market segment is a group of people with similar needs.

- Customers can be external, existing/new or internal.

In summary

- Customer service is concerned with meeting the needs and expectations of the customer.
- Customer service excellence involves exceeding customer expectations.
- Hospitality organisations often group their customers by market segment.
- Each market segment will have its own needs.
- Some needs are general, for example value for money or reliability of service.
- It is just as important to give good customer service to your internal customers as it is to your external customers.
- Providing good customer service benefits the customer, the organisation and the staff.

Key points

- Around 68 per cent of hospitality customers are lost because of the attitude of the owner or staff.
- Only 14 per cent are lost because they are dissatisfied with products.
- Good service benefits an organisation, its customers and its staff.

Practice assessment activity

Levels P1/P3

Working in pairs, visit two hospitality organisations and interview a member of the management team about their customer service provision. Observe how they provide customer service.

Make a presentation to your group:

P ■ defining customer service and highlighting its benefits to the organisation, the staff and the customers (P1)

P ■ describing how the two organisations meet the needs and expectations of their internal and external customers. (P3)

2.2 Know how consistent and reliable customer service contributes to customer satisfaction

This section covers:

■ consistent and reliable customer service

■ customer satisfaction.

Consistent and reliable customer service

To uphold the concept of customer service excellence all staff must understand their individual responsibilities. They should:

■ be aware of the benefits of providing good customer service

■ be motivated enough to want to provide good customer service.

Quality of service and products

A service or product is of good quality when it meets the customers' needs. For example, if your hotel is advertised as 'family friendly' there should be facilities for children.

No matter how large or small, expensive or otherwise, all hospitality organisations need to ensure that the quality of their services and products is consistent and reliable. Customers will measure quality by how well a product or service meets their needs and expectations and whether it provides value for money.

The type of service offered will obviously vary according to how much the customer is paying. In more expensive hospitality organisations customers will expect higher levels of service and much more interaction with staff.

Talking point

In groups discuss how you judge the quality of a restaurant.

However, whatever end of the market your organisation is operating in the service should be courteous, reliable and friendly.

There are many things which influence the quality of hospitality services and products:

■ product and service knowledge

■ staff training and standards

■ staff presentation, attitude and behaviour

■ availability, cost and value for money

■ ability to meet specific needs

- appearance and comfort of the restaurant
- standards of service.

Product and service knowledge

If they are to provide customer service excellence, staff must have a good knowledge of the products, services and service standards of the organisation. Good product and service knowledge will help staff to:

- answer customers' questions
- suggest products which match the customers' needs
- increase sales
- build customers' confidence in the organisation and win their loyalty
- suggest alternative products or services.

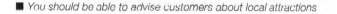

■ *You should be able to advise customers about local attractions*

Customers generally expect staff to know everything about the organisation they work for, but sometimes a customer may ask a question which surprises you. It may be about the work of another part of the organisation, or a new development you do not know about. If this happens you should always try to give some kind of helpful answer to the question, for example by suggesting someone else that they could ask to get the information they need.

Training and standards

Good customer service doesn't just happen. Staff must be provided with training that will develop their customer service skills. The purpose of training is to ensure that all staff:

- understand the vision, goals, plans, standards and practices related to the delivery of excellent service
- understand their roles and the expectations regarding the delivery of excellent service.

All the time spent understanding and planning a service is wasted if it can't be delivered to customers in a consistent and efficient way. Therefore everyone involved in serving customers must know exactly what they should be achieving. There should be standards of performance that all members of staff are aware of. All staff must also have the capability and resources available to them to deliver service to the standards set.

Dealing with problems

Customers may partly judge your customer service skills on your ability to deal with problems that might arise.

If you deal with a customer's problem efficiently and sympathetically, you can give a very good impression of your skills. It really is an opportunity to show customers that you care about them and that you are willing to 'go the extra mile' to meet their needs.

Staff presentation, attitude and behaviour

Customers will judge an organisation on the image the staff present. So it is vital that staff present a professional image and follow the guidelines laid down by the organisation with regard to personal presentation. You will learn more about presentation in section 2.4.

The attitude and behaviour of staff also has an enormous influence on customer service. No matter how nice the food tastes or how comfortable the hotel room, the whole customer experience can be spoiled if staff are rude, disinterested or uncaring.

Availability, cost and value for money

Organisations must ensure that products and services are provided in a timely fashion. This can be a bit of a balancing act as, although customers will not expect to be kept waiting, they will not want to be rushed either.

- If there is going to be a delay in service customers should be informed and told how long they might have to wait.

- If products and services are not available for any reason you must inform the customer as soon as possible.

Unfortunately telling customers of a delay or that a product or service is not available may result in them going elsewhere, but this might be better than upsetting them. If you do this, you risk losing them as customers for ever.

You may offer to compensate customers in some way to make up for poor service.

- If they are eating in your restaurant and their main course has been delayed, you might offer them a free drink.

- If a guest wants a meal that is not available, you could recommend something else.

- If a customer arrives at your hotel to check in and their room is not ready, you might offer them the use of another room to freshen up.

Activity

Make a list of services that you might expect in a five-star hotel that will not be provided in a budget hotel.

Talking point

While in a restaurant, you are served by a waiter or waitress wearing dirty clothes and with lank and greasy hair. Discuss how this would make you feel.

Customer satisfaction will be influenced by the cost of your products and services because customers expect value for money.

Meeting specific customer needs

You have already learned that customers' needs vary. What satisfies one customer may not satisfy another. It is therefore important to find out as much as you can about your customers.

In order to find out exactly what the customer wants or expects you will have to ask questions and listen to the answers. You will learn more about questioning and listening skills in section 2.4.

The most obvious way to find out if your customers are happy is to ask them. Research has shown that twice as many customers feel like complaining as those who actually do complain. Therefore, unless you ask the customer if they are happy you may never know that they are not.

Over to you

A guest has queued for a long time at your bar for a particular drink only to discover it is not available. What could you do to compensate the guest?

Working under pressure

The demand for hospitality products and services is not always consistent. There may be periods of very low or very high demand. In addition, organisations often have to cope with staff shortages. This can put enormous pressure on the staff and make it difficult to provide a consistent level of service.

It is more important than ever to work as a team on these occasions. Effective communication is vital, as is an appreciation of how other members of staff are affected by the high level of demand.

■ *Demand for hospitality products and services is not always consistent*

Customer satisfaction

Customer satisfaction is a measure of how products and services meet or exceed customer expectations. It is the key to success for if your customers are not satisfied they will not be happy. In order to achieve customer satisfaction with all customers it is vital that customer service is consistent and reliable. This section looks at how to achieve consistent and reliable service.

We have seen how organisations can provide consistent and reliable service. If they do this, then their customers are likely to be satisfied. This can be seen in the following ways.

■ **Confidence in service** –A satisfied customer will be confident that every time they visit an organisation they will have an experience which meets or exceeds their expectations and provides good value for money. They are more likely to return to the organisation if they feel this confidence.

Talking point

In your group, discuss how a pub can provide service excellence to its customers.

- **Exceeding expectations** – Organisations exceed customers' expectations when they provide customers with something they appreciate but do not expect. Exceeding your customers' expectations is critical if you are to deliver service excellence.

At one time or another most of us have experienced exceptional customer service. As customers, we remember the organisations that provide this service and how it made us feel.

Repeat custom and word-of-mouth reputation

At the beginning of this chapter you learned that one of the benefits of providing customer service excellence is that it increases customer loyalty. Customers will return and they will also tell their friends and family about your organisation.

The importance of this cannot be underestimated. Research has shown that it costs five times as much to win a new customer as it does to keep an existing one. Word-of-mouth is a powerful tool to encourage new customers to use your business.

Internal customer satisfaction

As you have learned, looking after internal customers is just as important as looking after external customers.

In looking after internal customers you are taking a vital step towards achieving customer satisfaction. Staff who are satisfied in their job are more likely to work well and form effective teams. This will have an impact on the service they provide to external customers.

Unfortunately, there are numerous reasons why staff may not give good service.

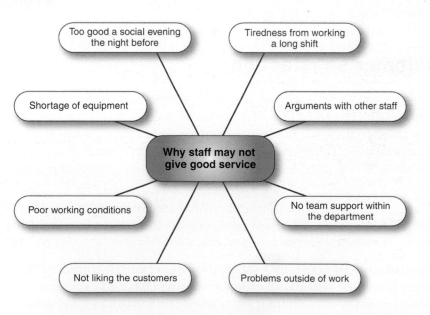

Too good a social evening the night before — Tiredness from working a long shift — Shortage of equipment — Arguments with other staff — **Why staff may not give good service** — Poor working conditions — No team support within the department — Not liking the customers — Problems outside of work

Case studies

It is the day after the Christmas party at the Swan Hotel, a 150-room city centre property. Four of the room attendants due to work that day have called in sick. The hotel was full the night before and is fully booked for the coming evening.

How can the housekeeper, the room attendants and other members of staff work together to provide the best level of customer service despite being understaffed?

In summary

- Customer service must be consistent and reliable if it is to satisfy customer needs.
- Many factors contribute to reliable and consistent customer service, including product knowledge, staff attitude and behaviour and the quality of service offered.
- Because of the nature of demand and the problems caused by staff shortages hospitality staff must learn to work under pressure.
- If customers are consistently satisfied they will develop confidence in your product.
- Exceeding customer satisfaction will encourage customers to return and to tell their friends and family about you.

Practice assessment activity

Levels P2/M1/D1

Using your findings from your visits to the two hospitality organisations (see section 2.1), make a presentation to your group:

P describing how consistent and reliable customer service contributes to customer satisfaction (P2)

M comparing the extent to which the two organisations provide customer service to internal and external customers (M1)

D evaluating the customer service provision in the two organisations, making suggestions for improvement. (D1)

2.3 Know how hospitality organisations monitor and evaluate customer service

This section covers:

■ monitoring customer service

■ evaluating customer service.

Monitoring customer service

Seeking and monitoring the opinions and views of customers and staff helps organisations provide a more effective customer service. This is important for a number of reasons.

■ To remain competitive, you need to provide service to your customers that is at least as good as, and preferably better than, your competitors.

■ The more you know about your customers' likes and dislikes, the more you can adjust the service that you provide to suit them.

■ Your products and services need to change as your customers' needs change, and **feedback** gives you a chance to do that.

Customer feedback

Feedback from customers can be informal (spoken or observed) or formal (written down). You might informally gather feedback from three major sources:

■ customer comments

■ observation

■ talking to customers.

Remember that those customers who make complaints or offer compliments are generally in the minority. If they are dissatisfied most external customers will simply not do business with you again.

Therefore informal feedback from customers may only tell you part of the story. However, when you have contact with customers you can encourage them to pass on comments that relate to your organisation's service. You can do this by asking them questions and checking that they have enjoyed themselves.

■ *You can gain feedback by chatting to your customers*

You should listen to what customers are saying, and use their comments to improve the service that you give.

Talking point

You do not always need direct contact with customers and staff to form an opinion of the service that you provide. In many situations, you can simply observe the reaction of customers to get a feel for their views on your organisation's products and services. In particular watch out for:

Activity

In pairs, take it in turns to show a feeling through body language rather than words. Try to guess what the other person is feeling.

- **body language** – do customers raise their eyebrows when they see the price? Do they walk out without being served? See page 64 for more on body language.
- **comments** – particularly loud remarks about the products or service.
- **queues** – long queues at checkouts are a major source of customer discontent.

Questionnaires and comment cards

Although informal feedback is extremely useful, you should not rely on it as the only means of monitoring customer service. More formal methods of feedback such as **questionnaires** and **comment cards** should also be used. These will enable you to:

- measure something specific such as the customers' reaction to a new menu
- determine if customers' needs are being met
- check that standards are being kept
- evaluate written feedback more easily.

Questionnaires and customer comment cards are an increasingly common way of getting feedback from customers. Hotels and restaurants have used this type of approach for some time, and other sections of industry and commerce are making more use of both types of feedback.

- Comment cards tend to be short and useful as a source of instant feedback.
- Questionnaires are often sent to or given to customers in the hope of getting more detailed information.

Customers are generally asked to complete comment cards while they are being served, or immediately afterwards. Because of this, they are designed to be brief, and may provide a limited range of information.

Questionnaires should be well laid out, easy to complete and should reassure the customer that any information they give will be treated confidentially. A letter sent with a questionnaire can act as an introduction for the customer, explaining the purpose of the questionnaire. It may offer some incentive (such as a free gift or entry in a prize draw) if the completed questionnaire is returned by a certain time.

In both cases, considerable care needs to be given to the phrasing of the questions. They should be:

- easy to understand
- unambiguous – both the customer and the organisation must have the same understanding of what is being asked.

To establish facts (how long it took to be served, the gender of the customer etc.), **closed questions** requiring a brief answer such as 'yes', a date or something similar can be used.

If the customer's feelings or opinions are required, the questions can be more open. (See page 63 for more on open and closed questions.)

Questionnaires and comment cards will often use rating scales and tick boxes to make it easy for customers to complete.

Customer Feedback Questionnaire

We value your opinion. Please use the questionnaire below to make any comments following your visit.

Quality of food/drink
☐ Very good ☐ Good ☐ Average ☐ Poor ☐ Very Poor
....

Menu
☐ Very good ☐ Good ☐ Average ☐ Poor ☐ Very Poor
....

Comfort
☐ Very good ☐ Good ☐ Average ☐ Poor ☐ Very Poor
....

Ambience
☐ Very good ☐ Good ☐ Average ☐ Poor ☐ Very Poor
....

Service
☐ Very good ☐ Good ☐ Average ☐ Poor ☐ Very Poor
....

Thank you for your feedback

Complaints and compliments

Feedback can come in the form of complaints or compliments. If a customer takes the time and effort to feed back their feelings about your organisation, you should take notice of what they say.

They might give their feedback in person or by letter. In either case, the feedback should be acknowledged to let the customer know that their efforts are appreciated.

Customer complaints give you a chance to put a problem right. The key to customer complaints is to have a positive attitude towards them and to treat them as an opportunity to improve the reliability of customer service.

Customer compliments are equally important to the organisation as they highlight areas where the service provided meets the needs of the

Over to you

Next time you go shopping or to a restaurant become a mystery shopper. You should evaluate the:

- promptness of service
- product knowledge of the staff
- general appearance of the outlet
- availability of products and/or services
- attitude and behaviour of the staff.

How could the company use your findings?

Seaview Hotel Brighton: Internal Mystery Visitor Audit

Area: Restaurant (Breakfast) 1 = satisfactory 0 = unsatisfactory

Time of Visit: AM	Location: Seafront Road, Brighton		
Items Checked	**Customer Satisfaction**	**Standard Achieved**	
Acknowledgement of guest (30 seconds)	1	1	**Notes:**
Assistance with seating and satisfaction confirmed		0	No assistance with sitting and no explanation of breakfast was offered
Service style explained/ order taken		0	Man who met at front door did not have a name badge
Promptness of breakfast tea/coffee (3 minutes)	1	1	Fresh fruit was missing
Friendliness of staff	1		
Use name at least once during meal or greeting		0	
Appearance of staff (including name badge)		0	
Cleanliness of restaurant	1		
Cleanliness of cutlery & crockery	1		
Satisfaction checked during meal or offer of any replenishments		0	
Quality of food – Taste, temperature and freshness	1		
Tables cleared of plates as required			
Bill & payment processed correctly	1	1	
Customer acknowledged and thanked on departure	1	1	
Rating (%)	**100%**	**44.4%**	

customer. Sometimes these comments are used in publicity for the organisation. Permission should be sought from the customer if their name is to be used.

Complaints and compliments should always be fed back to the staff concerned.

Mystery customers

When you work in hospitality, you will often be urged to mentally 'put yourself in the place of the customer'. **Mystery customers** are paid to do this in practice. Working with a checklist of points to consider, a mystery customer will behave just like an ordinary customer, noting the service that they get. This means an anonymous assessment of the service provided, with feedback from an informed yet impartial source. It is simply another way of getting feedback about the service that your organisation provides.

Staff feedback

Members of staff can provide feedback from customers that will be just as valuable when it comes to getting an overall picture of the service that your organisation provides.

Talking to staff and observing how they interact with customers will encourage them to give feedback on standards of service that they find difficult to uphold. It will also encourage them to give their ideas for improving service.

Evaluating customer service

As you have learned, feedback can be collected from customers in a number of different ways.

In most customer service situations, there is the potential for a lot of information to be generated. However, collecting all the feedback in the world is useless unless you can use it properly! When organisations make a decision to collect customer feedback as a basis for updating and improving customer service, they need to be clear about what information they want and what they will do with it. This could include:

- making improvements – in terms of product quality, reliability or value for money
- evaluating procedures
- monitoring job satisfaction.

The following types of quantitative information are often used to evaluate performance:

- level of sales
- repeat customers
- number of new customers
- level of complaints and compliments
- **staff turnover** – how long staff remain with an organisation.

Case studies

The following is an extract from a recent mystery shopping report for Spencer's restaurant:

Service standard	Average score
Food delivered within 15 minutes (target 90%)	75%
Telephone answered within 3 rings (target 85%)	60%
Smile when greeted (target 99%)	100%
Food quality satisfaction (target 99%)	76%

Identify two actions the manager can take with the staff to address these findings.

Making improvements

Seeking the opinions and views of your customers helps provide a more effective customer service. Always bear in mind the objective of collecting customer feedback is to improve the customer service that your organisation provides. Time and money spent gathering feedback is wasted if the feedback is not used to make improvements. Improvements can generally be made in the following areas.

Quality of product and service

- Feedback will often help to improve the quality of service.

- Both formal and informal feedback should indicate areas of service that customers are not happy with.

- Employing mystery shoppers is an excellent way of gauging the quality of service because they are taking a customer service journey.

Value for money

- Value for money goes hand in hand with customer service excellence.

- The most obvious indication that you are not offering value for money is that customers do not buy anything from you!

- Informal and formal feedback will also identify individual products or services that your customers avoid.

Reliability

- An excellent indication that customers feel that an organisation is reliable is that they visit you time after time.

- The level of customer complaints is a reliable way of measuring problems.

- Customers are much more inclined to fill out questionnaires or comment cards if they are particularly satisfied or dissatisfied with an aspect of your service.

Over to you

Suggest four questions that you could ask a customer to gauge the reliability of service in a city centre wine bar.

Evaluating procedures

As you have learned it is wise to set standards of performance for customer service and to train staff to follow them. Formal and informal feedback will allow you to determine which internal procedures are not being followed and to make an action plan to correct this.

It is worth noting here that staff must be consulted if they are not following internal procedures. The procedures might not be workable and they made need to change.

Compliance with legal obligations

Compliance with legal obligations is obviously vital and obtaining customer feedback is an excellent way of checking that this is happening.

Job satisfaction

Formal and informal feedback from staff can show if they are satisfied with their job. Many hospitality organisations regularly survey their staff to check that they are happy.

If staff are involved in the collection of feedback they will be interested in the results of evaluation exercises and motivated by any changes resulting from their involvement.

Talking point

How can you gauge whether staff are satisfied with their job by observing them?

In summary

- It is important to monitor customer service.
- Customer service can be monitored by informal and formal feedback.
- It is important to include staff in the feedback process.
- Collecting all the feedback in the world is useless unless you use it properly.
- Feedback can be used to improve quality of service, value for money, reliability, internal procedures, compliance with legal obligations and staff job satisfaction.

Practice assessment activity

Levels P4/M2

In pairs, investigate the means by which two hospitality organisations monitor and evaluate customer service.

In a presentation to the rest of your group identify:

P the methods used to monitor and evaluate customer service (P4)

M an analysis of the above, identifying the strengths and weaknesses of each method. (M2)

2.4 Be able to demonstrate appropriate customer service skills

This section covers:

■ presentation skills

■ interpersonal skills

■ communication skills

■ communication situations.

Presentation skills

Whenever you come into contact with customers you will influence how those customers think about you and your organisation. This is especially important if it is the first contact with the customer.

First impressions

You will never get another chance to make a first impression. A customer's opinion of you and of the organisation you work for will be formed within a few moments of meeting you. If the first impression is a poor one, it will be very difficult to turn this around and to impress them. On the other hand, if the first impression is good, they are more likely to approach the rest of their time with you in a positive state of mind.

Customers will be confident about your whole organisation if they are presented with a positive image of you. Presentation skills relate to:

■ personal hygiene and appearance

■ work areas and equipment.

Staff who are slovenly, scruffy, untidy and (worst of all) dirty will convey that image about themselves and the organisation they work for. This will not give the customer confidence. Staff who are smart and presentable are already halfway to satisfying customers. Their appearance says 'I am a professional. I know my job and I am ready to do business.'

Personal hygiene and appearance

Good personal hygiene is obviously essential in the hospitality industry. You should:

■ wash or shower daily

■ keep hair neat, tidy and clean

■ keep fingernails short

■ avoid wearing too much make-up or jewellery

Talking point

How can you create a good first impression to a group of customers arriving at your restaurant for their Christmas party?

- avoid bad habits such as chewing or playing with your hair
- keep your uniform clean and in good repair
- keep all cuts and wounds covered with appropriate, clean waterproof dressings.

■ *A smart appearance creates a good impression of you and your organisation*

Case studies

One day when you are on duty you notice a waitress has had her nose and tongue pierced.
- What impression will this give the customers?
- What should you advise the waitress to do?

Over to you

You are working on reception and a guest asks to borrow a pen, but you cannot find one. What impression will that give?

Presentation of work areas and equipment

The first impression that customers get of an organisation is formed not only by the presentation of the staff but also by the presentation of their work area. If your work area does not look well organised, customers may assume that you and your organisation are not organised either. Make sure that:

- your work area is neat and tidy
- you have all the equipment and supplies that you need when you first start a shift so that the service you offer guests is not hindered.

Interpersonal skills

Excellent customer service depends on you being able to demonstrate a high level of **interpersonal skills** when dealing with customers. This means that you should be able to:

- get along with the customer
- show that you care about them and recognise their needs.

Attitude and behaviour

A positive attitude and appropriate behaviour are essential when dealing with customers. Your attitude should let the customer know that you care and that you are trying your best. A negative attitude will affect how you communicate with the customer. They may even think you are being deliberately rude.

Greeting customers

Greeting customers is one of the most important duties that you will perform for your organisation because it is where the customer's first impressions are formed.

Hospitality organisations will often have their own performance standards for greeting customers. They will usually mention that the customer should be greeted with eye contact and a warm smile.

Respect for customers

The way in which you interact with customers will give an impression of how much you care! Customers will expect you to show them respect by:

- being courteous
- showing an interest in what they are saying
- trying to help them.

The experiences that they have had will affect their mood. This is great if they are happy, but more difficult to deal with if they are not. If customers are not happy with the service you are providing they may become aggressive and rude. If they do, it is important to stay in control and to get assistance if necessary.

■ *Greeting customers is often where the first impression is made*

Over to you

Two children have been staying in your hotel for over a week. How would you greet them?

Dealing with complaints

It is particularly important to show respect to customers who have cause to complain. Customers are far more conscious nowadays of what they should expect with a product or service and they can be very quick to complain if there is something wrong.

When dealing with a complaint you must:

■ Remember that the customer is likely to be angry, which might make them impatient, unhappy and sometimes rude.

■ Act in an efficient and diplomatic way or the customer may become very short with you.

■ Remain calm and polite no matter how angry the customer gets.

■ Remember not to take the customer's anger personally.

It is important to comply with the complaint's policy of your organisation. This may vary from one business to another. However, generally you should follow the course of action outlined below.

■ Acknowledge the customer immediately and say you are sorry that they are unhappy with the service they have received.

■ Listen carefully to their complaint without interrupting. You must let the customer finish what they are saying. Otherwise you may stop them from fully explaining what is wrong.

■ Summarise the complaint by repeating back its main points to the customer. This way you can make sure there is no misunderstanding about the nature of the complaint.

■ Explain what action will be taken and how quickly.

Besides keeping customers informed when there is a problem, your other priority is to maintain the highest possible service at all times. This means doing your best to:

■ reduce inconvenience to customers while the problem lasts

■ get back to normal service as quickly as possible.

Sometimes this requires you and other team members to be flexible and agree to do things outside your normal routine activities. It always requires extra effort from one person, if not the whole team.

Over to you

Visit a local hotel and find out their policy for dealing with customer complaints.

Communication skills

Accurate and effective communication with customers is essential if you are to meet their needs. You will need to show good listening skills as well as verbal and non-verbal skills. You must also be able to adapt your method of communication to suit different situations.

Listening

According to an old saying you should:

'Hear twice before you speak once.'

We often listen with 'half an ear' because we are worrying about what to do or say next. Do not be tempted to do that. Listen carefully to what is being said otherwise you may not get a full picture.

Listen also to how the customer is speaking. The way in which they say something and the level, pace and strength of their voice may also give you clues to their feelings.

Verbal communication

Verbal communication is an important skill to develop when you work in the hospitality industry.

- The effectiveness of your verbal communication is affected by the tone and pitch of your voice.

- A varied pitch and tone will demonstrate interest in the customer and enthusiasm for your subject. A flat pitch and tone demonstrates boredom.

- If you do not speak clearly customers will not be able to understand you and they will become dissatisfied.

- Customers must be able to understand what is being said to them. This means that you should be careful about the type of language you use.

- Do not use slang or jargon, or specialist terms such as no-show, ETA or rack rate that the customer may not understand.

Asking appropriate questions

Using sensitive questions may help you understand better how your customer is feeling. There are two main types of questions that you could use when trying to identify and interpret a problem affecting a customer.

Open questions

Open questions are used to get the other party talking. They often begin with 'Who?', 'What?', 'Where?' and 'How?', and can also take the form of an invitation, such as 'Can you describe the problems you have been having?'

Closed questions

Closed questions are used when you do not want or need the customer to go into detail. The answer is often confined to 'Yes' or 'No'. 'Would you like a large, medium or small?' is a closed question because it needs only a one-word answer.

Key points

Try not to use slang or jargon that the customer may not understand, for example:

- no-show – guests who make a booking and do not arrive
- ETA – estimated time of arrival
- rack rate – the full price of a room.

Body language

Body language is the gestures, poses, movements and facial expressions that a person uses to communicate. It is sometimes called **non-verbal communication**. Our body language is conveyed through:

- eye contact
- facial expressions
- body posture and movement
- hand gestures
- touching
- physical distance.

Body language accounts for nearly 55 per cent of our communication, so it is very important that you are aware of your own body language when dealing with customers. You should always make sure that your body language gives a positive and confident image.

■ *This waiter is not building a rapport with the customers*

Body language can convey a powerful message to the customer. If a customer comes to the reception desk and the receptionist continues with what they are doing without acknowledging them in any way, the customer will feel ignored and angry even if the receptionist is busy. On the other hand, if the receptionist smiles at the customer they will feel noticed and welcome.

Communication situations

People use different methods of communication for different situations. It is important to assess the situation and choose the most appropriate method of communication. The choice could depend on:

- with whom they are communicating
- the message they are communicating
- the mood of the person with whom they are communicating.

Face-to-face

Communicating face-to-face has many advantages over other forms of communication.

- You can observe the customer and get an idea of how they are feeling.
- It is easier to find out exactly what the customer wants because you can have a conversation with them and gauge their reaction to what you are suggesting.
- It is much easier to build a rapport with customers when you can see them.

When communicating face-to-face with a guest you should:

- maintain eye contact
- smile
- practise the art of listening
- try to gauge the mood of the customer.

On the telephone

The only thing that will create an impression of you when you are on the telephone is your voice. Therefore it is very important to remember that the impression you make comes from the words you use and the pitch and tone of your voice.

Here are some tips for answering the telephone.

- Answer the call within three or four rings or apologise for the delay.
- Use an appropriate greeting. Many hotels insist upon their staff answering the telephone in a certain way, for example 'Good afternoon. The Swan Hotel, Bournemouth. Suzanne speaking. How may I help you?'
- Sound confident and pleasant.
- Smile while you are talking. Your smile will transfer to your voice.
- Speak clearly.
- Ask the caller's name and use it.
- Ask the caller if there is anything else you can help them with before ending the call.
- Thank the caller for their enquiry.

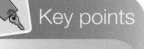

Key points

- Communication skills include listening as well as speaking.
- Communication can be verbal or non-verbal.
- Body language accounts for nearly 55 per cent of our communication.

Over to you

How would you talk to customers who:

- wanted to make a complaint about your food
- had just arrived at your hotel after a long and tedious journey
- had a happy holiday experience?

Good afternoon. The Albany Hotel, Exmouth. Michael speaking. How may I help you?

■ *Your voice should create a good impression*

■ Do not hang up until the caller has put the telephone down in case they remember something else they wanted to say.

In writing

You can communicate in writing by letter, fax or email. It is essential that you think very carefully about what you want to say. This is because once the communication has been sent to the customer you have no influence over how they interpret it and no chance to change the tone of your message. For many potential guests the written communication they receive will be their first contact with the establishment.

A letter or fax that is badly written or typed, with incorrect spelling or bad grammar, gives a very bad impression. Many customers will equate the standard of letter writing with the service provided by the organisation.

Many establishments have adopted a standard form of letter for **mailshots** or confirmation of bookings.

Urgent and non-urgent

Communication can be urgent or non-urgent, which could influence your action and method of communication.

Urgent communication includes:

■ complaint handling

■ telling guests of a change in products and services

■ informing other departments of a change in levels of business or customer requirements.

Non-urgent communication includes:

■ promoting products and services to customers

■ making 'small talk' (chatting) with customers

■ telling other departments about things that will be happening in the future.

Difficult or routine

Most of the communication that you deal with will be routine. An example of this would be taking a customer's order in the restaurant. However, sometimes communication is more difficult or complex. This may involve dealing with angry, aggressive, drunk, distressed or upset customers.

It is important in these situations to stay calm and try to identify the exact needs of the customer. You may need to seek help from a more senior member of staff.

Dealing with this kind of communication requires a basic knowledge of the organisation's policies and procedures.

Over to you

Visit a local hotel and ask about their procedures for dealing with:

■ fire

■ bomb alert

■ aggressive visitors

■ people who are drunk.

In summary

- Personal presentation is very important as it is often how the customer forms their first impression of your organisation.
- Body language is conveyed through eye contact, facial expressions, body posture and movement, hand gestures, touching and physical distance.
- It is important to have good interpersonal skills when working in hospitality.
- You must remember to listen when communicating with guests.
- The tone and pitch of the voice and the language used is very important in verbal communication.
- Written communication must be accurate and well presented.
- Communication can be urgent or non-urgent, difficult or routine.

Practice assessment activity

Levels P5/M3/D2

In groups of three, work on the following scenarios:

- taking a booking for a Christmas party consisting of 25 guests in your restaurant
- explaining to a young family on a weekend break what leisure activities there are in the area
- dealing with an irate customer who has checked into a room that has not been cleaned.

Take it in turns to be the customer, the employer and the observer.

P **M** 1 Role play the scenarios using the customer service skills learned in this unit. (P5/M3)

D 2 Bearing in mind the feedback of the observer, evaluate your own performance, making recommendations for improvement. (D2)

Test your knowledge

1 Define 'customer service'.

2 Who are the internal customers in a hospitality organisation?

3 Identify four benefits of customer service to a hospitality organisation.

4 Explain why hospitality organisations categorise their customers into 'market segments'.

5 List six words that describe consistent and reliable customer service.

6 Name three ways of collecting customer service feedback.

7 Give three reasons why it is important to gain customer feedback.

8 What is an 'open question'? Give an example of an open question you may ask a customer who has just eaten a meal in your restaurant.

9 Describe the process you would follow if a customer complained to you about a meal they had just eaten in your restaurant.

10 Explain how studying this unit has helped you to improve your customer service skills.

3 Safety in Hospitality

Introduction

Whether you are an employee in the hospitality industry or a visitor to an organisation or business your safety is of utmost importance. When you visit a hospitality outlet you will expect a safe environment, where you are not at risk of harm.

The hospitality industry employs around 2 million people and this number is increasing all the time. The points which follow give statistics of safety problems for the year 2005/2006 and indicate that improvements can be made in terms of safety in the hospitality industry:

- 1,863 people received an injury that kept them off work for more than three days

- 640 people suffered a major injury (many resulting in broken bones)

- 55 per cent of major injuries to employees were as a result of slips or trips

- 26,000 people suffered from an illness which was caused by their job

- half a million working days were lost due to workplace injury and work-related ill-health.

This unit introduces you to safety in hospitality. After completing it you will be able to identify the common hazards found within hospitality outlets. You will learn about the different safety legislation that applies to the hospitality industry, and you will also learn how to carry out risk assessments and identify safe working practices.

How you will be assessed

Unit 3 is assessed internally, so the Centre delivering the qualification will assess you against the criteria. On completion of this unit you should:

3.1 understand common hazards within hospitality outlets

3.2 know key safety legislation that regulates safe working practices

3.3 know the common types of safety information used in hospitality

3.4 be able to identify and follow safe working practices.

Assessment grades

The Edexcel Assessment Grid for Unit 3 details the criteria to be met. In general, to gain a Pass (P) you are asked to identify, describe, plan and prepare material; to gain a Merit (M) you are also asked to explain and compare; and to gain a Distinction (D) you are also asked to evaluate and analyse.

3.1 Understand common hazards within hospitality outlets

This section covers:

■ hazards

■ health and safety hazards.

Hazards

A **hazard** is anything that can cause harm, that is injury or hurt. You need to be aware of hazards within hospitality so that you can protect yourself and your customers.

■ *A kitchen can be a dangerous place*

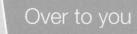

Over to you

In pairs, look at the illustration above and make a note of all the different hazards you can spot in the kitchen. Then combine all the hazards noted from each pair to make one list.

You will have noted many hazards. Most of them are very common in the hospitality industry and all could cause harm to the staff working in the kitchen.

A good way of monitoring hazards is to have a checklist, completed by a responsible employee who checks on safety throughout the working day.

Such a checklist could look like the one below.

Safety checklist

Person doing the check:	
Date/time:	
Location:	Hotel kitchen
Signature:	

Checks to be made	Tick once checked	Comment	Initial
No knives are in the sink			
Saucepan handles are not jutting out or over heat			
Hot oil in deep-fat fryer is not unattended			
Heavy saucepans are carried by two persons			
All food not being used is stored correctly			
Spillages are cleaned up immediately			
Yellow warning signs in use if floor is wet			
Equipment is fitted with effective safety guards			
Equipment is in good working order			
First aid boxes are adequately stocked			
No chemicals are left out or unattended			
Correct protective clothing is worn			

Using such a checklist will help reduce the number of hazards found in a kitchen. Such checklists can be set up and adapted for different areas of any hospitality outlet, for example the restaurant, housekeeping and reception, as they will have different safety hazards.

Case studies

A serious kitchen accident

Amy had only been working in the kitchen at the White Hart Hotel for two weeks. Amy's uniform consisted of chef's trousers, an apron, a white chef's jacket and flat sandals. On this particular day Amy was walking by the drinks dispenser which, unbeknown to her, was leaking. Amy slipped on a pool of water and instinctively reached out to stop her fall. In the process she plunged her arm into boiling oil.

1 Identify what hazards led to the accident occurring.
2 What could have been done to prevent it from happening?

Slips like Amy's are the most common type of accident in the hospitality industry and could, as you will have identified, be easily avoided.

From the case study you can see how hazards can be a danger to staff, but hazards can also be a danger to customers.

Hazards are likely to be present in all areas of hospitality. The diagram shows the common types of hazards that might be found in a restaurant. You will probably have more ideas of your own to add to this list.

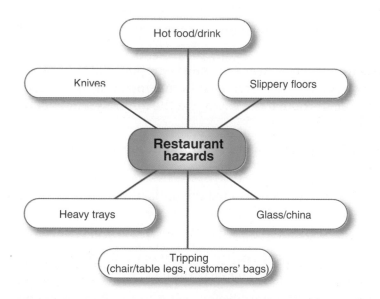

Due diligence

Nowadays people are increasingly suing companies for accidents that have happened in the workplace. Therefore employers must make sure that they do everything that they reasonably can to keep their customers and their staff safe.

Over to you

Working in small groups, take one of the areas listed below and identify all the different hazards that could cause a danger to customers and staff. Make sure all the settings are covered.

- reception area
- accommodation
- bar
- cellar.

When all groups have completed the task share and discuss the lists with the other groups.

You will have found that some hazards are found in more than one area, while others only occur in certain departments. Employers and employees are responsible for ensuring that all hazards are eliminated or controlled.

Due diligence is the term used when employers can prove that they have done all they can to avoid an accident caused by a hazard.

Consider this example of when due diligence has not been practised:

- You are the owner of a small coffee shop. An elderly customer enters your shop and promptly slips on some spilt coffee, badly breaking their hip.

It is likely that as the owner you would be responsible for that accident because you could have prevented it from happening. If the elderly person decides to sue the outlet, this could cost the business hundreds or even thousands of pounds.

Now look at the same example, but this time when due diligence *has* been followed:

- As the employer you had noted the spillage and immediately put up a large yellow sign indicating that the floor area was wet. When the elderly person entered the cafe they knew to avoid the area.

By practising due diligence in this way, there would be less chance of the customer being able to sue you successfully.

Employers can practise due diligence to protect staff by providing:

- instruction and training on all pieces of equipment
- personal protective equipment (PPE) where necessary
- training on the safe use of chemicals
- training on health and safety and food hygiene

- training on employees' responsibilities under health and safety legislation
- instruction and training on how to lift heavy loads safely.

You will learn more about these areas later in this unit.

Consider this final example.

- If a member of staff who has been trained in lifting heavy loads damages their back because they have not lifted the load properly, it is unlikely that the employer will be blamed. However, if the employer *had not* provided the training, then it is likely that they could be blamed.

Health and safety hazards

You have learned about the many different hazards that can be found in the working environment of a kitchen, restaurant and bar. All of these hazards have the potential to cause an accident if they are not eliminated or controlled.

Accidents

An accident is an unplanned, uncontrolled event that leads to actual or potential injury. For example, a wet floor could lead to somebody slipping over; a knife left in a sink could lead to somebody cutting their hand. The consequences of an accident could be:

- major injury
- fatality (death)
- damage or loss (for example of a limb)
- minor injury.

It is impossible to prevent all accidents, but many can be avoided by following good health and safety practices. These will be discussed in more detail later.

Fire

Another hazard – and a very serious one – that can occur in the working environment is fire. There are many hazards in the hospitality industry which could cause fires, including:

- arson – the deliberate setting of a fire
- faulty electrical equipment/wiring
- smoking
- naked flames on cookers
- gas
- explosions
- hot substances such as oil
- hot equipment or machinery, for example ovens.

Case studies

Accident with a dough machine

A young man started work in a bakery at around 6 p.m. Company policy allowed staff to finish early if they had completed an agreed quota.

It was well known that the seals on one of the dough machines deteriorated (became worn out) over time to a point where dough could seep into the mechanical drive area. When this happened, it became accepted practice to take off a fixed guard at the rear of the machine and remove the dough that had got through. This took a long time.

The fixed guard was interlocked with the dough machine's controls, so that when it was removed the power to the machine was cut off.

On the day of the accident the young man was rushing to finish, so that he could join his friends at a late-night party. The seals on the dough machine had deteriorated so much that he had to remove the rear guard every 20 minutes to extract the dough. Because of this and his eagerness to finish work, he decided to try to override the safety interlock switch so that he could keep the machine running while he removed the dough. He was able to do this quite easily.

Unfortunately the young man's loose clothing got caught in the gears and dragged him into the machine, killing him.

1 Identify as many of the causes/factors which led to the accident as you can.

2 Who should be held responsible for this accident?

The dangers associated with fire are:

- burns
- smoke
- toxic fumes
- loss of consciousness
- suffocation
- possible deaths
- property collapse.

The diagram below is known as the fire triangle. Fires can start if all three sides of the triangle are present. Let us look at an example.

- One of the waiting staff in a restaurant is on their break.
- They go outside into the fresh air (**oxygen**) and light a cigarette (**heat**).
- While they are smoking they are called back to the restaurant.
- They throw their cigarette down into an area where there is lots of rubbish (**fuel**).

The actions of this employee are likely to result in a fire. However, this potential fire could be avoided if the staff member had put out their cigarette, thus removing the **heat** element of the triangle.

■ *A fire is likely if all sides of the triangle are present*

Over to you

Consider the following statements and identify which element of the fire triangle has been removed in order to prevent or put out a fire:

1 A fire in a hotel room was prevented from spreading by shutting the door and by putting damp towels around the bottom of the door.

2 A fire that had started in a cellar was put out using the sprinkler system.

3 A lit match was thrown into a bin containing a small amount of paper; the fire died away quickly.

4 A fire in a section of a kitchen was put out using a fire blanket.

5 A deep-fat fryer containing oil was turned off at the end of a shift to prevent a fire from occurring.

6 A fire in a corridor was prevented from spreading by keeping the fire door closed.

Check each other's answers to see if everyone got them right.

Employers can practise due diligence in terms of helping to prevent fires by:

■ checking fire alarms regularly

■ conducting planned fire drills

■ ensuring that all staff are able to recognise the sound of the fire alarm

■ by making special arrangements for people with hearing problems or those wearing ear protection

■ ensuring that fire-fighting equipment is checked regularly and properly sited

■ identifying and controlling fire hazards

■ ensuring good housekeeping, for example keeping areas clean and tidy

- turning off electrical equipment when not in use
- emptying bins regularly
- providing evacuation procedures and training.

If a fire does break out it can be controlled by:

- workplace cleanliness and tidiness
- safe storage of waste
- avoiding blocking fire exits/escape routes
- keeping internal fire doors closed
- checking external fire doors for ease of opening
- fire-fighting equipment such as fire blankets, sprinkler systems and extinguishers.

When you start work with a new employer you should be told what to do in the event of a fire. You will be shown:

- fire exits, doors and escape routes
- assembly points
- the location of fire alarms
- the location of fire-fighting equipment.

You may also be given training on how to fight fires. However you will be told that in the event of fire your safety comes first, and that you must not tackle a fire unless you feel it is safe to do so.

Employers can take additional measures to protect customers in the event of a fire. These might include:

- making sure there are fire notices on the back of hotel bedroom doors
- providing good smoke-detection systems
- having well-signed exits.

Security

Security is another aspect of the working environment that could threaten staff and customers' safety. Crime costs the UK approximately £19 billion per year and the hospitality industry is a contributor to this.

Security in the hospitality industry can be quite difficult. The photo below is of the London Hilton in Park Lane. As you can see this hotel is huge. Its main entrance is a large revolving door with two additional side doors. This makes it very difficult to monitor people coming in and out of the hotel.

The Hilton has over 450 bedrooms, numerous meeting rooms, restaurants and bars, a fitness room, barber shop, beauty salon and gift shop. Therefore the people walking through the entrances are there for many different purposes and may not be guests staying at the hotel.

■ *It can be difficult to monitor all visitors to a hotel*

Despite the Hilton's size, compared to hotels in the USA it is quite small. The Bellagio Hotel in Las Vegas is spread over 49 hectares (122 acres) and has numerous facilities, including:

- 3,933 bedrooms
- 17 restaurants
- casino
- ballroom
- shopping centre.

The Bellagio's many different entrances are used by thousands of visitors, not to mention the hotel's 9,000 employees. You can imagine how difficult it must be to manage security in such a large establishment.

Businesses try to prevent threats to security as much as possible. Ways of doing this include:

- checking work references for all staff to help ensure they are honest and trustworthy
- regularly training employees in crime and security procedures
- making a manager or a team of people responsible for security.

■ *The larger the outlet, the more difficult it is to manage security*

Security of premises
To help prevent threats to security both outside and inside a building there are various steps that can be taken.

Outside the building
- Strengthen or replace doors and windows.

Over to you

Working as a group, make a list of all the potential risks associated with security in the hospitality industry.

- Install alarm systems.
- Install CCTV (closed-circuit television).
- Light up entrances.
- Use anti-climb paint on drainpipes.
- Secure boundaries.
- Remove graffiti.
- Secure vehicles and goods stored outside.

Inside the building

- Protect valuable stock by issuing keys and restricting access.
- Consider till location – don't place tills where there is easy access.
- Use a safe for storing cash and valuables.
- Have a clear key policy.
- Remove high-value equipment or stock from windows at night.

Case studies

The kitchen thief

As the security manager of a high-class restaurant you have been asked to comment on the following incident, noting how such an incident could have been prevented.

A chef in your restaurant has been caught stealing. One of the security guards was carrying out a random check of staff's bags. In the chef's bag in the locker room the guard found a copper saucepan, hand-made crockery and expensive cutlery, altogether worth several hundred pounds. The chef admitted to stealing the items during his break and hiding them in the bag with the aim of taking them out when his shift finished in the early hours of the morning.

If a business gains a reputation for bad security customers and employees are likely to go elsewhere. Employers must therefore do everything they can to protect all staff and customers from security threats.

Food safety

All hospitality outlets are likely to offer food to customers and staff. Outlets include, among many others:

- restaurants
- workplace cafeterias
- school or college canteens
- coffee shops

- takeaways
- bistros
- pubs or clubs.

When customers and employees use the catering services provided they expect the food to be safe to eat. Unfortunately this is not always the case.

Food poisoning

If someone becomes unwell after eating food it is likely that they have got **food poisoning**. Food poisoning is a general name given to illnesses that are caused by eating and/or drinking contaminated (bad) food or water.

- On average 2 million people a year suffer from symptoms such as vomiting and diarrhoea due to food poisoning.
- Food poisoning can cause serious illness.
- Some types of food poisoning can lead to permanent disability or even death.

Food poisoning occurs when the food that is eaten is not safe to eat. Food poisoning can be caused in various ways

Physical contamination

This is when food or drink has been spoiled by something unwanted falling into it, for example a hair, a nail or an insect. This contamination could come from:

- the person preparing the food
- machinery the food is in, for example part of a mixing machine
- packaging – it can be very easy for insects and vermin to enter food packaging
- contaminated food coming into contact with clean food
- dirt from kitchens, work premises or equipment.

Micro-organisms

The micro-organisms responsible for food poisoning are bacteria, viruses and fungi. These organisms contaminate the food and cause illness. There are many different types of food poisoning bacteria. One of the most common is *Salmonella*, which can be found in contaminated chicken, cream and milk. The symptoms of *Salmonella* food poisoning are:

- fever
- headache
- abdominal (stomach) pain
- nausea and sometimes vomiting
- diarrhoea.

Key points

- Hospitality businesses must keep their premises, staff and customers safe and secure.
- Security is more difficult to manage in large outlets.
- Security must be maintained both inside and outside.
- Hospitality outlets will lose business if customers do not feel safe.

In order to ensure that neither customers nor staff get food poisoning, hospitality employers and employees must be aware of the **bacterial danger zone** shown below.

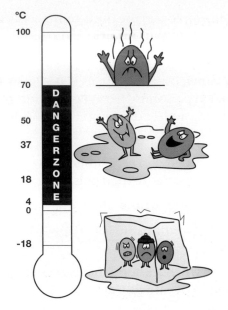

■ *Keeping food at temperatures bacteria don't like will help prevent food poisoning*

Employers can avoid the danger zone and help prevent food poisoning by making sure that:

■ all foods stored in refrigerators are covered and chilled to 4°C (Celsius)

■ all food handlers always wash their hands after visiting the toilet

■ cooked and reheated meat, especially poultry, reaches a temperature of above 70°C

■ all food handlers wash their hands after handling raw meat or eggs before they handle other foods.

Case studies

Food poisoning outbreak in schools

A contract caterer who supplied food to 27 schools in Wales was forced to close by health inspectors after 75 children suffered food poisoning. It was believed that the food poisoning was caused by *Salmonella*.

1 Identify all the points that could have led to the outbreak of *Salmonella* poisoning.

2 List the types of foods which may have been contaminated.

3 State how the outbreak of food poisoning could have been avoided.

In summary

- There are many hazards in the hospitality industry that could cause harm to customers and employees.
- The three elements of the fire triangle are oxygen, fuel and heat.
- The signs of food poisoning include vomiting and diarrhoea.
- The temperature danger zone in which bacteria can grow is between 4°C and 70°C.

Practice assessment activity

Level P1

P   Visit three hospitality outlets and identify at least five different hazards in each. Give examples of what types of accidents the hazards could cause. (P1)

3.2 Know key safety legislation that regulates safe working practices

This section covers:

- current safety legislation
- implications for hospitality businesses.

Current safety legislation

One definition of legislation is 'Laws which are made'. The hospitality industry has much safety legislation in place to protect employers, employees, visitors and customers. In this section you will learn about a selection of legislation covering areas such as:

- health and safety
- food safety
- fire
- handling of equipment and substances
- first aid
- protective clothing.

Health and safety

The main legislation regulating health and safety is the **Health and Safety at Work Act (HASAWA) 1974**. The aims of this Act are to:

- secure the health, safety and welfare of persons at work
- protect other people from health and safety risks caused by work activities
- control the storage and use of explosive and dangerous substances.

Under the HASAWA both employers and employees have responsibilities.

Employers' responsibilities:

- ensure the health, safety and welfare of employees
- provide and maintain safe equipment and systems of work
- make arrangements for the safe use, handling, storage and transport of articles and substances
- provide information, instruction, training and supervision
- provide a safe place of work and safe entrance and exit
- provide a safe working environment with adequate toilet, washing and changing facilities.

Employees' responsibilities:

- take reasonable care for their own health and safety and for others who may be affected by them

- cooperate with their employer and follow safety instructions

- not to tamper with anything provided in the interests of health, safety or welfare. This is illegal and can lead to prosecution.

Under this Act employees could be liable (blamed) should their actions result in a health and safety incident. The accident with a dough machine case study in section 3.1 (page 76) is a good example of an employer not meeting their responsibilities under the HASAWA by not maintaining the machine properly, and an employee not meeting their responsibilities because they illegally tampered with the machinery.

Food safety

Research has found that about 2,000 objects such as animal hairs, glass and metal are found in food and medicines each year. Section 3.1 looked at food safety in terms of food poisoning, physical contamination and bacterial danger zones. All of these points fall under the **Food Safety Act 1990** legislation. This aims to protect consumers by:

- preventing illness from the eating of food

- preventing them being misled as to the nature of the food they are purchasing.

In section 3.1 you also learned how food poisoning can be prevented by the correct storage, handling and cooking of food (see pages 81–82). The following cases illustrate how food safety legislation can protect consumers from being misled about food purchases

Case studies

Tainted food news stories

1 In February 2005 an Essex company was fined £2,000 after admitting selling curry powder containing the illegal cancer-causing dye Sudan 1. The company also had to pay £3,000 costs. The offence under the Food Safety Act 1990 concerned the sale of food not of a standard demanded by the consumer. It was stressed that 'Food companies have a legal responsibility to ensure that the food they sell is safe and fit for human consumption.'

2 In 2001 a woman found a chunk of something unusual in her jar of pickle. This turned out to be a metal cube inserted by the manufacturer as a way of checking whether its own metal detecting equipment was working properly.

Source: BBC go to www.heinemann.co.uk/hotlinks, insert the express code 5285P and click on this case study.

Talking point

In your group, discuss any unusual items you have found in food you have purchased and what you did about it.

Key points

- The main legislation covering health and safety is the Health and Safety at Work Act (HASAWA) 1974
- Employers and staff have responsibilities under this Act.
- About 2,000 unwanted objects (for example, animal hairs) are found in food items and medicines each year.

Employers must prove that they took every step to prevent such incidents (due diligence), otherwise they will be prosecuted under the Food Safety Act 1990. In order to meet the requirements of this legislation employers must take every measure to prevent food illnesses from occurring. They must ensure that the food they sell does not mislead the customer in any way in terms of its content.

Fire safety

The legislation concerning fire safety is the **Fire Safety Regulations, Regulatory Reform (Fire Safety) Order 2005**. It deals with general fire precautions and requires businesses to put in place fire precautions as far as practicable. These include:

- means of detection and giving warning in case of fire – fire alarms
- the provision of means of escape – fire exits
- means of fighting fire – fire extinguishers
- training staff in fire safety.

Employers are responsible for complying with the Act and they must carry out separate fire risk assessments. You will learn about risk assessments in section 3.4. Some of the responsibilities of employers and staff under this Act are as follows.

- Employers must let their employees know of any risks to them which have been identified in the risk assessment.
- Employers must give new employees fire training when they start work. This should include fire prevention and the location of fire equipment and assembly points.
- Employers must ensure that fire-fighting and detection equipment (for example smoke alarms) and emergency routes are fully maintained regularly to make sure that they are in good working order.
- Employees must cooperate with employers to ensure the workplace is safe from fire, and must not do anything that will place themselves or other people at risk.

All hospitality businesses will have a range of fire detection and fire-fighting equipment for different situations, including:

- smoke alarms
- fire extinguishers – the five main categories are water, foam, powder, carbon dioxide and vaporising liquids.
- fire blankets
- hose reels
- sprinkler systems.

Over to you

Using the illustration of five blank fire extinguishers, colour in the extinguishers so that they meet the Fire Safety Regulations, Regulatory Reform (Fire Safety) Order 2005 legislation in terms of appearance. Write alongside each one what type of extinguisher it is and what fires it can be used on.

Manual handling

Manual handling is about ensuring that employees do not harm themselves by lifting and carrying heavy objects. The legislation concerned with manual handling is the **Manual Handling Operations Regulations 1992**. It is designed to protect employees from hurting their back and upper limbs (arms, hands) through incorrect lifting.

There are many risks associated with manual handling in the hospitality industry. For example each department within a hotel will have risks associated with lifting and carrying, pushing and pulling.

- Kitchen area – carrying heavy saucepans
- Restaurant – lifting and moving tables and chairs
- Bar – moving heavy casks and kegs
- Housekeeping – changing and making beds.

Employers in practising due diligence must train employees in correct lifting techniques and carry out a manual handling risk assessment. Measures must then be put in place to either remove or control any risks.

The illustrations below show the right and wrong way to lift objects. If the correct way is not followed the person doing the lifting is likely to suffer from upper limb injuries and/or back pain.

Most risks can be avoided by proper training and by the use of lifting aids such as trolleys. Often the most important action an employer can take is informing and training their employees on how to lift safely.

Talking point

In small groups discuss other manual handling risks that you might find in the hotel departments shown below.

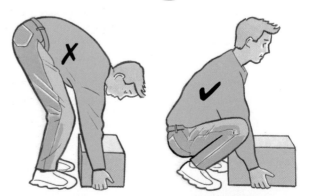

■ *It is important to follow correct lifting and handling techniques to avoid injury*

Safe handling of dangerous substances

Most departments within hospitality businesses will at some point use what is classed as a hazardous (dangerous) substance. Examples include:

- oven cleaner in a kitchen
- strong bleach in housekeeping
- fluid used to clean the beer lines in a bar.

The effects of hazardous substances can range from mild eye irritation to lung disease or sometimes even death. It is therefore essential that employees who have to use such substances are protected as far as possible.

The legislation which controls the handling of these substances is the **Control of Substances Hazardous to Health Regulations 2002 (COSHH)**. Under this legislation the employer is responsible for:

- assessing the risks to health from hazardous substances used in workplace activities
- deciding on what precautions are needed, for example masks and goggles
- preventing or adequately controlling exposure to dangerous substances. This could mean prevention by using safer chemicals or control by using chemicals for short periods of time.
- ensuring that employees are properly informed, trained and supervised in the use of substances
- ensuring that locked storage areas are available for substances
- ensuring that all substances are clearly labelled to show what they are, what they are to be used on and instructions on their safe use.

Case studies

The hidden dangers of drinking

Roger and Carol Banley own the Jack and Jenny pub where Chris has been working behind the bar for three weeks. Friday night is karaoke night and is always very busy. At about 10 p.m. Chris was extremely thirsty and got himself a pint of lemonade. Chris went into the kitchen and downed his drink very quickly. Instantly he felt a terrible burning sensation in the back of his throat and mouth. He was having difficulty breathing and then collapsed.

Chris was rushed to hospital where they found that, instead of lemonade, he had drunk very strong bleach which had been put into a lemonade bottle. Chris did regain consciousness, but due to the severity of his burns he was never able to taste food or swallow solid food again.

- How could this accident have been prevented?
- Who would be held responsible under the Control of Substances Hazardous to Health Regulations 2002?

First aid

The **Health and Safety (First-Aid) Regulations 1981** deal with first aid in the workplace. This legislation requires employers to provide the necessary equipment, facilities and personnel in order to be able to give first aid to employees if they are injured or become ill at work. The purpose of the legislation is to:

- prevent injuries
- prevent other conditions getting worse
- save lives.

Under these regulations employers must provide a first aid kit. Depending on the size of the organisation and the nature of the work they may also have to provide trained first aiders and a first aid room.

The minimum equipment a first aid kit must include is:

- guidance leaflet
- individually wrapped sterile plasters
- sterile eye pads
- triangular bandages
- safety pins
- sterile dressings of various sizes
- disposable gloves.

First aid kits should never contain any tablets or medicines because patients could have allergic reactions to such items.

Employers must tell all members of staff the names and locations of the trained first aiders, as well as where the first aid kits are kept.

Employees who are not trained must not give first aid themselves, but they are responsible for contacting a first aider if first aid is required. First aiders will provide the help and care that is necessary until qualified medics arrive.

Protective clothing and equipment

In some areas of the hospitality industry employers are required to supply protective clothing to their employees. The legislation that covers the provision of protective clothing is the **Personal Protective Equipment (PPE) at Work Regulations 1992**.

PPE must be provided by employers and must be worn by staff to protect them from risks to their health or safety. Some of the hazards and types of PPE required for the hospitality industry are shown below.

- Eyes – hazards include chemical splash and gas. The PPE required are goggles, face shields or visors.

■ *Staff must wear the correct protective clothing in the workplace*

■ Head – hazards include hair getting tangled in machinery. The PPE required are hairnets and hats to ensure that no hair is at risk of being caught in machinery.

■ Hands and arms – hazards include burns, cuts, chemical splash, skin infections. The PPE required are gloves and chef's long-sleeved jacket.

■ Feet and legs – hazards include slipping, cuts and chemical splash. The PPE required are chef's trousers and aprons and safety shoes with steel toecaps.

When an employer provides its staff with PPE the employer is practising due diligence. If an employee when cleaning an oven decides not to wear the PPE provided and as a result loses the sight in an eye the *employee* will be held responsible.

If, on the other hand, the employer in this case had not provided goggles or suitable eye protection, then the *employer* would be responsible under the Personal Protective Equipment (PPE) at Work Regulations 1992.

Injuries, diseases and dangerous occurrences

The final safety legislation we will look at here is the **Reporting of Injuries, Diseases and Dangerous Occurrences Regulations 1995 (RIDDOR)**. There are many different types of major injuries, work-related diseases and dangerous occurrences that by law must be reported. All of these are noted in the RIDDOR guide supplied by the **Health and Safety Executive (HSE)**.

Under RIDDOR legislation employers *must* report:

■ work-related deaths

■ major injuries – this includes amputation (loss of all or part of a limb) and loss of sight

■ any accident which results in an employee being off work for more than three days

■ work-related diseases – includes some skin and lung diseases

■ dangerous occurrences – includes collapse of building and explosion.

Employers have to report such occurrences so that the HSE can investigate these accidents, identify where they are happening and then take action necessary to help prevent them from happening again.

Implications for hospitality businesses

For employers who comply with all health and safety legislation and who follow safe working practices there can be both benefits and costs.

Over to you

Look at the photo and state how the PPE the chef is wearing can protect her from the typical risks associated with working in a kitchen. What additional PPE might the chef have to wear when cleaning ovens?

Safety in Hospitality 91

Benefits of complying:

- personal safety of employees and customers
- good reputation for the business
- low staff turnover
- happy staff
- less chance of legal action against them
- their business is legal – they 'abide by the law'.

Costs of not complying:

- poor reputation for the business and the employer
- loss of life
- increase in accidents
- high staff turnover
- high levels of sickness
- prosecution
- imprisonment
- fines
- loss of custom
- closure of business
- negative publicity.

These two lists show how much a business could suffer by following poor health and safety practices. It is therefore in the employers' best interest to comply with the different legislation and provide their staff with safe working practices as far as possible.

In summary

- There is a lot of health and safety legislation that applies to the hospitality industry.
- The legislation covers health and safety, food safety and storage, fire, manual handling, COSHH, first aid, PPE and RIDDOR.
- It is important for everyone's safety that employers and employees comply with the legislation.
- Some of the benefits of complying are a safe environment, a good reputation and a happy workforce.
- Some of the costs of not complying are accidents, prosecution, fines and imprisonment.

Practice assessment activity

Levels P2/M1/D1

P You have recently been employed as the health and safety manager in a three-star hotel. The general manager has asked you to inform him of the different legislation that he must comply with in order to provide a safe working environment for the hotel's employees and customers. State how the compliance can be enforced. (P2)

M Explain to the general manager how compliance with the legislation is used to control hazards and prevent ill-health or injury to staff and customers. Explain the benefits this compliance will bring to the organisation. (M1)

D Evaluate the benefits and costs to the general manager of complying with health and safety legislation. (D1)

3.3 Know the common types of safety information used in hospitality

This section covers:

■ safety signs

■ safety information

■ safety training.

Safety signs

All businesses need to display safety signs of some sort. There are many types of safety signs that are used across a range of different industries, including hospitality.

The most commonly used signs fall under the following categories.

■ **Warning** signs – these have a black symbol on a yellow background inside a black triangle.

■ **Prohibition** signs – these have a black symbol on a white background inside a red circle with a red diagonal line across the circle. These show things that *must not* be done.

■ **Mandatory** signs – these have a white symbol on a blue circular background. These show things that must be in place or done.

■ **Emergency** signs – these have a white symbol on a green rectangular or square background.

■ **Fire-fighting** signs – these have a white symbol on a red rectangular or square background.

One of the most common signs in hospitality and other industries is the yellow triangular sign – floor cleaning in progress.

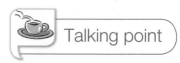
Talking point

In pairs match each sign in the illustrations to the correct category. Then discuss when each safety sign might be used in the hospitality industry. For example, a 'wet floor' sign must be used for spillages on the floor.

Key points

Common safety signs can be:

■ warnings

■ prohibitions

■ mandatory information

■ emergency information

■ fire-fighting signs.

Safety information

Health and safety can be very confusing for employers, as there is so much information they need to understand in order to protect everyone on their premises. The Health and Safety Executive (HSE) is there to protect people's health and safety by ensuring that risks are properly controlled.

To help employers, the HSE offers many free information guides and leaflets about different legislation. These include:

- first aid books
- COSHH leaflets
- PPE literature
- information on Hazard Analysis of Critical Control Points (HACCP) in food production (see section 3.4).

The HSE, along with local government, enforces the regulations associated with health and safety. HSE inspectors can visit and inspect premises whenever they choose; this may not be at a convenient time for the employer. If the inspectors notice that any requirements of health and safety legislation are not being met, for example a fire risk assessment has not been carried out or hazardous substances are not clearly labelled, they could:

- issue an informal warning – in this case employers are not obliged to follow the advice but would be wise to do so.
- issue an improvement notice – this will state what the breach of the law is, what needs to be done and by when.
- issue a prohibition notice – this will tell the employer to stop the activity. For example if a mixing machine is faulty they may stop its use until it has been fixed.
- prosecute individuals or the company.

Safety training

The Health and Safety Executive strongly recommends that employers give all employees comprehensive health and safety training. This is essential in the hospitality industry.

One way an employer could cover this is through a health and safety induction programme. This should include all the health and safety aspects of the working environment that the employee needs to know.

An induction programme could look like the one shown below.

Topic to be covered	Method	Name and signature of person delivering topic	Employee's name and signature	Date topic was covered
Lifting and carrying	Demonstration in the kitchen			15 January

Over to you

Draw up your own induction training programme to cover the following areas:

- health and safety
- food safety
- manual handling
- COSHH
- first aid
- fire drills.

It is very important that staff training is recorded so that employers can prove that they have practised due diligence and employees cannot deny that they have received training.

Employers should carry out and review safety training regularly. Employers should not assume that staff who have received induction training no longer need any safety training. Training will need to be reviewed and updated if necessary when:

- new equipment is bought
- premises change
- new legislation is passed.

Employers should also review the effectiveness of their training to make sure employees know all they need to follow safe working practices. Sometimes employers may choose to send their staff on a health and safety training course. Such a course would cover:

- health and safety at work
- health and safety legislation
- prevention of accidents and ill-health
- risk assessment
- first aid at work
- personal protective equipment (PPE)
- workplace health, safety and welfare
- work equipment

- fire prevention
- hazardous substances
- manual handling.

When employees attend this type of training course, employers will need to ensure that the knowledge they have gained can be applied in their actual workplace.

In summary

- There are many different safety signs that apply to the hospitality industry.
- Safety signs fall under different categories, including warning, prohibition and mandatory.
- The Health and Safety Executive (HSE) provides lots of safety information free of charge to employers.
- All employees should receive induction training on aspects of health and safety.

Practice assessment activity

Levels P3/M2

P You are the health and safety manager of a three-star hotel. Your general manager has asked you to draw up a poster describing the common safety signs used within the hotel. Include on your poster the types of information and documentation that is available regarding health and safety. (P3)

M On completion of your poster give a short presentation to the general manager explaining how four different types of safety information should be used within the hotel. For example, one type of information could be what is necessary in order to carry out a risk assessment. (M2)

3.4 Be able to identify and follow safe working practices

This section covers:

■ risk assessment

■ health and safety

■ food safety and storage.

Risk assessment

You have already learned about hazards in section 3.1 of this unit, but it is important to know exactly what we mean by a hazard and a risk.

■ **Hazard** means anything that can cause harm, for example cleaning chemicals.

■ **Risk** is the *chance* that the hazard may harm somebody.

According to the Health and Safety Executive (HSE):

'A risk assessment is nothing more than a careful examination of what, in your work could cause harm to people, so that you can weigh up whether you have taken enough precaution or should do more to prevent harm.'

The aims of risk assessments are to make sure that no employees are hurt or become ill in the workplace. Employers have a legal obligation to assess the risks in their places of work. The easiest way to do this is to carry out a risk assessment, which is a straightforward process.

Completing risk assessments

The HSE has devised five steps to follow when completing a risk assessment.

Step 1 Look for any hazards.

Step 2 Decide who might be harmed and how.

Step 3 Evaluate the risks and decide whether the existing precautions are adequate or whether more could be done to prevent the risk from causing harm.

Step 4 Record the risk assessment on an appropriate form.

Step 5 Review your risk assessment and revise it if necessary, for example when a new piece of machinery replaces an old one.

Using a kitchen as an example, the information below explains in more detail the steps for someone carrying out a risk assessment.

Step 1

■ The easiest way to spot and identify hazards is to walk around the work area being assessed, in this case the kitchen.

■ Ask all the employees who work in the area what hazards they feel are present.

■ Record all the hazards that have been identified.

Step 2

■ Identify all personnel who might be harmed by these hazards and how.

Step 3

Evaluate the risks and decide if existing precautions are enough to prevent the risks from causing harm or if more should be done. It is good practice for the person carrying out the risk assessment to actually rate the level of the risk.

■ If a hazard is very likely to cause harm it would be classed as high risk,

■ If the hazard has a low likelihood of causing harm it would be classed as low risk.

Hazards that might be classed as high risk in the hospitality industry include:

■ wet floors

■ heavy saucepans

■ hot substances

■ dangerous substances, for example oven cleaner

■ machinery

■ knives.

Low-risk hazards might include:

■ swinging doors – entry into the kitchen and restaurant

■ tripping over customers' bags or chairs.

Employers ideally need to try to classify every hazard as low risk. They can do this by getting rid of all the high-risk hazards if possible or by controlling the risks. You will always get wet floors in a kitchen but this risk can be controlled by informing and training employees to clean up spillages immediately and by placing 'wet floor' signs around the area. Other ways of controlling risks are to use PPE such as goggles and gloves when handling dangerous substances (see section 3.2).

Step 4

Having evaluated the risks and put in place as many control measures as possible, the next step is to record the findings of the risk assessment.

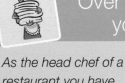

Over to you

As the head chef of a restaurant you have been asked to complete a risk assessment on the kitchen. Identify all the people who might be harmed and how they could be harmed.

Legally only employers with five or more employees have to record risk assessments. However, it is best practice to record all risk assessments regardless of the number of staff.

A risk assessment could be recorded on a form like the one below.

Risk assessment for	Assessment undertaken	Assessment review
Company name and address:	Date: Signed:	Date:
Step 1: Significant hazards found	**Step 2:** People at risk from the hazards	**Step 3:** List existing controls, risks which are not controlled and what action is needed

Talking point

In pairs, select an area of your school/college and carry out a risk assessment. Make sure your findings are recorded (step 4). In your pairs discuss when and why you think the risk assessment might need to be reviewed (step 5).

Step 5

Set a date for reviewing the assessment. Be prepared to change it if circumstances change, for example if new equipment is installed.

Some legislation requires employers to have separate risk assessments for different situations. These include:

- fire risk assessment – the person doing the assessment will only be noting hazards that could cause a fire
- COSHH risk assessment – the assessor will only be looking at hazards to do with dangerous substances.

Health and safety

As you have learned in section 3.2, it is important for all employers and employees to:

- understand what the safe working practices are for their work place
- follow those safe working practices.

Here we will look at examples of procedures and precautions that could help employers and their staff follow safe working practices.

Procedures

Employers will have documented health and safety procedures for staff to follow. Such procedures will cover areas such as:

- the safe use of equipment
- manual handling
- other general health and safety precautions.

Safe use of equipment

In a kitchen there are dangerous pieces of equipment such as slicing machines and food mixers. It is important therefore when someone starts working in a kitchen that they are shown the machinery they will be using and that they are told clearly how to use it.

It should be noted that certain types of catering equipment have age restrictions on their use. For example a meat slicer can only be used by a person aged 18 or over.

The employee should then be supervised on its use until they feel confident that they can work the machine safely. The employer might put up a notice beside a machine detailing the safe procedure to follow when using the machine, such as the one below.

Procedure for using the food mixer

- Check all guards are in place and secured.
- Check the machine is switched on at the socket.
- Locate the emergency red button.
- Put the ingredients into the mixing bowl.
- Ensure the mixing bowl and mixing implement are inserted securely.
- Turn the on switch to a low setting to start.
- If required turn up the setting.
- When the mixing is complete switch off the machine on the machine itself and at the socket.
- Release the mixing implement into the bowl and carefully remove the bowl.
- Clean the machine down, returning the bowl and the mixing implement when clean.

Simple procedures like these can be displayed beside all equipment across the hospitality setting so that employees are always aware of the steps they need to take in order to use equipment safely. Employers should make and store records of workplace safety procedures that are used for different tasks.

Manual handling

Another common safety procedure, and one which also is often displayed, is for manual handling (see section 3.2). The illustration below shows the steps to take when lifting a heavy item.

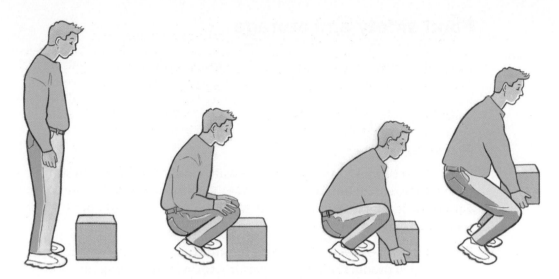

■ *Simple instructions like these shown in pictures are easy for all employees to understand and to follow*

Employers may provide special equipment to help with manual handling, for example:

■ trolleys

■ ramps

■ lifts

■ hoists and other lifting equipment.

Employees must also be trained in the safe use of any equipment to ensure they do not harm themselves when lifting heavy items. If special equipment is provided staff must then use these resources.

Protective clothing

You have already learned in section 3.2 about the provision and use of protective clothing under the Personal Protective Equipment (PPE) at Work Regulations 1992 health and safety legislation.

Continuing with our kitchen example, employers should provide the following PPE for safety and protection:

■ chef's whites (trousers and long-sleeved jacket) and shoes with steel toecaps

■ goggles and masks – to anyone using dangerous substances such as cleaning fluids

■ overalls and face guards – to protect staff carrying out maintenance work that could involve flying debris.

Fire-fighting equipment

In section 3.2 you learned about the different types of fire-fighting equipment. It is essential that employers provide this equipment so that if a fire does break out the correct equipment is available to fight the fire safely.

> **Over to you**
>
> *Draw up a procedure (written and/or illustrated) for use by staff in a hotel restaurant detailing how to lift a heavy box of wine. The aim of the procedure is to help ensure that the waiting and bar staff do not hurt their backs when lifting heavy boxes.*

Food safety and storage

Food safety and storage is extremely important in the hospitality industry, as you have learned in section 3.2 covering food poisoning. Employers will have written safety procedures detailing the best ways to handle and store food.

Procedures

HACCP stands for Hazard Analysis Critical Control Points. This is similar to a risk assessment but for food. The HACCP process is set up to help employers look at how food is handled, with the aim being to produce food that is safe to eat.

HACCP focuses on identifying every hazard that may be present at every stage of food production, from harvesting through to serving the food. After employers have identified any hazards, systems then need to be put in place to control those hazards and prevent them from causing harm.

Like risk assessments, in general HACCP has steps to follow:

- identifying the hazards
- noting how the hazards could cause harm
- putting control measures in place
- monitoring the measures to ensure they are working
- keeping relevant records.

HACCP plans also need to be kept up to date and reviewed, especially if there are any changes to food operations. In addition to HACCP, employers may also set up procedures that cover:

- personal hygiene
- workplace cleanliness
- pest control
- reporting illness.

Personal hygiene

Food handlers play a vital role in ensuring that prepared food is safe to eat. To help in this task food handlers need to follow a personal hygiene procedure such as shown below.

- Ensure all chefs' uniforms are clean and ironed.
- Ensure hats are worn and cover hair; long hair must be tied up and kept in a hairnet under the hat.
- All body piercing must be removed.
- No jewellery (including watches) except a wedding band may be worn.
- No make-up is to be worn.

- Hands must be washed when coming into the kitchen, after going to the lavatory, after handling different foods, after handling raw and cooked foods.

- No smoking is allowed in any of the kitchen areas.

A procedure such as this lets employees know exactly what is expected of them in terms of their personal hygiene.

Workplace cleanliness

Departments within the hospitality industry also need to be kept clean. One of the easiest ways to monitor cleaning is to set up a **cleaning schedule**. Employers should produce procedures for cleaning that:

- provide training for the staff

- show how to clean areas

- provide appropriate equipment and cleaning materials.

Schedules to monitor cleaning for the different departments of the business will also be available. A sample cleaning schedule is shown below.

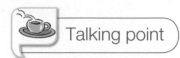

Talking point

In pairs, draw up a cleaning schedule for a kitchen. You can base your schedule on your school/college kitchen.

Restaurant cleaning schedule

Area to be cleaned	Frequency	Method	Name of employee carrying out cleaning	Signature and date of employee carrying out cleaning
Floor	Twice daily	Vacuum cleaner	Jon Jones	
Bar counter	Before, during and after service	Cloth and sanitiser	Claire Lye	
Glasses	During and after service	Glasswasher	Chris Porter	
Tables and chairs	Before and after service	Damp cloth for chairs; damp cloth and sanitiser for tables	Amelia Black	

Pest control

Another factor that can affect food safety is the risk of contamination by pests. Employers will have procedures in place to help prevent pest infestation. The main types of pests that are likely to be found in the hospitality industry are:

- rodents – rats and mice

- insects – beetles and flies.

■ *Hospitality staff should be aware of the signs of pest infestation*

The procedures to follow to help prevent pests might be as follows.

- Check all dry goods (flour, rice, lentils) at the time of delivery for pest infestation or damage.
- Transfer dry foods to pest-proof containers.
- Ensure all dry goods are stored off the ground and clear of walls.
- Clear up all spillages immediately.
- Make sure bins in the kitchen have close-fitting lids; outdoor bins must have pest-proof lids.
- Report any signs of a problem to the pest control contractor immediately.

Employers may also inform staff of the signs to look for in case of pest infestation. These include:

- gnaw marks
- droppings
- smear marks from grease
- holes and nesting sites
- footprints, tail marks in dust etc.
- the animals themselves
- webbing on food packaging, storage shelves or equipment, or in the food itself
- small tunnels or holes in food packaging
- bad smells.

Reporting illness

Section 3.2 covered the importance of reporting illness in the hospitality industry, particularly when the illness is reportable under Reporting of Injuries, Diseases and Dangerous Occurrences Regulations 1995 (RIDDOR). All employees should be told about the procedures required under RIDDOR during their health and safety induction training.

Procedures for reporting illnesses that are not covered by RIDDOR will also be in place and would include the following information.

In the event of illness:

- Contact your employer as soon as possible detailing the nature of the illness.
- If possible advise your employer when you will be returning to work.

■ If you are off work for more than three days, on return to work bring a
  doctor's certificate.

Employees should always inform their employer when they are unfit for
work so that the employer can decide whether they need to report the
illness under RIDDOR.

Food storage

In section 3.1 you learned about the bacterial danger zone in terms of the
temperatures that bacteria like and don't like. Temperature control is a
vital part of food safety and good kitchens will have procedures in place
for monitoring the temperatures of hot and cold foods.

The procedure will include the following temperatures (in degrees
Celsius):

■ fridges should be 0°C–5°C

■ freezers should be -18°C (minus 18 degrees)

■ hot food should be cooked to at least 70°C.

One way of checking temperatures is to have a procedure in place that
requires the monitoring of temperatures during kitchen opening hours.
This could be drawn up into a form like the one below.

Kitchen Temperature Monitoring Form for Monday 12 February				
Area to be checked	Recorded temperature	Time	Person responsible	Signature
Fridges				
Freezers				
Ovens				
Hot food				
Cold food				

By following these simple procedures employers can ensure that no food
falls within the bacterial danger zone, and provide food that is safe to eat.

In summary

■ There are five easy steps to follow when carrying out a risk assessment.
■ Separate risk assessments must be carried out for fire and COSHH.
■ Employers will provide written procedures for using equipment and
  manual handling.
■ HACCP stands for Hazard Analysis Critical Control Points.
■ Evidence of pest infestation includes gnaw marks, droppings and
  footprints.

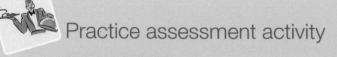

Practice assessment activity

Levels P4/D2

Demonstrate to your tutor two safe working practices in different hospitality settings. They should show:

P
1 manual handling techniques in a kitchen

2 safe handling of the correct chemical in order to clean an oven. (P4)

D Following on from the task above, assess how using safety information and safe working practices can improve the safety in these two settings. (D2)

Test your knowledge

1   What is the definition of a hazard?

2   Explain the term due diligence.

3   List the three elements of the fire triangle.

4   What is the bacterial danger zone?

5   List three items that should be in a first aid kit.

6   What does COSHH stand for?

7   What legislation has been broken if you find a nail in your sandwich?

8   Detail the benefits to employers of good health and safety practices.

9   What are the five steps of risk assessment?

10 What is the legislation associated with RIDDOR?

4 Planning and Running a Hospitality Event

Introduction

This unit enables you to be involved in planning, organising, running and reviewing a hospitality event. You will investigate all aspects of planning a variety of events before using this knowledge to plan your own event. This might include a restaurant service, an open day or maybe an event generated especially for this unit, such as a religious celebration, a barbecue or a charity dinner.

After learning about the purpose and types of promotional material, you will produce material to promote your event. Following this, you should be able to put your planning into practice and take part in running an actual event. Finally, you will design methods of reviewing the success of the event using information collected from the people involved.

How you will be assessed

Unit 4 is assessed internally so that the Centre delivering the qualifications will assess you against the criteria. On completion of the unit you should:

4.1 know the planning process for a hospitality event

4.2 be able to participate in the organisation of a hospitality event to meet customer or client requirements

4.3 be able to promote a hospitality event

4.4 be able to contribute to the running of a hospitality event to meet customer or client requirements

4.5 be able to review the success of a hospitality event.

Assessment grades

The Edexcel Assessment Grid for Unit 4 details the criteria to be met. In general, to gain a Pass (P) you are asked to produce, participate, contribute and review; to gain a Merit (M) you are also asked to design and analyse; and to gain a Distinction (D) you are also asked to review and make recommendations.

4.1 Know the planning process for a hospitality event

This section covers:

- the planning process
- hospitality events.

The planning process

Planning is the process of setting goals and targets and working out what tasks and activities you need to complete to meet those targets. Planning is the most important stage of the event process. Without it the event is unlikely to succeed.

In this section you will learn about the factors that influence the planning of a hospitality event and the process you will need to follow to plan your own event.

There are many things to consider when organising an event. We will look at these in more detail below. They include:

- the nature of the event
- location
- the target audience
- timing
- budget and resources.

Roles and responsibilities

When planning an event different members of the organising team will have different jobs and responsibilities so that, by working together, everything gets done.

It is important to create a shared, balanced workload and that each member of the team is given a role that they feel comfortable with. In section 4.2 we will look more closely at what those roles and responsibilities might be.

The nature of the event

Before you start the planning process you must consider the nature of the event – what type of event it is. This is very important as it will help you to make plans.

- Is it a conference, a party, a lunch or dinner?

- Why are you holding the event? Is it to celebrate, to inform, to teach, to reward?

- Will there be entertainment?

- How many people is it for?

Once you have decided on what type of event you are going to run, you can start to organise it. It is a good idea at this stage to write a list of all the tasks you have to complete, and to set a target date for their completion. You will also need to determine who is responsible for each task.

Here is an example of a table you could use.

Date	Activity	Progress
September	Select the event Design the event format Outline planning for the event Set the aims and objectives Confirm the budget for the event Look at suitable venues	

Date	Activity	Progress
October	Book the venue Identify and allocate roles and responsibilities of the team	

Monitoring progress

It is important that the event organisers meet regularly to check on the progress of the plans and to resolve any problems that may arise. Some guidelines for running successful meetings are as follows.

- Consider carefully what the purpose of the meeting is.
- Set out clear and precise objectives for the meeting.
- Set out a formal agenda (schedule) outlining exactly what you will be talking about in the meeting and in what order.
- Keep a written record of what was said and done. These records are called minutes.
- Set a date for the next meeting if necessary.

Location

A very important stage of the planning process is finding a suitable venue. You should ask yourself the following questions.

- Is the venue the right size for the type of activities planned and the number of people expected? It has to be large enough to accommodate everyone, but it is equally important that it's not too big as the guests may feel uncomfortable if it is.
- How much does it cost to hire the venue?
- Is it accessible, convenient and easy for the guests to get to?
- Is there enough parking for everyone?
- Does it have facilities for people with special needs, for example ramps or wide doors for wheelchair users?
- Are there facilities for cooking and food storage if needed?

Target audience

The type of event you plan, the activities, food and drink will depend on who is attending – the target audience. Throughout the planning process it is vital to bear in mind your target audience as the event must meet their needs and expectations.

Talking point

In small groups, discuss what type of event you might hold to celebrate the following occasions:

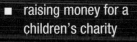

- raising money for a children's charity
- celebrating the 40th anniversary of your school or college
- promoting a range of new courses at your school or college.

■ *Make sure you consider the needs of your target audience*

Timing

You will obviously need to schedule a date and time for your event. Here are some of the things to consider.

- Are there any other events happening at the same time?
- Is your chosen venue available when you need it?
- How much time do you need to plan the event? Some venues are booked up a long time in advance.
- What is the weather likely to be at the proposed time of year?
- Is it an expensive time of year, day of the week or time of day to hire the venue?
- What time of day is most likely to suit your target audience?
- How long should the event run for?
- Is transport available at the time of day you plan to run your event?

Staffing

Staffing an event can be a problem because it is sometimes difficult to know how many guests you will have. It is important to get the right balance of staff and guests.

- Too many staff will cost too much money.
- Not enough staff will result in poor customer service.
- The right number of staff will give good customer service and meet the needs of the guests.

The planning process here involves not only working out how many staff you need, but also making sure that the right people are doing the right job.

Budget and resources

For all events, the event organiser may be given an amount of money to spend. This is called a **budget**, and it is very important that you do not spend more than the budget. There may be one overall budget or separate budgets for different resources.

Identifying resources

With your budget in mind, make a list of what you need to run your event and their cost. Resources may include:

- hire of the venue itself
- technical equipment, for example a public address (PA) system
- administration and promotional materials – posters, flyers
- stationery, for example invitations
- food and drink – or catering services
- payment for guest speakers
- transport – taxis, minibuses.

It is important when you make your list to think about the cost and availability of each item.

Constraints

A constraint is something you cannot do because of a limit or difficulty with an objective you have been set. The diagram shows some common constraints.

Key points

Important points to consider when organising an event include:

- the type of event
- the target audience
- timing
- location
- budget and resources
- staffing.

Key points

A budget is how much money is available to spend on an event. Separate budgets are often set up for specific resources such as:

- promotion and administration
- food and drink
- equipment.

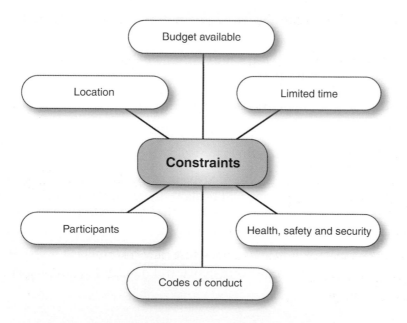

It is important to identify possible constraints in the planning stage so that you can think about how you might be able to overcome them.

Health and safety

The health and safety of everyone involved in the event – organisers, staff and participants – is of prime importance. It is important for organisers to identify any potential health and safety risks as early as possible.

One way to do this is to complete a risk assessment, as you learned in *Unit 3: Safety in Hospitality*. By carrying out a risk assessment at the planning stage you can look at possible hazards and put in place controls to avoid them or minimise their effect.

Hospitality events

For this unit you will need to organise, promote and run your own hospitality event. The list of possible events is endless, but this section gives an overview of a range of events you might consider. Hospitality events and functions that need organising can be:

- promotional
- business
- social.

These groups are just a guide as some events can belong to more than one category. For example, lunches or dinners could be promotional or business events.

Promotional events

These events give a venue or organisation the opportunity to showcase the goods and services it offers. Promotional events could include Open Evenings/Days, craft fairs and exhibitions.

Open Evenings/Days

An Open Evening or Open Day is usually held to attract more customers to a venue or organisation. For example:

- a college will want to attract new students
- a leisure club will want to attract new members
- a restaurant will want to attract new customers.

Visitors will usually be given a tour of the premises. They will expect to meet staff from the venue who will explain the services offered. There may also be an opportunity to sample the facilities, services or food the venue can offer.

As the Open Evening is all about attracting new customers, it is essential that visitors have a favourable experience and that they are impressed with what they see.

Activity

In small groups, make a list of activities that your local leisure centre could offer if it were to put on an Open Day.

Business events

Companies often hold events, either at their own premises or at outside venues. They might involve a few staff or the whole organisation, for example for their annual general meeting. Reason why businesses might organise hospitality events include:

■ to promote their business and attract new customers

■ conferences, meetings and seminars

■ exhibitions

■ training sessions

■ formal lunches/dinners for governors

■ social events for staff.

Governors' reception

Many organisations have a Board of Governors, which is responsible for ensuring the effective management of the organisation and its development. Every school, college, university and hospital has a Board of Governors, which holds regular meetings. Occasionally the governors will attend a reception, which is an opportunity for them to meet socially and for the organisation to thank them for their help. Usually food and drink are served and part of the evening is set aside for speeches.

Social events

Social events can take many forms, and the most important thing to consider is whether it is the right event for your guests (see section 4.1). For example, you will need to consider the ages, likes and dislikes of your guests when deciding whether to have:

■ a formal sit-down meal or a buffet

■ a disco or a string quartet

■ party games or no party games.

Social events can include:

■ parties

■ discos

■ sports events

■ lunches/dinners

■ receptions

■ charity fundraisers.

Parties

A party is intended primarily for celebration and could be organised for lots of reasons and take many forms, for example:

- wedding reception – this could be a buffet in a local pub or a formal sit-down meal in a large hotel
- birthday/anniversary – perhaps a children's party with entertainer
- religious festival – this might need special food or decorations.

Barbecues

A barbecue is a very popular type of party held in the summer when there is less risk of a downpour. Many organisations, business and clubs, such as scouts and guides, hold barbecues so that their members can get together and have fun.

The main considerations for anyone holding a barbecue are:

- that the equipment available can cook the amount of food needed
- that the organisers have a thorough knowledge of how long everything takes to cook so that food is ready on time and does not pose a health risk. See Unit 3.2 for detailed information on food safety.
- that there is a contingency plan in case it rains. See section 4.2 for more on contingency plans.

Charity fundraisers

Organising an event can be a great way to raise money for charity. Whether you are planning a sporting event, a picnic, a fashion show or a meal you will be taking part in a worthwhile activity which can bring you a lot of personal satisfaction.

When organising a charity event you need to:

- consider the target market.
- decide how the money will be raised – through ticket sales, a raffle or an auction. See if local companies will support you by donating prizes.
- see whether the charity you are supporting will supply publicity material for the event.
- make it clear to your customers what proportion of the money they are spending is being donated to the chosen charity.

Activity

You can make a lunch or dinner much more interesting and fun by adding a theme. There are lots of different ways that you can theme your event. The main considerations in all cases though are choosing the right food, drink, decorations and clothes to reflect the theme. Here are some suggestions:

- a historical period
- the food and culture of a different nationality
- a film or television programme
- promoting foods such as organic products, chocolate or local produce
- a sporting event.

Choose a theme for a dinner party and list all the things you might need.

In summary

- When organising an event it is important to make a plan.
- You must always consider the needs and expectations of the guests when deciding on the type of event to organise.
- The plan will identify the tasks and timing involved in running the event.
- The planning process must be reviewed regularly.
- It is important to have a contingency plan in place in case of problems.

Practice assessment activity

Level P1

You have been asked to plan a talent show for a group of children in year six of the local junior school. The show will be performed in front of the whole school the day before it breaks up for the Christmas holidays.

P Outline the planning process that you will need to follow to organise the event. (P1)

4.2 Be able to participate in the organisation of a hospitality event to meet customer or client requirements

This section covers:

■ client or customer requirements

■ resources

■ roles and responsibilities

■ contingencies.

For all events, whether large or small, the secret to success is in the planning. This section will help you to plan your own event so that all the necessary jobs are carried out on time and you can keep track of your progress.

Client or customer requirements

The requirements of clients or customers will vary enormously according to the type of event that you are running. It is the organiser's responsibility in the planning stage to ensure that the customers' needs are identified and that the event is structured to meet those needs.

Objectives

Every event will have a purpose, and once the purpose has been established the organisers can begin to plan. One of the first stages of planning an event is to set out the objectives of the event. Objectives state what the organisation aims to achieve, how success will be measured and the timescales for achievement. Planning is needed to meet those objectives.

When setting objectives they must be **SMART**:

■ **Specific** – The objective has to be written so that everyone involved in meeting it understands what they need to do. For example, the objective 'To raise money' is not specific and doesn't tell people how much money they need to raise.

■ **Measurable** – You need to be able to work out whether or not the objective is being met and to what extent. For example, if your event is a college Open Evening and you are trying to recruit students on to a particular course, your objective should state how many people you want to recruit.

■ **Achievable** – Do not be tempted to be overambitious and set yourself targets that you cannot achieve. If it becomes obvious that you will not achieve your objectives the event team will become demotivated and disheartened.

■ **Realistic** – Make sure you have adequate resources to meet your objectives. This could include staff, equipment, money or premises.

■ **Time-bound** – You need to state when you will achieve the objectives by.

Resources

Every event needs resources to run, and it is the responsibility of the events team to organise these resources. You must make sure that the resources meet the needs of the customer and do not cost too much money. Resources cover items such as:

■ venue

■ budget

■ transport

■ staffing

■ equipment

■ catering.

You will need to deal with a lot of different people when organising the resources for your event and it is important to ensure that:

■ everyone understands your exact requirements

■ everyone is reliable.

Venue

One of the most important resources is the venue for the event. In section 1 of this unit you learned about the considerations that must be made when choosing a suitable venue.

Before you make a decision you should visit possible venues to make sure they meet your needs. Take with you a list of the information you need to find out and the questions you need to ask.

On the visit:

■ Ask to see the room(s) you will be using.

■ Check the public areas, parking and access to the building.

■ Try to get a feel for how friendly and welcoming the staff are.

Activity

This is a whole group exercise. Once you have chosen an event to organise, decide what the objectives of your event are.

Key points

Objectives must be SMART:

■ **s**pecific

■ **m**easurable

■ **a**chievable

■ **r**ealistic

■ **t**ime-bound.

- Make sure you know how much the venue will cost to hire and what will be included in the price, for example furniture.
- Check that the venue has the correct licenses and insurance for your event. (You will probably need to seek help from your tutor with this.)

Once you have decided on the venue you will need to make a formal booking. At this stage you will be entering into a contract, so you must make sure that you understand exactly what you are committing yourselves to.

Budget

At the early stages of planning you should establish how much money you have to spend and what this needs to be spent on. You need to create a budget and stick to it (see page 113).

Shop around to make sure you are getting a good deal when buying/hiring equipment or materials. However, the cheapest may not be the best deal; you want quality as well as good value.

Remember to keep a check on what you are spending so that you do not go over budget. It is essential to keep all receipts and invoices relating to the event.

You could try to find some kind of sponsorship for the event to help you raise or save money.

■ *It is important to create a budget and stick to it*

Transport

It is important to consider how people will get to the event.

- How you will transport your equipment?
- How will the customers or guests get there?

It may add to the costs considerably if you have to hire taxis or minibuses. You therefore need to check bus and train routes and the availability of parking at the venue.

Staffing

As you have have learned in section 4.1, the success of an event partly depends on having enough trained and competent staff to meet the needs and expectations of the customers. You will need to work out:

- what the jobs are
- what skills are needed for those jobs
- how many people you will need to do the jobs.

Before the event you need to draw up a staff schedule. Everyone involved should know what they are doing and who their points of contact are in the lead-up to and during the event. Keeping staff informed is very important to the success of the event.

Equipment

Every event needs a variety of equipment and materials such as:

- stationery for advertising
- catering equipment for food and drink
- audio-visual equipment
- prizes
- decorations to suit a theme.

Identifying exactly what you need, how to get it and how much it costs is essential. The equipment needed will obviously depend on the type of event, but you must consider:

- how easy it is to get
- how much it costs
- how easy it is to use
- what equipment is already available at the venue
- what you need to buy or hire
- what you can borrow.

You may be surprised at how willing local businesses are to support or sponsor your event. They might provide food, drink, prizes or decorations.

Catering

You must decide what kind of food and drink is best suited to your event and think carefully about how to cater the event, for example as a fork buffet, finger buffet or a sit-down meal.

- How much money do you have to spend?
- What are your customers' preferences?
- What equipment is available at the venue for catering?
- What skills do you have as a team?
- Will you or the venue provide the food and drink? Some venues will not let you bring your own food.
- How will the food be served? For example, plated, a buffet or silver service?
- How much time will the guests have for eating and drinking?
- Is the venue licensed to serve alcohol?

Key points

- Set a budget for your event and stick to it.
- Visit and check potential venues carefully before making a decision.
- Make sure you have enough trained and competent staff to meet customer needs and expectations.

■ *Local businesses are often willing to support events*

Over to you

Write a letter to send to local businesses asking them to donate a raffle prize for your event.

- Are there any food safety regulations to be considered?

- Are there any special dietary requirements to consider, such as allergies, cultural or religious requirements and dietary restrictions?

- Seasonal or regional factors. For example, which items are in season? Can you use popular food items from the region or location of the event?

You will learn more about menu planning in *Unit 7: Basic Culinary Skills*.

Roles and responsibilities

Every member of the event organising team will have their own role, which will come with specific responsibilities. Examples of the different roles and responsibilities are:

- coordinator – organises other members of the team

- marketing – to advertise and promote the event

- finance – keeping control of the budget and spending

- administration – important for correspondence and keeping paperwork in order

- food and beverage – responsible for catering

- health and safety – making sure all relevant legislation is followed.

Teamwork

A team approach is essential if the event is to be a success. It is important to make the best use of the skills of team members. When a team is working well all its members will be clear about what they are trying to achieve.

Over to you

Using the list above, choose roles for each member of your event team and list the responsibilities that go with each role. Bear in mind the individual skills of your team when allocating roles.

■ *Good teamwork is important for a successful event*

Meetings and communication

You have already learned how important it is to hold regular meetings to:

- monitor progress
- evaluate each person's input
- make changes to plans if necessary.

When organising an event you should schedule a series of meetings and put the dates and places in your diaries. Make sure the whole team knows about the meetings:

- what they are for
- when they are taking place
- where they are taking place.

Customers and potential guests also need to be kept informed about the event. This will be looked at in section 3 of this unit.

Activity

Organise, conduct and record a series of formal meetings for your event.

Health and safety

The importance of ensuring the health and safety of your guests was discussed in section 1 of this unit. Remember that you must:

- identify the risks of different elements of your event
- have a plan to minimise those risks and deal with problems if they occur.

Check the legal requirements (legislation) related to what you are doing, for example:

- insurance
- food safety
- fire regulations.

Over to you

Complete a risk assessment for your event. Look back at Unit 3.4 for guidance if necessary.

Contingencies

A plan is a guide, a sequence of tasks and activities to be completed. It is not set in stone and so it will need to be monitored and changed as necessary. However well your planning is going, you must always be prepared for unforeseen situations. Therefore, as well as planning what you need to do to run a successful event, you must also make plans for what you will do if something goes wrong. These are called **contingency plans**. You will need to think about such things such as:

- what to do if it rains during a barbecue or fete
- coping with accidents or emergencies
- changes to numbers of people attending
- how you will cope with staff shortages

- what to do if you cannot get hold of certain equipment.

It is important to have written contingency plans in place for each part of your event so that you are ready to deal with any problems that arise. Make sure that everyone knows the contingency plans.

Bad weather

If you're holding an outdoor event, such as a barbecue, you must decide what to do if it rains. If you have to postpone the event think about ways of letting people know as soon as possible what has happened.

Accidents and emergencies

Your risk assessment should have identified potential accidents that are most likely to occur and measures should be in place to prevent them.

Unfortunately accidents cannot be completely prevented and do still happen despite safeguards. You will therefore need someone responsible for first aid and for recording accidents so that the causes can be investigated. Also make sure everyone knows what to do in case of fire.

■ *The weather need not ruin everyone's enjoyment*

Changes in numbers

If the number of guests changes at the last moment you may need to alter your plans to deal with this. You may not be able to run the activities you had planned.

Over to you

What contingency plans have you made for your event? Who needs to know what they are?

Staff shortages

A staff member may be ill or absent for other reasons on the day of the event. If this is the case you may need to reallocate their duties. It is a good idea to have two or three volunteers to call on in case of staff shortages.

Equipment not arriving

You should arrange for equipment to arrive in good time for the event. If it is delayed for any reason, make sure you have telephone numbers with you so that you can find out what has happened to it.

In summary

- It is very important to set clear, SMART objectives for your event.
- It is essential to set a budget for the event.
- It is the responsibility of the event team to organise the resources within budget.
- The venue must be suitable for the event, accessible and within budget.
- Event organisers should know their roles and responsibilities and work as a team.
- A meetings schedule should be planned and monitored.
- It is important to have contingency plans in place to deal with unexpected situations.

Practice assessment activity

Levels P2/M1

As a group, decide on the event you will run for this unit.

P Take part in planning the event. Explain the roles and responsibilities you undertook and support this with evidence. (P2)

M Explain the process you used, as a group, to plan the event. Describe the contingencies that you put in place to deal with deviations from your plan. (M1)

4.3 Be able to promote a hospitality event

This section covers:

- purpose of promotion
- promotion.

Purpose of promotion

With the target audience defined, objectives set and plans well under way, details of the event now need to be communicated to your customers. The purpose of promoting an event is to make people aware of it, to inform them about it.

Raising awareness

In order to raise awareness you need to answer the following questions.

- Does the promotional literature reflect the 'image' the target customer group is looking for?
- Have advertisements been placed where the target customer groups will see them?
- Does the material give a clear message about the purpose of the event?
- Is there enough information about the event within the material to allow people to decide if they want to take part or attend?

Informing customers

It is important to give customers detailed and clear information about the event. When deciding on the message you want to give out, think about:

- what you want to say
- to whom you want to say it.

Anyone attending the event will need to know:

- the date and time of the event
- where it will take place
- how much it costs – this could include the ticket price, any extra charges for activities or for refreshments
- what food and drink will be available
- the purpose of the event – to have fun, raise money or to celebrate
- what will be happening at the event – any entertainment or activities.

This information could be given to the target customers in stages. For example, the date, time, location and theme of the event could appear on a poster or in advertisement announcing that the event is going to happen. Further details, such as the food available and itinerary, could be communicated by means of an information or delegate pack given out at the event itself.

Promotion

By promoting an event you are trying to publicise it and make it appealing to your target audience. You will need to consider factors such as:

- advertising – how customers will be informed about the event
- timing – when the promotion will begin and end
- cost – how much will be spent on it.

The trick is to adapt your promotional material to appeal to your target market.

Timing

The timing of your promotional campaign is very important. You need to decide when to start promoting the event and the time frame for each promotional activity.

- If you start to promote the event too soon people may lose interest.
- If you leave it too late, they may have booked something else.

Cost

As with other aspects of planning the event, a budget must be set to cover the cost of promoting it. The amount of money you have to spend will affect what method of promotion you can use. For example, you could not afford television advertising on a small budget.

Advertising

How you advertise your event will depend on things such as cost, the type of event, the venue and the target audience. However, all promotional material must be effective to attract customers.

Impact and design

Promotional material should have immediate impact because the customer will not want to read too much before finding the main message. When designing your promotional material you should follow the **AIDA** model.

Attention – The material must be placed where it will be most visible and must attract the attention of the reader. This might be achieved through the colours, pictures or words used.

■ Make sure your promotional material has all the information needed

Interest – The material must create interest in the event and encourage the reader to find out more.

Desire – The material must make the reader want to come along. You need to make the customer feel that the event is too good to miss.

Action – If people are ready to come to your event, they need to know what to do about it. Information such as 'Tickets are on sale NOW at main reception' should be clear.

Materials and methods

The materials you use and the methods of promotion are also important. For example, you might decide to:

- put an advert in your local paper

- design posters to place around your school or college

- post flyers to local houses.

Depending on your budget, you might even be able to run an advertisement on your local television channel or local radio station.

The materials and methods that you use will depend on:

- the target customer group

- the message to be communicated

- the budget available.

Using newspapers, national television or radio can be very expensive, but some local radio and television stations might promote your event free if you give them a **press release**. A press release is produced by organisations to provide the press with a public interest story or information about their products. It is usually written in the form of a newspaper story. If your event aims to raise money for charity it is very likely that the local media will support it.

You may be able to use other free services such as:

- your local council website

- local radio stations, which often have regular 'What's on' bulletins

- listings websites – for example, those that list family events, leisure activities or just local events

- the 'What's on' section in your local newspaper.

Activity

Your local drama school, Fantasy Land Drama School, has asked you to design a campaign to promote a drama workshop. Prospective students will be invited to spend a day at the school to get a taste of the kind of things drama students do. The budget is small.

The school wants to know the best promotional method to use and wants a flyer for the event.

In summary

- Promotional material must make sure an event appeals to the target audience.
- Timing of the promotion is very important – too early and people may lose interest; too late and they may have made other arrangements.
- Use the principles of AIDA when designing promotional material.
- Local media advertising can be very expensive but if you are running a fundraising event your local newspaper may not charge.
- Research places where you can advertise your event for free.

Practice assessment activity

Levels P3/M2

Plan a promotional campaign for your chosen event.

Provide:

- a time frame for the campaign
- details of costs

P
- a copy of promotional materials. (P3)

M Analyse the impact of your campaign. (M2)

4.4 Be able to contribute to the running of a hospitality event to meet customer or client requirements

This section covers:

■ setting up
■ during the event
■ clearing away.

Setting up

It is vital that the organising team is thorough when setting up the event because it will save a lot of work when the event is up and running. Walk through your event before any of the guests arrive and make sure you brief your team well. Some points that should be considered include:

■ signs
■ rooms
■ equipment.

Signs

It is really off-putting for customers and guests to arrive at an event only to find that they have no idea where to go. It is therefore very important to make sure that there are adequate signs to guide them to:

■ meeting rooms
■ toilets
■ the restaurant or refreshment service area.

Rooms

The rooms that are being used for the event will have to be fully prepared so that they are ready for use in good time of guests arriving. The furniture should be laid out with the customers' comfort in mind. You should consider the following.

■ *Time spent setting up an event can help things run smoothly*

- Is there enough room for customers and staff to move around comfortably?
- Are there enough seats?
- If they're expected to write, are there tables?
- Does the decor reflect the theme of the event?
- Is there adequate ventilation and lighting?

Food and drink service areas

Make sure you have done as much as possible to prepare for the event with regard to the service of food and drink. The preparation of the refreshment areas is called mise-en-place (preparation for service). Mise-en-place entails:

- making a plan for the event staff to show where they will be working
- going over the menu with staff
- ensuring that all equipment needed is available and clean.

Equipment

You may be confident that you have all the equipment you need because you sorted it out during the planning stage. You may be getting equipment from many different sources, and when you are busy it is easy to forget things. It is therefore useful to prepare a checklist of what you will need on the day of your event. This will include equipment for:

- entertainment
- food and drink service – crockery, cutlery and glasses.

At least one member of the event team should be responsible for ensuring that there are enough glasses, crockery and cutlery for the event, that they are clean and that they are where they should be.

During the event

If you have followed the advice given so far in this unit, everyone should know what their duties are on the day of the event. However, you still need to consider how you can make sure things run smoothly at this stage. One of the keys to the success of the event is effective communication. It is very important for the event team to communicate with each other throughout the event.

Food and drink service

If you have completed your mise-en-place and the event team know their responsibilities, the service of food and drinks should be relatively trouble-free.

Over to you

List the mise-en-place that would need to be completed to prepare for a finger buffet for 100 guests.

Over to you

Design an equipment checklist for your event.

In *Unit 8: Serving Food and Drink* you can learn all about the service of food and drink in general. However, when catering for an event there are special issues to consider.

■ It may be necessary to announce to the customers that the food and drinks are about to be served.

■ If a buffet is provided for large numbers, tables will need to be sent up one at a time to avoid long queues.

■ Communication with the chef is vital as speeches and activities may mean the food has to be delayed.

Meeting customer requests

It is a good idea to get as much information about your customers as possible before the event with regard to any special requests, such as special diets. However, it is highly likely that guests will have individual requests during the event. For example:

■ they might not like the food or drink being served

■ they might need a piece of equipment that they hadn't anticipated

■ they might simply want you to call them a taxi.

Even though these requests may come at a time when you are very busy, you must remember that customer satisfaction is vital if your event is to be considered a success.

Finally, remember your event team and make sure you thank everyone who made a contribution to the event.

Unexpected occurrences

In section 2 of this unit you learned about the importance of contingency planning to enable you to cope with unexpected situations.

However, *planning* for the unexpected and *dealing* with the unexpected are two different things. If something unexpected does happen it is vital that you stay calm and do not let the customers think that anything as gone wrong.

Clearing away

Clearing away or tidying up is likely to be the last thing that you want to do once your event is over, but it is just as important a part of successfully running your event as all the other tasks that you complete.

Waste disposal

The hygienic and safe disposal of waste is vital. If you are hiring a venue for your event you should check out the procedure for disposing of waste with one of the venue staff. If your event is likely to generate a lot of litter, it might be wise to clear up as you go.

Talking point

How can you ensure you provide customer service excellence at your event?

Activity

Draw up an order of work for your event.

Glasses, crockery and cutlery

The person with overall responsibility for this area (see Equipment, above) should make sure all these items are washed up, counted and returned to where they came from.

Surplus food and drink

If you have catered for your event yourself, it may be your responsibility to deal with any food and drink which is left over. Although it may be tempting to take the food home, you must ensure that you have considered whether it is safe to do so.

If food is to be returned to your college or school kitchen you must follow the food hygiene regulations you learned about in *Unit 3: Safety in Hospitality*.

Rooms, signs and equipment

If you are using a room in your own venue, you must ensure that it is left in a clean and tidy state. If you have hired a venue it is a good idea to check who is responsible for cleaning and tidying the rooms you have used.

- Equipment must be put away carefully and returned to the correct place. You must also make sure it is stored securely.
- Signs put up especially for the event should be taken down.
- The room should be tidied and vacuumed.

In summary

- If the organising team is thorough when setting up the event it will save a lot of work when the event is up and running.
- The team should be fully briefed before the event so that everyone is aware of their roles and responsibilities.
- Effective communication is one of the keys to a successful event.
- Clearing down or tidying up is as important to successfully running an event as all the other tasks.

Practice assessment activity

Level P4

P Participate in the running of your event. Explain what roles and tasks you undertook at the event and support them with evidence. (P4)

4.5 Be able to review the success of a hospitality event

This section covers:

- reviewing an event
- assessing success.

Reviewing an event

When an event is over it is necessary to review its success. This usually means determining to what extent the objectives have been met.

Although the review mainly comes after the event, you need to decide what you are reviewing and how at the planning stage. This is one of the reasons why it is so important to set SMART objectives. How can you measure if the event has been successful if you haven't decided beforehand what will make it a success?

The way in which you will review the success of the event also needs to be identified. It can be both formal and informal and should include feedback from a range of people: the customers, the staff and the organising team.

One of the best ways to make sure you have learned something from planning, organising and running an event is to evaluate your own performance. This can be a difficult process because you need to be very honest with yourself.

This section looks at possible sources of feedback and the documentation used to record that feedback. Sources of feedback include:

- you and your team
- your tutor
- the customer.

Documentation might include:

- questionnaires
- witness statements
- observation records.

Sources of feedback

The customer
The customer is probably the most important person to get feedback from because you have run the event for them. If you do not give them the

opportunity to feedback their opinions you will never really know if they are happy, satisfied or dissatisfied.

As you learned in *Unit 2: Customer Relations in Hospitality*, customer feedback can be formal or informal (see page 52).

You can get informal feedback simply by asking the customer if they have had a good time or by observing their behaviour.

Formal feedback can be gathered by a variety of means, such as questionnaires, comment cards and telephone surveys. Formal feedback should always be recorded, whether it comes from the customer, your tutor or from you.

■ *You can get feedback from a customer simply by observing their behaviour*

You and your team

The event team is obviously in a very good position to review the success of the event – both individually and as a team. You are the one best placed to answer the questions that need answering if you are to learn from your experiences. These questions might be:

- What objectives were met?
- Why were they met?
- How were they met?
- Who was responsible for meeting them?
- What objectives were not met?
- Why weren't they met?

In order to answer these questions you need to be honest and fair and to allow everyone involved in the team to give their opinions.

Your tutor

Your tutor will also be in an excellent position to review your event because:

- they know what you were hoping to achieve
- they will be reviewing your progress throughout the planning process.

Despite the fact that the success of the event can only be reviewed once it is over, it is wise to keep your tutor informed of decisions you are making throughout the planning process. This is because they will be able to make sure that you are on target to meet your objectives.

Although your tutor will have their own criteria when reviewing the success of the event and your performance as a team, you might like to produce your own questionnaire for them to use.

Talking point

As a group, discuss the advantages and disadvantages of gathering formal and informal customer feedback.

Over to you

As a team decide how you are going to evaluate your own performance. Draw up a form to record your findings.

Feedback Questionnaire

Event/Course Title:
National Association of Hotel Concierges Forrum 2008

Trainer/Host:
Mary Rees

Date:
21 April 2008

Venue:
Conference Room

We are always trying to improve the forum, events and courses we offer and would value your feedback to help us identify any improvements.

Please mark in the appropriate box your view of each of the following statements. Any additional comments would be welcome.

Question	Strongly agree	Agree	Neither agree or disagree	Disagree	Strongly disagree
1. The event was relevant to my needs	☐	☐	☐	☐	☐
2. I found the forum interesting	☐	☐	☐	☐	☐
3. The presentation was informative and applicable to my needs	☐	☐	☐	☐	☐
4. The Hospitality & Catering presentation was beneficial	☐	☐	☐	☐	☐
5. The information Technology presentation was appropriate	☐	☐	☐	☐	☐
6. The event was the correct length	☐	☐	☐	☐	☐
7. The event was the correct pace	☐	☐	☐	☐	☐
8. The room was comfortable (e.g. lighting, temperature, surround)	☐	☐	☐	☐	☐
9. The facilities were accessible and purposeful (e.g. car park, toilet facilities, lift)	☐	☐	☐	☐	☐
10. I enjoyed the forum and would recommend it to others	☐	☐	☐	☐	☐

Comments: Please include any topics and/or future courses you would like to hear about at the next forum

....

■ *A sample of a questionnaire*

Documentation

Questionnaires

One of the most common ways of gathering customer feedback is by using questionnaires. These could be sent out as part of a marketing follow-up or given out at the event. They should be designed to obtain:

■ factual information that can be turned into statistics

■ the opinions and feelings of the customer.

An example of a questionnaire is given above. It could be introduced as follows:

'We would like to thank you for attending our event and we hope you have had an enjoyable evening. To help us in the organisation of future events, it would be extremely helpful if you would complete this form and return it to one of the event team before you leave.'

Comment cards

Comment cards are a very popular way of gaining feedback from customers in the hospitality industry. They are short questionnaires, often placed with products purchased at a hotel or between the salt and pepper pots at a restaurant.

Witness Statement		
Learner name:		
Qualification:		
Venue and Time:		
Description of activity undertaken (please be as specific as possible)		
Assessment criteria (to which the activity provides evidence)		
How the activity meets the requirements of the assessment and grading criteria, including how and where the activity took place		
Witness name:	Job role:	
Witness signature:		Date:
Learner name:		
Learner signature:		Date:
Assessor name:		
Assessor signature:		Date:

■ *A sample of a witness statement*

Witness statements and observation records

These can be completed by someone who is able to comment on your participation in the event first hand. The statement or observation record should include:

- the name of the person being assessed
- the date, time and venue of the activity carried out
- a description of the activities performed
- the name of the person writing the witness statement
- the signature and job title of the witness or observer.

Assessing success

Once you have gathered your feedback you can start evaluating it to see if the event you organised has been a success. There are three sets of criteria against which you can assess the success of your event:

- against objectives
- against budget
- deviation from plans.

Against objectives

Earlier in this unit you learned how important it is to set objectives for your event. You also learned that the objectives should be measurable. Once the event is over, you can make sure you have met these objectives. You can determine your successes and identify what could be done better next time.

Having reviewed your objectives you can consider whether you:

- charged the right price
- targeted the right market
- included the right activities
- promoted your event effectively
- served suitable food and drink
- held the event in the right venue, at the right time
- made the right amount of profit.

Answering these questions honestly will help you to learn. You should recognise what you have done well and congratulate yourself. But you should also recognise the things that did not go so well and think about how you could improve them next time.

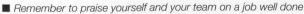

■ Remember to praise yourself and your team on a job well done

Against budget

It is all very well to pat each other on the back if your customers are happy and you feel that you have met your objectives. But before you start celebrating your success, you must make sure that you have not spent too much money.

In the planning stage of your event you should have determined how much money you had to spend (a budget) and what you were going to spend it on. It is too late to review your spending once the event is over. This is something you should have done throughout the planning process – every time you had a meeting.

However, your budget might have been worked out on the basis that your event would generate some money, for example through:

- ticket sales
- food and beverage sales
- raffle tickets
- customers paying for activities and competitions.

In this case you will not know if you have overspent until the event is over.

Deviation from plans

When you first started to plan for your event, you should have written a list of tasks that you needed to do, with target dates for their completion. However, you learned earlier in this unit that, for many reasons, you may need to make changes to your plans.

Even though it is acceptable to make changes, you will need to review why the changes were made.

- Were you too ambitious and set your sights too high?
- Did some members of the team not pull their weight?
- Did you discover that some things cost a lot more than you thought they would?
- Did you find that you were not selling any tickets?

There are endless reasons why your plans might have needed to be changed. The important thing to consider is whether the changes were due to weaknesses in your team's work or whether they were caused by events beyond your control.

If changes were made because of weaknesses in your original plans, do not feel too downhearted. Instead, you should congratulate yourself on recognising those weaknesses and discuss how you might overcome them if you were to run an event again.

In summary

- After an event you need to review its success to determine how far its objectives have been met.
- You can gather feedback from the customer, your tutor, yourself or others in your group.
- It is important to devise a means of recording feedback such as questionnaires, witness statements or observation records.
- The success of your event will depend on you meeting the objectives, staying within budget and dealing successfully with deviations to your plans.

Practice assessment activity

P5, M3, D1, D2

P Design and use at least three different methods to review your event. (P5)

M Use the feedback you have gathered to analyse the success of your event. (M3)

D Review the planning and organisation of the event, including your own role, and make recommendations on how these could be improved. (D1)

D Make recommendations for improving the success of your event based on feedback you have collected, including the success of the promotional materials used. (D2)

Test your knowledge

1. List four things you must consider when choosing a venue for an event.
2. What is a contingency plan?
3. Why is it important to set objectives for your event?
4. Identify three risks of holding a summer barbecue for a group of college students.
5. What does AIDA stand for?
6. Identify three ways of promoting your event.
7. What is mise-en-place?
8. Identify three ways of reviewing your event.
9. Name two ways you can show you participated effectively in the planning, organisation and running of your event.
10. Describe how you can determine if your event was a success.

5 Healthy Lifestyles

Introduction

There is a lively interest in healthy lifestyles at present, with programmes appearing on television and articles in the press with particular emphasis on healthy eating. In 2004 the government published a White Paper on public health, and few of us could have missed the debate started by chef Jamie Oliver's programmes about school dinners.

This unit looks at the idea of a healthy lifestyle, including diet, exercise and fitness, together with the positive and negative influences affecting a person's choice of lifestyle. As people involved in the hospitality industry we can make a positive contribution to a healthy lifestyle of others by menu planning which concentrates on healthy aspects for different types of people.

The hospitality organisations we work for can make a positive contribution to healthy lifestyles and also benefit from the changes made. Working through the unit will also help you make choices about your own lifestyle; you could gain skills and be healthier.

How you will be assessed

Unit 5 is assessed internally, so the Centre delivering the qualification will assess you against the criteria. On completion of this unit you should:

5.1   understand the concept of a healthy lifestyle

5.2   know the influences that affect healthy lifestyles

5.3   be able to plan a menu that contributes to a healthy lifestyle

5.4   understand how hospitality organisations can make a positive contribution to healthy lifestyles.

Assessment grades

The Edexcel Assessment Grid for Unit 5 details the criteria to be met. In general, to gain a Pass (P) you are asked to describe, identify, outline and design; to gain a Merit (M) you are also asked to compare, explain and analyse; and to gain a Distinction (D) you are also asked to assess and review.

5.1 Understand the concept of a healthy lifestyle

This section covers:

■ a healthy lifestyle.

A healthy lifestyle

A varied diet

Diet is all that we eat and drink. Most people build up a habit of what and when they eat. It is said that 'We are what we eat'.

Eating a variety of foods should give us all the nutrition that our bodies need. Food for a healthy lifestyle should be chosen from the five food groups. These are shown later in the unit.

Eating too much of any one food is not healthy. For instance we all know carrots are good for us, but a diet of only carrots would leave us lacking in other substances we need to be healthy. Foods sometimes need to be eaten together for the body to be able to use them effectively. Eating a variety of foods is the best way to achieve this.

Healthy weight

A **calorie** is a unit of energy in food. If we eat more calories than we spend in effort the extra ones are stored in the body as fat.

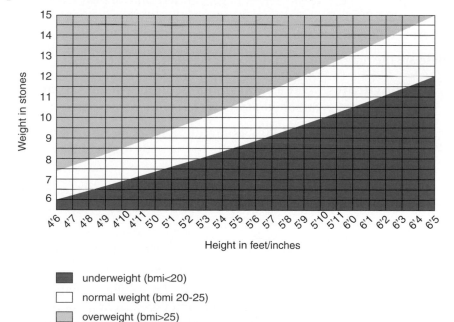

underweight (bmi<20)

normal weight (bmi 20-25)

overweight (bmi>25)

■ *Charts like this can help you work out your correct weight*

Over to you

Use the chart to check your own weight

Weight has become a big issue in the UK over the past few years with 23 per cent of men and almost 25 per cent of women now classed as clinically **obese**. There is a national debate about the obesity explosion as more of the population becomes obese and the problems this will cause for the National Health Service (NHS).

We all need to be aware of what the healthy range of weight for our height should be. For more on weight guidelines see section 5.2.

Regular meals

Part of a healthy lifestyle is eating regular meals. If we do eat regularly we are more likely to think about what we are eating and its content. Also our energy levels will be more constant during the day if we eat regularly.

Regular meals mean:

- eating enough food for the stomach to feel comfortable three or four times a day
- *not* missing breakfast, snacking during the day and having a huge evening meal.

Eating breakfast is a habit that people need to develop as it kick-starts the day, giving the body energy to work with after a night's sleep. Breakfast should be followed by a meal at lunchtime and another one in the evening.

Nutrition

Our bodies need to gain a certain amount of nutrients or nourishment from our diets. These nutrients fall into different classes. The amount we need depends on factors such as our age, gender, state of health and how active we are. Each class of nutrient gives the body what it needs to perform certain functions.

These are the main classes of nutrients and their uses in the body.

- **Carbohydrates:** There are two groups of carbohydrates – sugars and starches (complex carbohydrates) – which are a major source of energy.
- **Fibre** (NSP – non starchy polysaccharides): There are two types of fibre, soluble and insoluble, which help the body digest and absorb food.
- **Fats:** There are two main types of fats, saturated and unsaturated; they give the body energy, prevent heat loss and aid the absorption of fat-soluble vitamins.
- **Protein:** Made from chains of amino acids, this is essential for the growth, repair and replacement of body tissue.
- **Vitamins:** There are two types of vitamin: fat-soluble vitamins (A, D, E, K) and water-soluble vitamins (B, C). They are essential for the release of energy from foods, fighting infection, the formation of new cells and promoting healthy bones and teeth.

Activity

Keep a food journal for a week. Write down what and when you eat and drink each day. Do you eat a variety of foods on a regular basis? Do you eat a lot of snacks? Discuss this in your group.

- **Minerals:** These are part of the body's structure and they help regulate body fluids.
- **Water:** Although not a nutrient, water is essential for the body to function.

These nutrients, together with some of the foods that contain them, can be found in the five major food groups shown in the table.

The five food groups and their main nutrients

Food group	Foods included	Main nutrients
1 Cereals, pulses, potatoes	Bread, pasta, couscous, rice, oats, polenta, wholegrains, breakfast cereals, yams, potatoes, sweet potatoes	Complex carbohydrates, dietary fibre, calcium, iron, B vitamins
2 Fruit, vegetables	Fresh, frozen and canned fruit and vegetables, dried fruit, vegetables, fruit juices	Vitamin C and K, B vitamins, calcium, magnesium, potassium, dietary fibre
3 Dairy foods (not butter and cream)	Milk, cheese, yoghurt, fromage frais	Protein, fats, vitamins A and D, B vitamins, calcium, magnesium
4 Protein foods: Meat, poultry Fish Eggs, pulses, nuts	Meat products – salami, bacon, sausages Fresh, frozen and canned fish Fresh, canned or dried beans, chickpeas, lentils	Protein, fats, complex carbohydrates, B vitamins, vitamin D (eggs), vitamin E, iron, zinc, magnesium
5 Fats and sugary foods	Butter, lard, margarine, ghee, other spreading fats, cream, chips, oil-based dressings and mayonnaise, pastry, biscuits, cakes, chocolate, fried foods, ice cream, jam, sugar, sweets, pickles, soft drinks	Fats, sugar, vitamin A, E and D

 Over to you

In a group, using the table of five food groups and your food diaries discuss whether your weekly diet contains all the classes of nutrients. Consider the following points:

- What is your diet lacking?
- What are you eating too much of?
- How might your diet affect your health and lifestyle?
- How might your diet affect you in the future?

Exercise and fitness

A healthy lifestyle is not only about diet and nutrition; the role played by exercise in keeping us fit is important as well. Staying physically fit is a vital part of a healthy lifestyle. It is recommended that we all do 30 minutes of exercise three times a week. You will find more information about the role of exercise in the next section.

Lifestyle choices

Smoking

Smoking is linked as a risk factor in illnesses such as cancer, asthma and heart and lung disease. Smoking can also cause red eyes and dry wrinkled skin. This can make smokers look older than they are.

Smoking makes the body less efficient at absorbing nutrients such as vitamins and minerals, so a smoker needs to eat more food in order to get the necessary amounts. However, as smoking also depresses the appetite the smoker is actually likely to eat fewer nutrients.

A Bill banning smoking in enclosed public spaces came into force in England on 1 July 2007, following similar bans in other parts of the UK.

Alcohol

We are recommended to drink alcohol in moderation. It can help reduce stress and blood pressure, and a daily glass of wine is often recommended to the elderly. While a little may be good for you, too much can cause major problems.

■ *Smoking is increasingly seen as antisocial*

The Health Education Authority (HEA) guidelines for over-18s are:

- 21 units of alcohol per week for women at the most
- 28 units of alcohol per week for men at the most
- a couple of alcohol-free days a week.

One unit of alcohol is considered to be a small glass of wine, a pub measure of spirits or half a pint of standard-strength beer or lager.

In summary

A healthy lifestyle includes:

- a diet with a variety of foods eaten on a regular basis
- maintaining weight within a healthy range
- ensuring we eat all the necessary nutrients
- taking enough exercise
- making correct lifestyle choices such as not smoking and drinking alcohol only in moderation.

Talking point

In a group discuss what you think are the effects of smoking and drinking on the body and people's behaviour.

Practice assessment activity

Level P1

P In a group, discuss what you think a healthy lifestyle is. (P1)

5.2 Know the influences that affect healthy lifestyles

This section covers:

■ positive influences

■ negative influences.

Positive influences

There are many positive influences that affect our ability to have a healthy lifestyle. This section explains what these influences are and their possible effects on people. The positive influences we will look at here are:

■ a balanced diet

■ mental and physical fitness

■ image and social awareness

■ personal hygiene

■ government initiatives.

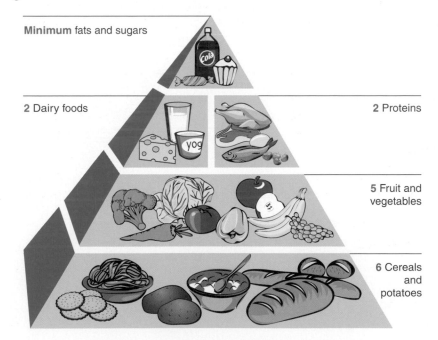

Minimum fats and sugars

2 Dairy foods

2 Proteins

5 Fruit and vegetables

6 Cereals and potatoes

■ *A food pyramid like this one is a useful tool to help plan a healthy, varied diet*

A balanced diet

One of the most important influences on a healthy lifestyle is a **balanced diet**. We have a balanced diet when we eat a mix of foods to supply us with necessary nutrients in the correct proportions to maintain our health. We do not necessarily need to have three carefully planned meals a day but should have at least one. This should help to provide a balanced diet over a week.

Mental and physical fitness

Mental and physical fitness are closely linked. Both are important for a healthy lifestyle. A good way to see how fit you are is to calculate your Body Mass Index (BMI). This is a method of measuring body fat in relation to weight to height.

To calculate your BMI:

- divide your weight in kilograms by your height in metres squared.

Example: Someone 1.7 m tall and weighing 70 kg would have a BMI of 24.2.

As a general guide, the BMI levels are:

- below 20 = underweight
- 20–25 = normal weight
- 25–30 = overweight
- over 30 = obese (dangerously overweight).

Allowance has to be made for someone with a lot of muscle because muscle is heavier than fat. It should be noted that the BMI is a guide for adults only.

Exercise

Whether we want to become healthier, lose weight or gain weight, exercise is an important part of a healthy lifestyle and has many benefits for the body. For many people exercise is also an enjoyable and social activity.

It is generally accepted that at least 30 minutes of exercise three times a week is essential for well-being. The type of exercise we take should be:

- Load-bearing, where weight should be on our limbs. This includes hiking, jogging and dancing.
- Aerobic, which is sustained for a long period such as 50 minutes and is moderately intense. Examples include running, swimming and cycling.

Talking point

Discuss ways that different people could fit exercise into their everyday lives.

■ *Exercise should be enjoyable*

Case studies

A group of people aged between 18 and 65 plan to improve their levels of fitness. Using websites with up-to-date information, find out what the latest recommendations are for exercise.

Talking point

In a group, discuss how much and what sort of exercise you do each week. How do your exercise levels compare with recommendations?

There are many benefits of exercise:

■ It can help us feel better and healthier and it boosts our immune system.

■ It keeps bones strong and helps prevent bone thinning as we get older. We start to lose bone mass from the age of 20.

■ It tones our muscles and improves blood circulation, body systems and body shape.

■ It prevents us from putting on weight by balancing calorie intake and expenditure.

■ It can boost our energy – as we breathe deeply we push more energy round the body.

■ It can enhance our moods; there is a feel-good factor after exercise.

■ It can help to relieve stress.

Fitness classes

These have become increasingly popular and more common. Leisure centres, youth groups, private companies, gyms and adult education centres now offer a wide variety of classes to suit all tastes and age groups. These include:

- gym classes for babies and toddlers
- classes in homes for the elderly
- fitness dance classes
- aerobics and step classes
- yoga for all levels
- swimming classes.

■ *There are fitness classes to suit all ages, tastes and abilities*

Image and social awareness

With so much emphasis on diet, health, image and exercise in the media, healthy lifestyles are now becoming much more socially acceptable and indeed desirable. For example, socially aware people now tend to see smoking as antisocial and a bad habit. The image that people have of themselves can be positively influenced in a variety of ways.

Self-esteem: We need to have positive self-esteem and feel good about ourselves from both a physical and mental perspective. This will be helped and continually boosted by living a healthy lifestyle.

Body image: This has become an important part of life for young and old of both sexes. Designer clothes are seen on people of all ages, and to look good we need to keep ourselves in good shape and to be aware of our body image.

Peer pressure: Most people are influenced by how others see them. Some people like to look like others in their age group so that they feel part of the group and not left out.

Media advertising: Glamorous images of slim, fit and healthy looking people of all ages are often shown in adverts in all areas of the media. These images give us the message that this is a desirable way to look. We are also given ideas of how to attain this body image and look. Adverts for clothing from some major companies use models of different ages and sizes to show what we can aspire to.

Weight-watching clubs

These are very big business in the UK, with most areas likely to have at least one club. They can have a positive effect as they encourage people not only to lose weight but

Activity

Investigate how many different fitness classes there are in your local area and share the information within the group. Are any focused on a particular age group? Did you find any for elderly people or children?

■ *Many television adverts use models to create an ideal to which we can aspire*

also to live healthier lifestyles by suggesting exercise regimes. The clubs use positive images of people who have lost weight to advertise themselves. They also use peer pressure from other members in a positive way to keep everyone on track and to try to develop a social atmosphere.

Their diets work by trying to retrain people's eating habits through various methods, such as counting points or calories. Whatever method is used they are based on eating less but more healthily. The regimes include lots of fruit, vegetables and water in the diet.

Personal hygiene

Much information is given in the media on how to keep ourselves, our clothes and our homes clean. Television programmes and articles in the papers and in magazines all give a positive image of cleanliness and aim to show us how to reach these goals with regard to cleanliness in our lives.

Government initiatives

Over the past few years the government has put a lot of emphasis on encouraging people to adopt a healthy lifestyle. The government and its agencies such as The Food Standards Agency (FSA) have made recommendations and offered initiatives. These include:

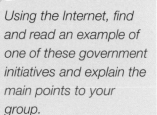

Using the Internet, find and read an example of one of these government initiatives and explain the main points to your group.

- encouraging healthy eating in schools
- advice about food and feeding in homes for the elderly
- the use of legislation to prevent smoking in enclosed public spaces
- publishing guidelines on how much alcohol we should consume
- the '5-a-Day' campaign to encourage us to eat more fruit and vegetables (see section 5.3).

Negative influences

While there are many positive influences to help us achieve a healthy lifestyle, there are also many negative influences that need to be overcome. Those we will look at here are:

- smoking, alcohol and drugs
- inactivity
- medical problems
- low self-esteem
- time pressure
- peer pressure
- media advertising
- isolation
- income.

In your group, discuss why people smoke.

Smoking

Smoking is a danger to the health of smokers themselves and to anyone who breathes in the smoke (passive smoking). As you have learned in section 5.1, smoking:

- makes clothes, hair and breath smell
- contributes to diseases such as cancer, lung and heart conditions
- ages the skin, making people look older than they are.

Alcohol

One negative effect of drinking alcohol is to lower a person's self-control, perhaps leading them to have another drink and then another. We have seen that drinking, if done in moderation, is considered acceptable and a small glass of wine can be good for our health. But too much alcoholic drink can cause terrible effects.

- Too much alcohol can gradually destroy the liver.
- It can make people behave very badly, getting into fights, being sick and taking up ambulance, police and hospital time.
- Alcohol can contribute to weight increase. There are many calories in alcohol without any nutritional value. These are called 'empty calories'.
- Alcohol is an addictive drug. Someone who regularly drinks too much will become dependent on it. Many alcoholics lose control of their lives and risk losing their jobs and their families.

Drugs

Many drugs have a negative affect on lifestyle so it is always a good idea to steer clear of them. Some drugs are marketed as helping you to become more healthy looking. An example of this is slimming pills which are supposed to help you lose weight. Different types act as appetite suppressants so that you don't feel like eating, or to prevent the digestion of fats. Slimming pills always have a negative affect on a healthy lifestyle. Because they do nothing to change bad habits, they don't help towards achieving a healthy lifestyle.

Inactivity

If you sit on the couch all the time and do nothing, you will become a 'couch potato'. Because couch potatoes take no exercise they have many problems associated with inactivity, such as:

- weight gain (getting fat)
- laziness
- the brain does not work as efficiently as it might
- poor self-esteem
- poor body image
- depression.

Eventually other health problems associated with lack of exercise also appear.

Medical problems

Obesity is one of the medical problems that negatively influence lifestyle. Once someone is obese it is very difficult to start a healthy lifestyle, exercise and lose weight. They therefore keep adding to their weight.

Other medical problems associated with an unhealthy lifestyle are eating disorders such as anorexia and bulimia. Anorexia is when people starve themselves by eating far too little, although they may think they are eating healthily and see themselves as being too fat. Bulimia is when a person binge eats (eats a lot in a short time) and makes themself sick to get rid of the food so that they don't gain weight.

Disorders such as anorexia or bulimia can often be the result of low self-esteem or peer or media pressure (see below).

Low self-esteem

When a person is suffering from low self-esteem they may find it difficult to exercise or watch their weight. They may prefer to sit on a couch and 'comfort eat' chocolate, or go on a fad diet to try to achieve massive weight loss quickly (see page 155). Low self-esteem can also lead to a person developing anorexia or bulimia (see above).

Time pressure

Nowadays people have busy lifestyles. They may spend a lot of time at work or travelling, or they may work shifts. There is pressure on their time and sometimes convenience and processed foods seem a good alternative to preparing and cooking fresh foods. You will learn more about these types of food in *Unit 7: Basic Culinary Skills*.

You may have noticed how people often 'graze' in the street and when travelling, buying and eating food from booths at the station or shops in the high street. These foods contain large amounts of fat, sugar and salt – all the foods that we are told to eat little of. They are often more expensive than if bought from the supermarket, lead to litter and can annoy others if eaten on buses or trains.

Peer pressure

Has someone ever said to you 'Just have one, it won't hurt','Have another to finish the plate' or 'I'm having one why not join me'? It could be a cake, ice cream, drink, burger or the chips to go with it. Peer pressure can be very difficult to stand up to, especially as no one wants to be seen as a killjoy.

Media advertising

We have looked at its positive influences, but media advertising can also have a negative impact on a healthy lifestyle. Think of all of the examples of skinny young men and women in advertisements who are very underweight – the '0' size models. They influence young people to try to look like them. This can lead to much unhappiness and dissatisfaction.

Key points

- 'Grazing' in the street leads to unhealthy food choices, is expensive and generates litter.
- Food portions are getting larger than we need.

More seriously, some young people take dieting to extremes and become ill; some have even died.

There has been a shift in the acceptable size of a **portion** of food sold by restaurant companies. The customer likes to see a lot for their money, so menus and adverts now give the size of a portion of meat. This may be as much as 12 or 16 ounces (340 or 450 g), whereas the accepted size used to be 6 oz (170 g).

Foods are marketed to children by linking cartoon or other television characters to the foods. These foods are often high in fat, sugar and salt. Even after all the debate about obesity in children some breakfast cereals containing as much as 30 per cent sugar are still being marketed. This type of advertising relies on the 'pester power' of children in the supermarket.

A lot of negative or misleading advertising has now been stopped, such as sophisticated drink adverts and those connecting smoking and drinking with sport.

Fad diets

Fad diets claim that they can help achieve massive weight loss, often in a very short time. They all 'work' because they starve the body and show rapid results in the short term. They are sold by adverts, often in magazines, which claim 'Lose 18 lb in 4 days' or 'Lose 4 kg every 11 days'.

■ *Happy and healthy?*

Examples of fad diets are:

- the Atkins diet, which is mainly protein-based
- the grapefruit, the banana, the three-day, cabbage soup and bread and butter diets.

This last example tells you to eat a slice of bread and butter as part of each of your three daily meals, but overall the calories for the day only come to 850.

Fad diets are not recommended because the body tends to shut down and protect itself, so it begins to starve. As soon as you start to eat the weight goes on again. These diets have a negative influence on a healthy lifestyle and create nutritional problems by excluding many essential foods.

Isolation

Nowadays more and more people, both young and old, are living on their own. They often do not eat properly for a variety of reasons.

- Sometimes older people find it difficult to get to the shops.
- People on their own may think it is not worth cooking for one.
- Portions of fresh meat and fish available in supermarkets are generally for two.

Even within a family group many activities are solo – watching television in the bedroom, watching it for too long or playing computer games. Frequently meals are taken in bedrooms, in front of the television or

Talking point

How often do you sit at a table and eat a group meal? Why is a group meal important? Discuss why people nowadays don't eat as a group as often as they used to.

games console and not as a family round a table. This leads to snack meals and little exercise.

Income

It has been shown that some of those on a low income tend to spend less on fresh food but use convenience foods. They are more likely to purchase the cheapest brands of food, which may have less nutritional value and contain more additives than the more expensive brands. People on low incomes may also have less money to spend on exercising in leisure and fitness centres.

In summary

- There are many influences on living a healthy lifestyle.
- Positive influences include balanced diet, fitness and exercise, image, social awareness and government initiatives.
- Negative influences include smoking, drinking, inactivity, medical problems, eating disorders, fad diets and media advertising.

Practice assessment activity

Levels P2/M1

P Prepare a poster which identifies three positive and three negative factors that influence healthy lifestyles. Briefly outline each of these factors. (P2)

M Compare the positive and negative aspects of two lifestyles. (M1)

5.3 Be able to plan a menu that contributes to a healthy lifestyle

This section covers:

■ features of a healthy menu

■ recommendations for healthy eating

■ factors to consider.

Features of a healthy menu

This section of the unit looks at what should be considered when a healthy menu is planned, together with recommendations for healthy eating and different factors to consider. It should give you the toolkit to be able to plan a healthy menu for different types of people.

There is a lot of advice available about what should feature in a healthy menu and what contributes to a healthy lifestyle. Much of this advice comes from websites and free publications that are a big help to caterers. Suggestions for menus, recipes, brochures and posters are available to download when needed. Useful websites include the Department for Children, Schools and Families and Channel 4. Go to www.heinemann. co.uk/hotlinks, insert the express code 5285P and click on the link to this page. However a major source of advice comes from the government in the form of guidelines and initiatives (see also section 5.2).

Government guidelines

These set out what should be included in a healthy menu for certain age groups and types of people. The Caroline Walker Trust is a charity that has done a lot of work in the nutritional field and advises the government in this area.

Nutritional Guidelines for School Meals set out their recommendations as a percentage of overall daily requirements. These recommendations are available for children of nursery, primary and secondary school age. Free fruit is now offered to schoolchildren between the ages of 4 and 6, and breakfast clubs have been set up in some schools across the country. The whole issue of poor school meals was highlighted as a result of an investigation into obesity in children.

A national action plan has been set up by the Health Minister to tackle the issue of older people and nutrition. This was done after an investigation into the standards of nutrition of the elderly in hospitals and care homes found that many elderly people came into institutions well nourished but began to suffer from malnutrition (poor diet) once there.

Interested bodies such as the Food Standards Agency (FSA), the British Heart Foundation (BHF) and the private healthcare service BUPA have also issued guidelines recommending the daily levels of water, fat and salt we should have in our diets.

Recommendations for healthy eating

This section looks at the recommendations to follow to enable you to plan a healthy diet.

Water intake

The body is made up of 60 per cent water and this needs to be topped up daily to keep us healthy. We can survive for quite a long time without food but can only live for a few days without water.

Why do our bodies need water?

- to flush out waste products through the skin and kidneys
- to keep hair, skin and organs healthy
- because it produces digestive enzymes
- to helps nutrients flow from the food into the body
- it helps fibre to swell, stimulating the gut and preventing constipation.

Water is lost all the time from the body through the kidneys and the skin when we sweat, but it is lost more quickly when we are sick. A guide to tell whether we are dehydrated (lacking water) is to check the urine. This should be a pale straw colour; dark-coloured urine is a sign of dehydration, which can be very serious.

- Adults should drink 2 to 3 litres (4 to 5 pints) of water daily.
- The daily recommendation for a 3-year-old is 750 cl (1¼ pints).

Fat intake

It is fat that gives a lot of foods their flavour, but excess fat has been linked to many health problems such as obesity, heart disease and cancer. However it is an essential part of our diets as it carries the fat-soluble vitamins A, D, E and K. The problem is that many people eat too much of the wrong type of fat.

There are three different types of fat.

- **Saturated** fat is hard at room temperature and is found in meat, meat products, dairy products and coconut oil. Eating a lot of this will increase our risk of heart disease.
- **Polyunsaturated** fat is liquid at room temperature and found in cooking oils such as grapeseed, safflower, sunflower and corn oils, and oily fish such as salmon, trout, sardines and herring. Omega-3 fatty acids are also found in this type of fat, and these can help prevent heart disease and reduce the symptoms of joint problems.

Talking point

How much water do you drink daily? Do not include fizzy drinks, tea or coffee.

If not enough, perhaps you could carry a small bottle around with you.

- **Mono-unsaturated** fats are liquid at room temperature and found in olives, groundnut oil, nuts and avocados.

■ *Mono- and polyunsaturated fats are healthier than saturated fats*

All fats are high in energy-giving calories (9 per gramme) but as it is easy to eat a large amount of hidden fat it can contribute to a weight problem.

Salt intake

All of the foods we eat contain salt, but pre-prepared and convenience foods add a lot to our daily consumption. The recommended daily amount of salt is:

- adults – 6 g (1 teaspoon)
- babies – no more than 1 g; note that salt should never be added to babies' food.

A label on food might state that it contains 0.5 g of *sodium* per serving, but this can be misleading. To find the amount of *salt* in the serving you need to multiply by 2.5. Each serving contains 0.5 times 2.5 = 1.25 g of salt.

'5 a Day' fruit and vegetables

One aspect of a healthy menu is having enough portions of fruit and vegetables daily. Most people have heard of the government campaign to eat five portions of fruit or vegetables each day. We need to do this because:

- Eating a variety of fruit and vegetables gives us plenty of vitamins and minerals such as folic acid, vitamin C and potassium.
- They are a good source of fibre and antioxidants.
- They are generally low-fat, low-calorie foods which fill us up and help keep the weight off.
- They may help to reduce the risk of heart disease and some cancers.

Key points

- Nutritional guidance is freely available through government websites.
- Fat is linked to heart disease and obesity.
- We should aim to eat five portions of fruit and vegetables a day.
- Salt should never be added to babies' food.

Just Eat More
(fruit & veg)

Activity

In groups, discuss how many portions of fruit and vegetables you eat on a typical day. Discuss how this part of your diet could be improved.

What is considered to be a portion of fruit or vegetables?

- A portion of fruit or vegetables is considered to be about 80 g (3 oz).

- Canned (in its own juice), frozen and dried fruit and vegetables all count, as well as fresh.

- A portion of dried fruit is similar to what you would eat if it were fresh, for instance three apricots or a handful of sultanas (dried grapes).

- 100% juice (fruit or vegetable juice or smoothie) only counts as one portion however much is consumed. The recommended portion size is one medium glass of 100% juice = 150 ml.

- Potatoes do not count at all as they are a 'starchy' food.

- Fruit and vegetables added to foods such as pasta sauces, soups and puddings can contribute to 5 A DAY.

- Pulses such as lentils, beans and chickpeas count once a day, as they do not have the same mix of nutrients as other vegetables.

- To gain most benefit and essential nutrients, vitamins and minerals you should eat a variety of at least 5 portions of fruit and vegetables every day.

Case studies

Some children at a primary school have breakfast, lunch, mid-morning and afternoon snacks provided for them at school. Their parents pick them up from an after school club.

Their parents have become aware of the '5 a Day' campaign and are concerned how little fruit and vegetables their children eat. Once they get

home from school in the evening the children are tired and not inclined to eat much.

The parents have approached the school to discuss how more fruit and vegetables could be introduced into the meals the children have there.

What ideas do you have which could help the school caterer manage this problem?

2 broccoli florets

16 okra

2 halves of canned peaches

3 heaped table-spoons of peas

12 chunks of canned pineapple

1 cereal bowl of mixed salad

7 strawberries

1 medium apple

1 tablespoon of raisins

3 whole dried apricots

1 medium banana

1 medium pear

7 cherry tomatoes

1 medium glass of orange juice

1 handful of grapes

2 medium plums

1 handful of vegetable sticks

2 heaped table-spoons of sweetcorn

3 heaped table-spoons of cooked kidney beans

2 satsumas

Lean meat

Lean meat is a nutritious food which should feature on a healthy menu, but which should also be eaten in moderation. It provides diet protein, B vitamins, vitamin D, iron and zinc. Lean meats are:

- chicken and turkey without their skin
- pork without its fat and crackling.

We are told to eat less fat but a lot of fat is part of the meat we eat.

- Minced beef or lamb can be 25 per cent fat.
- Beef has fat throughout it called 'marbling' which gives it its taste.
- Bacon has fat, and lamb has a quite a lot of fat throughout.

Minced meat from supermarkets is now sold with labels that give the fat content, but it is more difficult to control how much fat is in mince when buying large amounts wholesale. All visible fat on meat should be removed.

Food labelling

Labelling plays an increasingly important part when we start to look at recommendations for healthy eating. Labels give the nutritional content of packaged foods and as they have become complicated to understand the Food Standards Agency has produced a set of guidelines. These are 'traffic light labelling' for packaged foods. They are a simple way of guiding a busy shopper to foods that have a more healthy nutritional content.

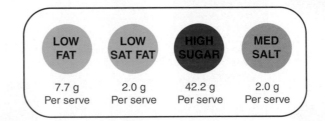

LOW FAT	LOW SAT FAT	HIGH SUGAR	MED SALT
7.7 g Per serve	2.0 g Per serve	42.2 g Per serve	2.0 g Per serve

- Green means a low amount of un undesirable nutrient such as salt or saturated fat.
- Amber means a medium amount.
- Red means a high amount.

The nutrients listed are fat, saturates, sugar and salt and the figures are given for 100 g of food and a portion serving.

Some supermarkets have devised their own schemes but use the same colour principle and may also give the nutritional amounts as a percentage of a portion. There is a lot to read on a label and the traffic light system allows people to make a quick decision when shopping.

There are also increasing concerns about allergies and the label will pinpoint the presence of known allergens such as nuts or milk.

Recommended daily allowances (RDA)

Throughout this unit you will find recommended servings of the different food groups, together with recommended limits on the amount of salt and fat in the diet. The following chart is to help you plan a healthy menu with the right number of calories.

Age	Male	Female
4–6 months	690	645
4–6	1715	1545
15–18	2755	2110
19–50	2550	1940
65–74	2330	1900
over 75	2100	1810

Source: Weight Loss Resources. Go to www.heinemann.co.uk/hotlinks, insert the express code 5285P and click on the link to this page.

Factors to consider

Many different factors need to be considered when planning a menu to contribute to a healthy lifestyle. These include:

- age groups
- special dietary needs
- cooking methods
- skills, time and costs.

Age groups

This section looks at the nutritional needs that people have at different stages of their lives.

Children

- Children learn their eating patterns from their parents, developing tastes and habits such as sitting at the table.
- Children need the same variety of food in their diet as adults but in smaller amounts
- Their bodies are growing so bodybuilding foods with calcium and vitamin D are essentials.
- Regular small meals to keep blood sugar levels steady are important.
- Avoid processed foods with additives such as colourings, preservatives and anti-oxidants – the 'E' numbers which may lead to hyperactivity.
- Most importantly use fresh foods.

Teenagers

There is something special about teenagers. Their bodies are still growing and they put on a spurt of growth in their teenage years when hormones really kick in and their bodies start to develop into adulthood. Hormonal activity can also affect hair and skin, with spots appearing.

A government report in 2000 on the nutritional intake and physical activity of young people found that:

■ 50 per cent of young people had not eaten any citrus fruit, leafy green vegetables, eggs or tomatoes in the previous week

■ teenage girls and boys are prone to iron deficiency

■ 25 per cent had less than the recommended level of calcium intake, just when bones are growing.

A lot of teenagers have big appetites and need lots of energy, which should come from starchy carbohydrates not fats and sugars.

■ Plenty of fruit and vegetables, lots of dairy products and enough protein should be eaten.

■ They should eat breakfast, preferably fortified cereal, semi-skimmed milk and fruit juice.

Adults

Much of the information in this chapter has been written about the adult population. It is important that adults look after themselves so they will be healthy as they move into the elderly age group. A healthy plan for adults includes:

■ watching weight levels – being neither over- nor underweight

■ eating a balanced diet to ensure they get sufficient nutrition

■ not eating too much of the wrong foods

■ drinking alcohol in moderation.

The elderly

Age does not tell us too much about health and activity. Someone of 65 may be very inactive, whereas an active member of an early morning swimming club is 101.

Our bodies change as we age and thought has to be given to how the elderly can be kept healthy. Some may be in homes or hospitals where all of their food and nutrition is supplied. Studies show there are levels of malnutrition in some homes and hospitals

■ The bodies of the elderly are slowing down; while they need fewer calories the level of nutrition has to be kept up.

■ They may need vitamin D to help prevent bone loss (osteoporosis), especially as they may not go outdoors as much. Vitamin D is made by the effect of the sun on the body.

Activity

With the help of your teacher, obtain examples of menus from institutions; your local hospital, college or school may help. With your knowledge, comment on whether the menus are suitable for a healthy lifestyle.

How could they be adapted for the elderly or for children?

- Small portions of attractively served fresh foods are needed.
- Some elderly people have difficulty swallowing.
- One-dish meals can be easy to eat and include a variety of foods.
- Attention should be paid to the inclusion of zinc in the diet.

Special dietary needs

People have special dietary needs for different reasons, these may be medical, cultural or from choice. The one thing these people have in common is the need for a healthy diet.

Medical

Diabetes: This is is a medical condition where an increased amount of sugar is found in the blood. The blood sugar level therefore has to be balanced, either by diet or medication, depending on the type of diabetes and how serious it is.

Allergies: If a person has a food allergy they can become ill even when a tiny amount of the food is eaten. This can lead to the person going into **anaphylactic shock** requiring immediate treatment. Many people are allergic to nuts.

Food intolerance: Some people's bodies react badly to certain foods, which can make them very unwell. Wheat gluten and dairy products are examples of foods that may not be tolerated. Serious wheat gluten intolerance is known as coeliac disease. A doctor can carry out tests to find out which foods are making someone unwell.

Other types of special medical diets might include low-fat, low-sugar, low-calorie and high-fibre.

Culture and lifestyle diets

- **Vegetarian** – no meat, poultry or fish.
- **Vegan** – does not use or eat any animal products.

Kosher

- follows Jewish food laws
- meat killed by a specialist
- only eat animals with split hooves and that chew cud
- no blood products or pork
- meat and dairy stored, cooked and eaten separately.

Halal

- follows the Muslim food laws
- animals slaughtered by having throat cut and blood drained
- no blood products or pork.

Healthy cooking methods

These are methods that do not:

- use too much extra fat in the cooking method
- overcook vegetables and fruit, thereby spoiling vitamins
- use large amounts of water that will remove water-soluble vitamins.

Examples of healthy eating cooking methods are:

- **Steaming** – food such as vegetables are cooked in steam so that nutrients are not boiled away in water
- **Baking** – in the oven without fat
- **Stir-frying** – vegetables, meat, fish and chicken can be cut into strips and cooked quickly using very little oil
- **Roasting** – in the oven with a minimum of fat added
- **Braising** – a method of slow cooking meat with a little liquid
- **Grilling** – a quick method of cooking where fat can drain away
- **Poaching** – a minimum of liquid and no fat added for fish and fruit
- **Boiling** – in water.

Ingredients available

Nowadays ingredients are available from all over the world. Fresh, chilled, frozen, tinned and bottled foods are brought in by air, road or ship and quickly distributed to suppliers. Foods now available out of season in the UK include:

- Lamb – chilled or frozen and shipped from New Zealand
- Fresh fruit and vegetables.

Over to you

Visit a supermarket and, looking at the fruit, vegetables and meat, see how many examples of these have been imported to fill a seasonal gap.

The availability of so many ingredients means caterers have a huge choice of dishes they can put on the menu. This should allow them to cater for everyone's taste and need.

Skills available

An important factor in planning a menu is the skill of the caterer and chef. The skills they need to have include:

- knowledge of food – to be able to recognise what a **commodity** (primary, raw product) is, know its taste and its nutritional values
- food preparation and cookery skills
- literacy and numeracy skills for designing and costing a menu.

One problem faced, for example, by the school meals service is that people without these skills have replaced fully trained chefs and cooks. There is now a move to provide cookery skills training for school meal staff.

Time available

How long you have to prepare and cook a meal is another factor to be considered. Normal working hours may not leave enough time for some foods to be prepared and cooked. In these cases preparation can be done on the previous day, but not in a five-day operation when the kitchen is closed over a weekend.

Costs

The cost factor is in every caterer's decision when menu planning, but costing may serve different purposes in different settings.

- In an upmarket, expensive restaurant the dishes need to be costed to decide whether they will have too high a price to sell.
- In a school, hospital or old people's home the dishes are costed to see whether they fit the budget.
- In any profit-making business products must be able to sell and make the required amount of profit

Cost should not prevent healthy menus being designed, but will lead to the caterer making a choice of dishes that fit the budget. You will learn more about cost in *Unit 7: Basic Culinary Skills*.

In summary

- Features of a healthy menu can be based on government guidelines.
- Healthy eating includes eating recommended amounts of foods daily and cutting down on salt, sugar and fat.
- Healthy cooking methods such as steaming or grilling should be used.
- People's ages must be taken into consideration when planning a healthy menu.

Practice assessment activity

Levels P3/M2/D1

P Design a healthy two-course menu, either starter and main course or main course and dessert, for adults at work. There should be a choice in each course. (P3)

M Explain the factors that make this a healthy menu. (M2)

D Assess how the specific needs of your client group have been met by the menu. (D1)

5.4 Understand how hospitality organisations can make a positive contribution to healthy lifestyles

This section covers:

■ positive contributions

■ constraints

■ benefits of change.

Positive contributions

Hospitality organisations are in a very good position to make positive contributions to people's healthy lifestyles. There may be some constraints on the organisation being able to make a contribution. But by making changes there are benefits not only for the customers in terms of their health, but also for the organisation itself.

Positive factors looked at in this section include:

■ menu design

■ staff training

■ pricing and promotions.

Menu design

As we have seen in the previous section, a healthy menu is an important factor in a healthy lifestyle. Whoever is responsible for menu design in an outlet will have a great deal of influence on people's lifestyles.

'Green' policy concepts

With growing awareness of 'green' issues such as 'carbon footprints' and 'sustainability' (making sure that stocks do not run out), there has been a move for different parts of the hospitality industry, including school meal providers and pubs, to source ingredients locally and support local farmers and growers. Many outlets use this as a marketing tool.

By using **organic** and locally produced foods the hospitality industry can check whether they have been produced in a healthy and humane manner. To be called organic, food production has to meet certain criteria, such as being grown in a natural way without the aid of chemicals.

The advantages of locally grown food are that:

■ the premises can be visited to check for cleanliness

■ the caterer can build a good relationship with the food producer

- checks can be made on whether humane methods of food production are used
- local products reduce the carbon footprint of food supplies as they do not have far to go to be delivered to the outlet.

Providing for special diets

A positive contribution is made by providing special diets for those either needing or choosing them. If a low-calorie, low-fat or other alternative main course is wanted then it can be provided. Vegetarian alternatives can be a popular option. We have already looked at the types of diets that may be needed in section 5.3.

Showing nutritional values

Menus can show the nutritional value of dishes, thereby allowing the customer to make an educated choice about what to eat. The nutritional value can be shown in a number of ways.

- A traffic light system can be used, similar to the one mentioned in section 5.3.
- In a hospital the menu shows the type of special diet the dish is appropriate for.
- On many menus a large V is put beside a dish to indicate its suitability for vegetarians.
- At a health farm or a local leisure centre the actual calorie value for a portion may be shown.

Staff training

Training can make a big contribution to healthy lifestyles. Catering staff who come into contact with customers at mealtimes can have an effect on what gets eaten. Staff may be trained to:

- be aware of the role diet plays in a healthy lifestyle
- advise on the nutritional content of foods, including health warnings of too much fat, sugar and salt
- serve a 'normal' portion
- suggest what might accompany a main course
- serve a children's portion
- look out for food left on the plate to see what is uneaten
- make the food look appetising
- observe whether a customer has difficulty eating
- cook and keep hot or cold meals so as not to lose their nutritional content.

Pricing and promotions

Healthy dishes should be priced as average on the menu, and not be more expensive than less healthy dishes.

When promoting foods caterers can make a deal of two healthy dishes to emphasise the good nutrition aspect. They could use the promotion to educate the customers by showing why the food is healthy.

Constraints

As you have learned in *Unit 4: Planning and Running a Hospitality Event*, constraints are limits. The main constraints that hospitality organisations face when contributing to healthy lifestyles are financial or customer-based.

Financial constraints

Financial constraints are a bigger factor in certain parts of the hospitality industry than in others. For example, a large chain hotel will have more to spend on catering than a small guesthouse.

Budget

For most caterers a major constraint is budget. When food has to be supplied to a limited budget then cheaper suppliers and dishes for the menu may have to be chosen. Parts of the hospitality industry more likely to suffer financial constraints include:

- hospitals
- school meal services
- care and residential homes
- prisons
- contract catering for people at work.

Budget constraints:

- can deter the caterer from making a positive contribution to healthy lifestyles; though this may not always stop them using local or organic produce
- may affect the total number of dishes which can be produced for the menu
- may limit the number of healthy options available on the menu
- may not allow for staff training.

Cost of production

When a menu is large and includes complicated dishes, the cost of producing those dishes is high. It may then be cheaper to provide a simpler menu with simpler dishes and cut down on the number of expensive chefs needed to prepare and cook them. We will look at this in more detail in *Unit 7: Basic Culinary Skills*.

Customer lifestyles and trends

Another constraint on the hospitality industry's ability to positively contribute to healthy lifestyles is the lifestyle the customer already has. Despite all the publicity about obesity and its possible causes, many people are still unaware of health initiatives and guidelines such as the '5 a Day' campaign.

Chips, chocolate and sugary fizzy drinks sell very easily and it is difficult for people to change their lifestyle habits. Some people are not aware of a problem; others are not prepared to do anything about it, as seen in the following case study.

Case studies

In one school under a new healthy eating regime where healthy food was being provided, the mothers of some of the students bought chips and hamburgers and passed them to their children over the school wall.

In that school the fashion was for a certain diet and the parents and children would not change!

Benefits of change

There are many benefits to the industry of making some changes towards a healthy lifestyle.

Bigger client base

The number of clients or customers will improve. For instance, a contract caterer may develop a reputation for producing healthy menus for schools with freshly cooked food.

- First the number of students eating school dinners is likely to increase.
- Another school will hear about the service being offered and approach the contractor to see whether they can also cater for them.
- All of a sudden the number of clients and customers is expanding.

Happier staff and lower costs

With training and increased skills, staff will feel more motivated and keen to produce new dishes and healthier food. Better-trained staff, with improved skills, are also quicker and more efficient, leading to lower employment costs.

■ *Well-trained staff will be happier and more helpful*

Recognition

One benefit of a change towards healthy eating is the recognition which the outlet might gain in the form of awards given to various parts of the industry. These include:

- Local Authority Caterer's Association (LACA) School Chef of the Year – for school meals
- Organic Food Award
- Healthy Living Award (Scotland).

In summary

- Through labelling showing nutritional values, good menu design, staff training and sourcing locally the hospitality industry contributes to healthy lifestyles.
- There are a number of constraints on the industry, including financial and the need to change people's habits.
- Benefits to the industry include more clients, recognition and better-motivated staff.

Practice assessment activity

Levels P4/M3/D2

P Visit a local hospitality business and write a report describing how healthy lifestyles could be promoted there. (P4)

M After making a visit to a local business, analyse how it is making both positive and negative contributions to promoting healthy lifestyles. (M3)

D Review the business's food and beverage provision and identify all good practices that they use to promote healthy lifestyles. Make suggestions as to how they might make improvements. (D2)

Test your knowledge

1   Give six benefits of taking exercise.

2   What are the five food groups?

3   How many portions of fruit and vegetables should be eaten daily? Give two examples of a portion.

4   Give three reasons not to drink alcohol.

5   Explain five healthy cooking methods and find two recipes using each method.

6   What is essential to life but not a nutrient?

7   What should be the maximum amount of salt intake daily for an adult?

8   What should be features of a children's healthy menu?

9   Why are teenagers special?

10 Give ways in which the hospitality industry can contribute to healthy lifestyles.

6 Developing Employability Skills for Hospitality and Related Industries

Introduction

This unit aims to make you aware of all the different job opportunities available in the hospitality and related industries. You will be able to identify the employability skills you presently have and plan how to develop other employability skills you may need. You will also look at a range of job roles and career opportunities and how you can start the process of applying for them, including the completion of application forms and CVs.

Hospitality and its related industries of retail, sport and leisure and travel and tourism offer many job opportunities. This unit aims to make you aware of these industries and the job opportunities available.

How you will be assessed

Unit 6 is assessed internally, so the Centre delivering the qualification will assess you against the criteria. On completion of this unit you should:

6.1 know the different industries related to the hospitality industry

6.2 understand the different job roles and career opportunities available in the related industries

6.3 know the sources of information related to job and career opportunities

6.4 be able to match your own skills to required employability skills

6.5 be able to undergo a job application process for employment in hospitality or a related industry.

Assessment grades

The Edexcel Assessment Grid for Unit 6 details the criteria to be met. In general, to gain a Pass (P) you are asked to identify, describe, plan and prepare material; to gain a Merit (M) you are also asked to explain and compare; and to gain a Distinction (D) you are also asked to evaluate and analyse.

6.1 Know the different industries related to the hospitality industry

This section covers:

■ hospitality-related industries

■ functions of related industries

■ links with hospitality

■ main competitors.

Hospitality-related industries

We have learned that the hospitality industry in itself is huge, and in any city, town or village you will find a mix of hotels, restaurants and bars. In addition to these industries there are others which relate to the hospitality industry. Hospitality-related industries include:

■ retail

■ sport and leisure

■ travel and tourism.

■ *Retail outlets can be part of major chains …*

■ *… or smaller independent shops*

Retail

By walking along your local high street you will find a variety of different retail outlets. Some may be part of big chains such as Marks & Spencer, Debenhams, Gap and Next, whereas others will be smaller independent shops owned by one or two people.

Sport and leisure

It is likely that within your local or surrounding area there will be a large health club, for example one which belongs to a chain like Fitness First, David Lloyd or Cannons; or you may have a smaller independent local gym. The large health clubs are usually open to members and guests only and offer a vast range of facilities, including:

- gyms
- studios for exercise classes
- swimming pools
- solariums
- beauty treatment rooms
- restaurants and bars.

Alongside these large private health clubs there will also be council-led leisure centres and sports clubs. These last two will offer a range of facilities for the general public to use. Unlike the private clubs, the council-led centres allow both members and non-members to use the facilities.

Travel and tourism

The third related industry comes under the umbrella of travel and tourism. Examples include:

- travel agents such as Thomas Cook, Thomson and First Choice Holidays
- airlines such as RyanAir and easyJet
- online tour companies
- caravan parks and campsites
- tourist information centres
- cruise lines and ferry operators
- local attractions, places of interest and theme parks.

Over to you

In groups, take one of the industries mentioned above and draw up a list of businesses which fall into each category. Share your findings with your group.

■ There are many opportunities in travel and tourism

From your own lists and the information above, you should see the huge number of different businesses which fall into the category of hospitality-related industries.

Functions of related industries

All the industries listed above have specific functions that are carried out in order to help make the business successful. The primary focus of most businesses is to make a profit – that is, to make more money than is spent. The best way businesses in these related industries can achieve a profit is to focus on the following three functions:

- providing goods and services
- satisfying customer needs and expectations
- providing entertainment.

Goods and services

There are a large number of different types of products and services offered in the different industries identified above. Some examples are:

- selling merchandise, for example sports clothes in health clubs
- providing changing and toilet facilities
- taking bookings
- selling holidays
- selling and serving food and drink
- selling beauty services and products
- providing fitness facilities
- providing accommodation.

Satisfying customer needs and expectations

If customers are not happy with the goods and services on offer then they are unlikely to return. An example of this is shown below.

If you were going to join a health club and the cost was £65 per month with a £150 joining fee, you would rightly expect a large, fully equipped modern gym, swimming pool, solarium, a variety of exercise classes, food and beverage outlet(s), good changing room facilities and crèche facilities. Imagine if you turned up and the only facility available was a small gym. Your expectations and needs would not have been met and it is likely that you would want your money back.

Providing entertainment

In some of the related industries, customers will expect entertainment. This is particularly true on cruise ships and in holiday parks, where customers may expect a casino, cabaret evenings, dance classes and various organised activities. If a business does not provide these services then once again customer expectations will not be met.

Links with hospitality

You will have realised that when exploring the hospitality-related industries there are clear links with hospitality industries. Many of the related industries require similar basic functions to be carried out. These include:

- customer-focused functions which include dealing with enquiries, solving customers' problems and selling to people
- revenue-focused functions such as cash handling, reducing costs and generating profits.

Main competitors

Over to you

Think about an occasion when you have had lunch in your local town. Then think about all the choices available to you.

We have already seen that there are products, services and functions that overlap between hospitality and its related industries. The result of this leads to a very high level of competitiveness both within and across industries. These could include a variety of restaurants and pubs, cafes, coffee shops, health clubs, takeaways and so on.

All these different companies are in competition with each other, all wanting your business, so they have to try to offer the best products and services available.

In summary

- Hospitality-related industries include retail, sport and leisure and travel and tourism.
- Each of these industries is focused primarily on providing goods and services to customers.
- Each of the related industries have links with the hospitality industry because they are all concerned with customers and making a profit.
- The overlap between hospitality and its related industries in terms of functions, products and services leads to high levels of competition.

Practice assessment activity

Level P1

P You have been asked to prepare a presentation identifying the different industries related to the hospitality industry found in your local area. Having identified each of the industries, give examples of businesses which fall into each category. Briefly explain the goods and services that they offer and how these businesses link to businesses within the hospitality industry. (P1)

6.2 Understand the different job roles and career opportunities available in the related industries

This section covers:

- job roles
- career opportunities
- skills
- teamwork
- problem-solving
- communication
- personal attributes.

In section 6.1 you learned about hospitality-related industries and the types of businesses which fall under each category. This section will focus on the types of jobs and career opportunities available in the related industries.

Job roles

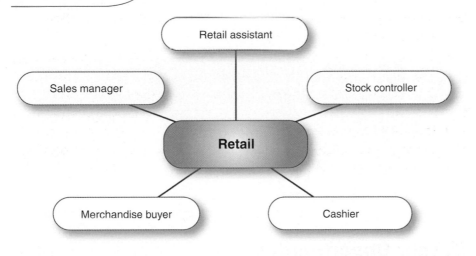

Each of the related industries has a number of possible job roles and career paths, some of which are shown below.

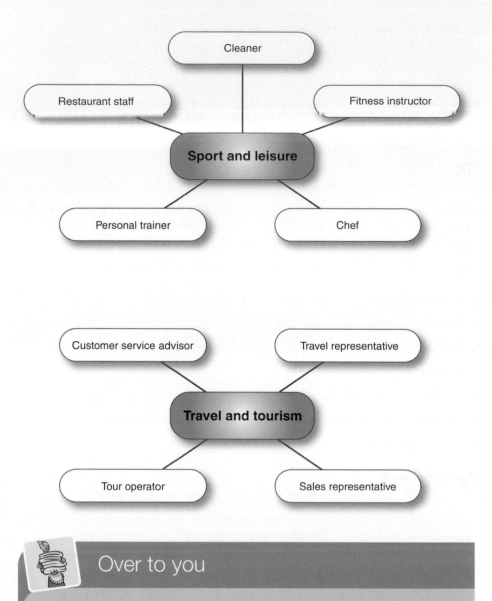

Working in groups, choose one of the diagrams above and try to add as many more job roles to it as you can think of. Once completed, come back together and feed back, noting where the overlaps are between the different industries.

Career Opportunities

All of the jobs shown in the diagrams will provide you with different career opportunities. During your working life you are likely to progress up the career ladder. There are three clear levels that you may progress through.

■ **Operational** – Many people start at this level when they enter the world of work. If, for example, you wanted a job in a retail outlet you would probably start off as a sales assistant.

- **Supervisory** – In time you may be promoted to a supervisory role. A job at this level in retail would be a sales supervisor. At this level you would have additional responsibilities such as being in charge of the sales assistants.

- **Management** – The next promotion could be into management. A job at this level could be a retail manager, who would be responsible for all aspects of the retail outlet.

Skills

Whatever the level of job you are in there are certain skills you need to have in order to be successful. Some of these skills are noted below, and many have been covered in *Unit 2: Customer Relations in Hospitality*.

As an example, skills a customer service advisor would need are:

- communication
- handling stress – being able to cope when busy
- listening skills
- teamwork
- problem-solving and complaints handling
- product and organisational knowledge
- commitment to the organisation.

Teamwork

You have already learned about the importance of teamwork in *Unit 1: Exploring the Hospitality Industry*. Most jobs in the hospitality-related industries will involve teamwork; there are very few jobs where you would be working totally on your own.

So what does teamwork mean? A group of people who are working at achieving the same goal can be classed as a team.

- You may be a part of a football team whereby all the players share the aim of wanting to win.

- You may be part of a chef's brigade whose goal is to ensure that all the meals are ready on time.

- You may be part of a team of retail assistants whose goal is to make the most sales.

Basically a team of people are united together and realise that their goal cannot be achieved without the help and support of the other team members.

Over to you

Think about a time when you were part of a team – this could be a sports team, a work team or a team you have been part of at school/college. Then think about the skills that you needed to make the team successful.

Problem-solving

Whether in an operational role or a management role, in most of the jobs that you do you will encounter problems. Skills which will help you with problem solving are:

- patience
- listening skills to enable you to fully understand the problem
- good product knowledge
- understanding
- flexibility – in order to solve a problem you may have to work in a different way.

Communication

As you have learned in *Unit 2: Customer Relations in Hospitality*, effective communication is one of the key success factors of any business. Communication skills include:

- listening skills
- speaking clearly at the right pace and tone – not too quickly or slowly and not too loud or too soft.

Communication is not only about speaking; you will also communicate via writing – by letter, email or fax. We also communicate non-verbally through body language, which can often be a good indication of what a person is feeling. For example, you can tell if somebody is happy, sad or angry just by looking at their face – usually the eyes and mouth give the game away. See *Unit 2: Customer Relations in Hospitality* for more on body language.

Personal attributes

Many of the skills listed above require a particular set of personal attributes if they are to be carried out successfully. Your personal attributes are the qualities which you bring to your job. They include such things as:

- patience, tact and diplomacy
- being a good team player
- honesty
- initiative
- self-motivation.

It is important to have all of these qualities if you are working in hospitality or other related industries.

Patience, tact and diplomacy

If you have patience, tact and diplomacy you are able to be sensitive when dealing with others who have difficult issues. These qualities are required particularly if you are solving problems or handling complaints.

Team player

The ability to be a team player is a personal attribute that is essential to the industries that we have mentioned. Being a team player does not come naturally to all people as some prefer to work on their own independently. However, as mentioned earlier, most jobs in the service industries need team players.

Honesty

Honesty is essential if you are going to have long-term success in your job. You will not make a very good employee if you are not honest.

Initiative

The *Oxford English Dictionary* defines the word initiative as 'The power or opportunity to act before others do'. So with initiative you are anticipating customers' needs and demands – thinking about them even before they have. Initiative is also very useful when solving problems. If you can solve a customer's problem quickly and efficiently without having to go and ask somebody else for advice, your customer will be very happy.

Self-motivation

Motivation is the reason, desire or enthusiasm to do something. Often we feel motivated by a reward and/or by praise. This is called **extrinsic motivation** and is when something in the external environment is motivating you. For example, an extrinsically motivated person will carry out a job because they have been promised a pay rise.

In contrast, an **intrinsically** motivated person is motivated by their own desire to achieve. This means they want to do really well in a job purely for their own sense of achievement. If you are intrinsically motivated then you are self-motivated.

From an employer's point of view, to have an employee who is self-motivated is very positive. A self-motivated employee will:

- not always have to be asked to carry out tasks
- work to a high standard
- have lots of energy
- turn up to work on time (or even early)
- have good personal presentation skills
- usually do over and above what is required of them in their job.

 Talking point

Imagine that you work in a retail outlet. It is Christmas time and late-night shopping has started. You are coming in to work for the late shift starting at 4 pm. The colleague you are taking over from tells you that the float in the till is accurate. You have a busy evening, taking lots of money. When you come to cash up you cannot get your takings to balance. Eventually you realise that the float was in fact incorrect and was down by £20.

Discuss with your group how would this make you feel and how it would affect teamwork.

If you have the personal attribute of self-motivation you are likely to progress quicker in your career than someone who is purely motivated by external rewards.

In summary

- There are many different roles and career opportunities available in hospitality-related industries, including cashier, retail assistant, gym instructor, receptionist, customer service advisor and tour operator.
- For all these jobs you might start at operational level but could then progress to management level.
- All the different jobs require certain skills such as teamwork, communication and problem solving.
- The personal attributes that you will need to bring to a job include patience, tact, diplomacy, honesty, initiative and self-motivation.

Practice assessment activity

Levels P2/M1

You work for the careers service and have been asked by your manager to prepare an informative careers leaflet for each of the hospitality-related industries mentioned in section 6.1.

P Your leaflet should describe five job roles, along with their career opportunities available in each of the related industries. (P2)

M In addition to the above, add to your leaflet an explanation of the skills and personal attributes necessary for at least two of the selected job roles. (M1)

6.3 Know the sources of information related to job and career opportunities

This section covers:

- sources of careers advice
- sources of job information
- suitability of different sources.

Sources of careers advice

Sometimes we would like to start the process of finding a job by actually talking to somebody to get some advice. Three different sources of career advice are looked at below.

Connexions

Connexions is an organisation specifically set up to help and advise young people between the ages of 13 and 19 who are trying to decide where they want to be in life.

- Connexions offices are scattered across the UK and you should have one local to you.

- You can arrange a private one-to-one meeting with a Connexions advisor who will help you to realise what you would like to do in the next stage of your life.

- They have all the up-to-date educational courses available.

- They advertise local job vacancies and have a dedicated website called Jobs4u.com which also has lots of job vacancies.

- The advisor can also help you to identify what jobs you would be most suited to.

Industry

People from industry may visit your school or college to discuss the various jobs available to you in their businesses. Some industries have open events where people are invited to visit the employer's premises to learn about the different job opportunities available in that company. See *Unit 4: Planning and Running a Hospitality Event* for more about Open Evenings/Days.

Tutor

Your tutor or college/school careers advisor will also be a valuable source of advice and are probably the most logical people to contact first. They may be able to offer to you more specific advice because they:

- will know you well
- will know your likes and dislikes
- will know your strengths.

Sources of job information

When you start to look for a job you may wonder where to begin. You may already have a part-time job which had been advertised in the window of a local business; or you may have just gone inside and asked if there were any jobs available.

Both of these methods are classed as sources of job information, but there are more sources available such as:

- newspapers
- trade magazines such as *Caterer* and *Hotelkeeper*
- company websites
- employment agencies
- local Job Centres.

An example of the type of advert you may have found is shown below:

Over to you

In pairs, find two jobs from each of the five sources listed above. The jobs need to link to hospitality-related sites.

Assistant Manager	Job id: 34709593
Location:	Settle, North Yorkshire
Salary:	£15–£20k Live-in plus bonus
Company:	The Falcon Manor Hotel
Job type:	Permanent
Date posted:	13/12/2007 13:00

Description: **Assistant Manager**

The Falcon Manor Hotel, Settle, North Yorkshire.

We are currently looking for an enthusiastic, experienced, hands-on, individual to work as part of a small team, in this privately owned 19 bedroom, 3 star country hotel. The Hotel has a restaurant and 2 bars and conference and banqueting up to 80 people. The Hotel nestles on the edge of the Yorkshire Dales with its wonderful countryside and relaxed way of life.

You will assume day to day responsibility for the running of the hotel and should ideally have experience in a similar role. Whilst you will be involved in the running of each department, you will be particularly involved in developing food and beverage sales and profits as well as setting and maintaining standards.

Source: http://www.totaljobs.com/JobSearch/JobDetails.aspx?JobId=34709593 (accessed 13 December 2007)

From your searches you will realise just how many jobs are available through the various sources.

Suitability of different sources

Not only is there so much choice in terms of the number of jobs available, there is also a lot of choice in terms of the advice you can get. The table below looks at the suitability, advantages and disadvantages of each source.

Source	Suitability (advantages/disadvantages)
Newspapers	■ Up to date ■ Reliable ■ National papers may not have many jobs suited to young people ■ Newspapers cost money to buy ■ Employers use local and national newspapers to advertise jobs, but there will be a cost involved
Trade magazines	■ Up to date ■ Reliable ■ Only advertise jobs in their specific industry ■ Advertise local and overseas jobs ■ Can be expensive to buy ■ Not easily accessible ■ Employers use trade magazines to advertise jobs, but there will be a cost involved
Company websites	■ Can be out of date ■ Job choice may be limited ■ Only jobs specific to the company are advertised ■ Can often apply online ■ Job adverts are free to view ■ Accessible to anyone with Internet access ■ Excellent for employers to advertise jobs as they have full control of the website and do not need to pay to advertise
Employment agencies	■ Lots of agencies available ■ Some may not be reliable and up to date ■ Access to agencies on the Internet ■ Some ask for lots of personal information before you can log on to job site ■ Many employers pay to advertise vacancies through agencies

Source	Suitability (advantages/disadvantages)
Job Centres	■ Many centres throughout the country ■ Up-to-date vacancies ■ Local to your area ■ Accessible ■ Advice available ■ Choice may be limited ■ Jobs may not be suitable for under-19s
Connexions	■ Lots of choice ■ Up to date and reliable ■ A free service ■ Meeting with a one-to-one advisor ■ Accessible via the Internet and the high street ■ Aimed specifically at the 14–19 age group so all jobs suited to those ages ■ Not suitable for all employers as the vacancies they have could be at too high a level for people over the age of 19
Industry	■ Can be difficult to access ■ Specific jobs for that industry ■ Up to date ■ Reliable ■ Jobs to suit different people and ages ■ May be able to visit and experience the actual workplace ■ Good for employers as they can invite people to visit their company at minimal cost
Tutor	■ Reliable ■ Trustworthy ■ Specific to you ■ Easy access ■ Free ■ If you have put your tutor down as a reference, employers may make contact. Employers may ask tutors if they can advertise job vacancies on the school/college notice board, and usually this is free of charge

The information in the table clearly shows that there are numerous sources you can draw on when you are ready to enter the job market. Your task is to make sure you use the sources which are right for you.

In summary

- The main sources of job information available to you are newspapers, trade magazines, company websites and employment agencies.
- Sources of careers advice are Connexions, the industry and your school/college tutor.
- When looking at the different sources, make sure you select the ones that are most suited to you – those with reliable and up-to-date information, accessibility and so forth.

Practice assessment activity

Levels P3/M2

You need to explain to a new employee within the careers service the different sources of information available for job and career opportunities.

P Identify the sources of information available to them for job and career opportunities. (P3)

M Compare three of the sources of information identified above in terms of their suitability. Suitability can be judged in terms of different audiences, different types of jobs (for example overseas), job requirements, part-time, full-time, for their up-to-date information, for their ease of access and so forth. (M2)

6.4 Be able to match your own skills to required employability skills

This section covers:

■ employability skills

■ matching skills.

The previous section focused on the sources of information available to you in relation to job and career opportunities when you reach the stage of looking for your first job. This section of the unit focuses on you, the skills that you already have and the skills that you may need to develop on entering the world of work.

Employability skills

Employability skills are the skills that an employer is looking for when trying to fill a job vacancy. They tend to fall under the following categories.

■ **Vocational skills** – The job holder must come to the job with some experience of the specific type of work, for example bar work.

■ **Personal skills** – attributes such as motivation, enthusiasm, personal presentation and so forth that you will bring to a job (see section 6.2).

■ **Qualifications** – Most jobs will require the job holder to have a certain qualification. Qualifications required will be stated in the personal specification and will range from GCSEs, vocational qualifications such as VRQs and NVQs, BTEC qualifications, A Levels, degrees and so forth. The level of job that you go for, whether operational or management, will determine the relevant level of qualification and experience. For example when you apply for a management job the employer is likely to expect you to have a degree and management experience.

■ **Courses and training** – Along with a qualification, some employers would like you to have attended certain courses. For example, if you apply for a job in a kitchen the employer might want you to have attended a Basic Food Hygiene course. Other courses or training employers in the hospitality-related industries like employees to have completed are Basic Health and Safety, First Aid and the Control of Substances Hazardous to Health (COSHH), referred to in *Unit 3: Safety in Hospitality*.

■ **Work experience** – Some employers will recognise that you may not be able to come to the job with any actual experience as you are applying for the job straight from school or college. In this case if you have had any work experience while at school or college then the skills you have learned will certainly make you more employable.

Essential and desirable skills

When you apply for a job it is increasingly likely that the advertisement will include not only a job description but also a personnel specification.

- The job description outlines all the duties you would have in that job role.
- The personnel specification will detail the requirements that the employer wants you to have in order to be able to carry out the job.

The personnel specification is usually broken down into two sections:

- **Essential skills** are the skills you must have in order to stand a chance of getting the job.
- **Desirable skills** are those that the employer would like you to have, but are not essential.

An example of a job description and job specification can be seen below.

Job Description
Position: Bar Person
Reporting to: Bar Supervisor

Main duties and responsibilities:

- Maintain the high company standards on every shift
- Maintain a high standard of customer service at all times
- Maintain product knowledge and ensure that all drinks and associated products are served and presented in accordance with company standards
- Ensure the bar and surrounding areas are kept clean at all times
- Ensure that empty glasses are cleared quickly and efficiently
- Be able to work the till and manage the float
- To be able to receive and store deliveries
- Assist the bar team in achieving all financial targets set for the pub
- Follow company security procedures
- Be aware of and adhere to licensing, data protection, Health and Safety at Work, COSSH and other legislation at all times
- Carry out any reasonable instruction given by any supervisor or member of the management team.

Personal Specification
Essential requirements:

- Have excellent customer service skills
- Be professional and well presented

- Have experience of working in a bar
- Have strong teamworking skills and people skills
- Have excellent communication skills at all levels
- Have a high level of motivation and enthusiasm
- Be able to remain calm under pressure
- Have a relevant qualification equivalent to NVQ Level 2
- Be over the age of 18
- Have proof of right to work in the UK
- Have a bank account
- Be willing to work unsociable hours.

Desirable requirements:

- Full driving licence
- Attended a one-day Cellar Training course
- Basic food hygiene qualification
- Basic health and safety qualification
- Attended and passed a one-day Personal Licence course.

You can see from the above that the employer is very clear on exactly what skills the employee *must* have if they are to carry out the job, and the skills that they *would like* them to have.

- If you apply for a job with all of the essential requirements but not the desirable requirements you are still likely to get an interview.
- If more than one person is interviewed for the job and one person has all the essential and desirable requirements, then they are more likely to get the job.

Matching skills

When you start to look for a job you need to carry out a matching exercise to see if you have the skills that an employer is looking for – the employability skills outlined at the beginning of this section.

By carrying out the *Over to you* exercise you will have identified some gaps between the skills you currently have and the skills the employer wants you to have. You have therefore started to review your own vocational and personal skills. This section will look at matching your skills and planning how to bridge the skills gap.

Over to you

Using the resources available to you (for example the Internet, newspapers), look for one or two jobs that you could realistically apply for. Look carefully at the job specification and see if the employability skills you currently have match those on the job specification.

Reviewing vocational and personal skills

By making a list of the skills you would need to have in order to apply for a particular job you are taking the first step towards identifying your strengths and areas for development.

Identifying skills development requirements

The headings below can be used as a guide to list your strengths, for example the skills you have and are good at, and the areas where you require some development.

Strengths

- good timekeeper
- good personal presentation
- enthusiastic
- self-motivated
- good written communication.

Development areas

- limited knowledge of food hygiene
- no till experience
- no vocational experience
- no experience of complaints handling.

To assist with the above exercise you may want to get feedback from your tutor, friends, family, part-time employers and so on – people who will tell you honestly what they think your strengths or areas for development are.

Over to you

Have a go at assessing your strengths and areas for development. These points will be added to and amended as your skills improve.

Personal development plans

After identifying your skills development areas, you should be ready to complete a personal development plan. A personal development plan is an exercise in which you list:

- all the areas of development you need to address
- when you will address these needs
- how you will address the needs
- whether it will cost you any money.

An example of a personal development plan for a 16-year-old school-leaver wishing to have a career as a receptionist in a health club is shown below.

Development need	How the need will be met	Time frame	Cost
To learn ICT skills: email, Excel and Word	Computer course, evening classes	Six weeks, one evening per week	£50
Reception experience	NVQ Level 2, part-time at local college	1 year	Free
Till experience	In my part-time job – will move on to working on the till	2 months	Free
Health and safety awareness	Health and safety course at local college	1 day	£60 as part of NVQ programme
Complaints handling	Covered in NVQ 2 Reception and on work experience	1 year	Free as part of NVQ

Over to you

Have a go at drawing up your own personal development plan in line with one of the jobs that you found earlier. Use the strengths and development areas form as a basis for your personal development plan. Having completed the plan, show it to your tutor, who will give you feedback and help with addressing your identified skill needs.

By carrying out this exercise:

■ you are identifying the gaps you have in terms of employability skills

■ you are planning how to address the gaps

■ once you have addressed the gaps you will be far more employable.

Your development plan can travel with you as you progress through your career. You will remove areas from it as skills gaps are met, and you will add to it as new skills need to be learned. Remember, we will continue to learn and develop new skills throughout our lives.

In summary

- Employability skills include vocational skills, personal skills, qualifications and work experience.
- It is a good idea to match the skills you presently have with employability skills to see if you have any developmental areas.
- A good way to address developmental areas is to draw up your own personal development plan, identifying your development needs, how they can be addressed, how long it will take to improve the skills and how much it could cost.
- As you progress through your career you will develop new skills and identify skills that need developing; this cycle of development is never-ending.

Practice assessment activity

Levels P3/P4/D1

You are approaching the time when you are ready to find a job. You know that at this time you may not have all the employability skills that may be required.

P Using feedback from others and your own self-assessment, draw up a table listing all your current strengths and your current skills areas that need developing. With this information, put together a personal development plan. Your personal development plan should match the personal skills you will need to have in order to progress with your career. Present your plan to your tutor. (P3/P4)

D Referring to your development plan and reflecting on your own personal development of skills and personal attributes, evaluate the changes in you that will need to take place in order to prepare you for employment. (D1)

6.5 Be able to undergo a job application process for employment in hospitality or a related industry

This section covers:

- documents
- interview and selection methods
- interview preparation
- interview skills.

Documents

The final section of the unit looks at compiling CVs, completion of the documents required when applying for a job and finally tips which will help you have a successful interview. In this section you will learn in detail about the various documents that form part of the application process, including:

- CVs
- letters of application
- application forms
- letters of acceptance or decline.

Often these documents will be the first impression an employer will get of you so it is essential that you get this stage right. Remember:

'You only get one chance to make a good first impression.'

CVs

CV stands for curriculum vitae, which translates to 'course of life'. A CV should provide a potential employer with a brief account of your career so far. CVs could be viewed as opportunities to market yourself to prospective employers.

CVs should have the following headings:

- Name
- Address
- Contact telephone number
- Email address
- Date of birth

- Schools attended
- Qualifications
- Employment history
- Personal skills and abilities
- Interests/hobbies
- Any special skills, for example driving licence
- Referees.

The following pointers will help when drawing up your CV.

- It should be no longer than two sides of A4 paper.
- It should be word-processed so that it can be amended and updated easily.
- Your CV should follow a logical order in terms of the above headings.
- Highlight your headings so that they stand out, that is bold, italics, underlined and indented.

CVs tend to fall into two different styles:

Traditional – This style lists everything in date order, starting with your education and qualifications, followed by your employment history, interests and so on.

Personal – This style starts with a picture of yourself, highlighting your skills and experiences relevant to the job you are applying for first.

Activity

Using the information given above and the two templates shown, draw up your own CV.

Letters of application

When you apply for a job, it is likely that you will be asked to either send a CV with a letter of application or to complete an application form with or without a letter of application. Like your CV, your letter of application is an opportunity to create a good impression. Letters of application generally contain the following information in the following structure:

- Personal address in the top right-hand corner of the letter with the date underneath
- Company address beneath your personal address on the left-hand side
- You should start the letter with 'Dear' (put the name if you have it) or 'Sir or Madam'
- Then add the title of the job that you are applying for

Traditional style CV

CURRICULUM VITAE

NAME: Peter Johns

ADDRESS: 1 High Street
Anytown AB1 CD2

TELEPHONE: 01234 567890

DATE OF BIRTH: 2nd April 1989

EDUCATION: Grovelands College of Food
Hallamshire High School

QUALIFICATIONS: NVQ Level 2 Food and Drink Service
6 GCSEs (English, Maths, Science, Geography, Art. History)

WORK EXPERIENCE: Waiter at Sunnyside Café, Anytown, 2006–7
Voluntary work at local homeless shelter, 2005

SKILLS AND PERSONAL QUALITIES: Excellent customer service skills, diligent and I
recognise the importance of attention to detail

INTERESTS: Cycling, swimming, computer games

OTHER INFORMATION: Full, clean driving licence
First aid qualificaion

REFEREES: Mrs D S Butcher, Head of Food Service, Grovelands College of Food

Mr F Smith, Headteacher, Hallamshire High School

Personal style CV

CURRICULUM VITAE

Name   Peter Johns

Address: 1 High Street
                 Anytown AB1 CD2

Telephone: 01234 567890

Email: peterjohns@abcmail.co.uk

Date of birth: 2nd April 1989

Personal profile
- I have a lot of experience of customer service and have very good people skills
- From my NVQ, I gained valuable knowledge of the hospitality industry
- I recognise the importance of attention to detail in the food service sector

Qualifications
- NVQ Level 2 Food and Drinks Service
- 6 GCSEs – English, Maths, Science, Geography, Art, History

Education
- Grovelands College of Food
- Hallamshire High School

Employment and work experience
- Waiter at Sunnyside Café, Anytown, 2006–7
- Voluntary work at local homeless shelter

Other interests
- Cycling
- Swimming
- Computer games

References
Mrs D S Butcher, Head of Food Service, Grovelands College of Food
Mr F Smith, Headteacher, Hallamshire High School

Activity

Have a go at writing a letter of application to accompany your CV for the job shown in the advert

- State why you want the job and why you think you would be a suitable candidate
- Give any information that would support your application in terms of relevant work experience
- If you know the name of the person the letter is going to, you should sign off the letter 'Yours sincerely'; if not you should sign off 'Yours faithfully'.

Restaurant Supervisor	
Salary:	£16,000–£18,000
Location:	Sudbury, Suffolk
Employer type:	Hotel
Recruiter:	The Grove Hotel
Job reference:	Caterer/swan140607
Job description:	A truly excellent opportunity for an applicant with a genuine interest in food, wine and restaurant operations. The successful candidate would help oversee the management of our 80-cover gallery restaurant and function rooms. We are looking for someone who is very customer focused and has a great passion for quality service.

Application forms

Some employers would prefer you to apply for a job by completing their application form rather than sending in your CV. The main reason for this is so that they can ensure they get the information they want from you. The application form may ask for information that would not normally be found on a CV. Some employers ask that the application forms be handwritten, providing them with an opportunity to assess the applicant's level of handwriting.

As with the CV and letter of application, an application form needs to be completed with care and thought. If this is what the employer has requested, this becomes their first impression of you.

Tips for completing application forms:

- Always try to have two copies, so that you have one you can practise on.
- Read through the whole form before you start, so you know exactly what information is expected.
- Follow the instructions carefully; some may ask for the forms to be filled in using black ink, capital letters and so on.
- Ensure you address the questions asked specifically and clearly.
- To avoid spelling mistakes, ask someone to check your form.

- Do not leave out any sections; if you feel that they do not apply to you then put N/A (not applicable) in the box.
- Always provide honest answers.
- Once accurately completed, take a copy for your own records.

Letters of acceptance or decline

Once you have applied for a job and had an interview, you will be informed either verbally or in writing whether you have been successful. Successful applicants would be expected to put in writing their decision to either accept or decline (turn down) the position. This is an important stage in the application process as it formalises your decision. In most cases if you have applied for a job one could assume that you want it, so if you receive an offer of the job it is likely that you will be writing a letter of acceptance. It might however be the case that your circumstances have changed since applying for the job and that you are no longer able to accept the new position.

Like all of the documents mentioned above, your final letter needs to look professional. The format of the letter would be the same as the letter of application but obviously the content will differ.

- It is important that the letter is sent promptly.
- In the letter be clear and succinct in either accepting or declining the position.
- If you are declining the position then you must notify the organisation immediately, so that they can either re-advertise or offer the job to another applicant.

Activity

Have a look on some hospitality or related industry websites for application forms. Choose two and have a go at completing them. Once completed, swap the forms with a peer to check for any spelling errors.

Interview and selection methods

Employers will use different interview and selection methods and they will probably inform you of this before you actually attend an interview. The different methods employers may use are shown below.

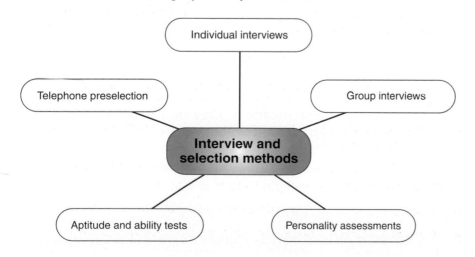

Individual and group interviews

These are the most common method and the types that you may have already experienced. If you are invited to attend an interview you can reasonably expect the following.

■ You will be invited to the prospective employer's business premises.

■ You will need to announce your arrival to a secretary or receptionist, who will inform your interviewer of your arrival.

■ The interview will take place in the employer's office or in a meeting room.

■ The layout of the room traditionally will be the interviewer(s) seated behind a desk with a chair for the interviewee (you) to sit in front.

■ There could be more than one interviewer (a panel) and there is likely to be a person who will be making notes.

■ At the beginning of the interview you will be introduced to all those present and their role in the interview will be explained.

■ After formal introductions the interview will start and questions will be asked.

■ A group interview would follow a similar sequence, but part of the interview process may involve a group activity.

Personality assessments

These are used to determine a person's typical reaction and attitude to a range of situations. Often they are used so that employers can identify how well you get on with others, how you react to stressful situations or your feelings about the kind of people you like to work with. There are many different types of assessment some of which are listed below.

■ BBC Personality Type Indicator Test

■ Team technology

■ The Keirsey Temperament Sorter

For links to these websites, go to www.heinemann.co.uk/hotlinks, insert the express code 5285P and click on the links to this page.

Aptitude and ability tests

These are structured, systematic ways of evaluating how people perform on tasks or react to different situations. They are often conducted in test conditions and may be in the form of multiple choice questions, or long answer questions. Such tests could be verbal or numerical reasoning. Ability tests can be focused more on testing a person's ability at a certain skill or task.

Telephone pre-selection

This type of selection method is used under a variety of circumstances.

Over to you

In small groups, try to add more interview and selection methods to those in the diagram and then discuss these with the whole group.

- As part of the screening process – Some employers may use this method to give the applicant the chance to make an early verbal impression on the employer. You should bear in mind though that at this stage the call may be unannounced.

- As part of the interview process – In this case the call will be prearranged at a time convenient to employer and applicant. If you are accepting a job overseas it may not be practical to have a face-to-face interview, so a telephone interview is more suited.

- As part of an ability test – particularly if the job you have applied for is in sales and marketing.

Some tips for telephone interviews are listed below.

- If possible ensure the call is on a landline rather than a mobile.

- Choose a quiet place to take the call, where there will be no distractions.

- If you know the time of the call ensure you answer the phone in a professional manner.

- Be prepared for the call – have all relevant information available (your CV, information on the company and so forth), plus pen and paper.

- Stand up or sit up straight – your voice will sound louder and more assertive than if you are slouching or lying down.

Interview preparation

Preparation for an interview is essential. You are unlikely to be successful at an interview if you don't plan carefully for it.

Your preparation needs to include research into the company to which you are applying. Often the first question an interviewer will ask is why you want to work for the company. Technology makes this research easy as most companies now have their own websites giving information about the business. If this is not the case, then it would be a good idea to ring the company before the interview and either ask some questions or ask for information on the company to be sent to you.

Be absolutely clear on exactly what the job is that you are applying for. If you have been sent the job description then refresh your memory before the interview. This will also help you to draw up any relevant questions you may wish to ask at the interview.

Plan your dress code before the day of the interview because you must dress appropriately. This will usually mean wearing a suit – either trousers and jacket or skirt and jacket with an appropriate top or shirt and tie.

Hair needs to be clean and tidy, as do hands and nails. Only a minimal amount of make-up, aftershave or perfume should be worn.

Use the photo to identify the positive and negative aspects of the person's dress code and personal appearance for a job interview.

Attitude and behaviour

Interviewers like to see interviewees who:

- are confident
- can speak clearly and knowledgeably
- can answer questions thoughtfully.

Being overconfident is seen as negative, as is being underconfident. With careful planning, you should be able to walk into the interview with confidence. Take the interview seriously; it is not a time to tell jokes and be silly. Your behaviour needs to be professional from the moment you enter the building until the moment you leave the building.

■ *Make sure you dress appropriately for an interview*

Interview skills

The planning has taken place; the next and final stage is actually attending an interview.

Below are two lists, one gives interview skills and the other a series of words and phrases. Both lists are needed in order to have a successful interview.

Interview skills

- body language
- social skills
- personal skills
- active listening
- presentation techniques
- responding to questions
- asking questions.

Matching words and phrases

- Sit up straight
- Speak clearly
- Be honest
- Good eye contact

- Use appropriate tone – not too soft or too loud
- Have a firm handshake
- Don't interrupt
- Paraphrase (choose different words to say something, to make it clearer)
- Don't chew
- Turn mobile off
- Be succinct
- Clear visual aides
- Confirm understanding by positive affirmations for example nodding
- Think before you answer
- Answer fully
- Be polite
- Knock before entering the interview room
- Open posture, that is hands and legs not crossed
- Dress appropriately
- Professional PowerPoint slides – bullet points not paragraphs
- Ask open questions
- Sit down when asked
- No nervous habits such as touching face or hair, tapping a pen
- Be sensible – no telling jokes
- Ask relevant and appropriate questions
- Wait until the question has been asked before giving an answer

Activity

Study these two lists, then match the words and phrases to the appropriate interview skills. Discuss with your tutor and others in the group why you feel these skills are important for a successful interview.

In summary

- The job application process could involve the completion of a CV, letters of application, application forms and letters of acceptance or decline.
- All of the above must be completed professionally and carefully, with no mistakes.
- Common methods of interview and selection are telephone interviews, individual and group interviews.
- Planning for an interview is essential; without planning you will reduce your chances of success.
- For any type of interview you must plan well, dress smartly and have good personal and social skills.
- Tips for attending an interview include: don't turn up late, don't tell jokes, don't look scruffy, don't lie and don't talk too much or too little.

Practice assessment activity

Levels P5/M3/D2

Using available resources – for example newspapers, Internet job sites, *Caterer and Hotelkeeper* magazine – select a relevant job that you would like to apply for. Ensure that the chosen job has an application form which you can complete. Then draw up the following relevant documentation that you would need to have in order to apply for the job:

- CV
- application form.

In preparation for the interview, gain company knowledge, be absolutely clear about what the job involves and decide on appropriate dress for the interview.

In pairs, role play the interview, ensuring that you use the appropriate interview skills.

Ideally the interview role play will be videoed so that both the interviewer and the interviewee can use it to evaluate their performance. As an interviewer you will need to feedback both verbally and in writing to your interviewee. To assist with this, in pairs, draw up assessment criteria to measure the success of the interviewee. These would include such pointers as body language, social skills, personal skills, listening skills and so forth. These assessment criteria can then form the basis of the written and verbal feedback. Your criteria could be graded on a scale of 1–5, where 1 shows poor interview skills and 5 shows excellent interview skills.

P Prepare a CV, complete an application form, prepare for interview and use interview skills in preparation for employment. (P5)

M Explain how CVs, application forms and interviews assist employers when making employment decisions. (M3)

D Analyse the effectiveness of your own performance in all aspects of the job application process and recommend improvements. (D2)

Test your knowledge

1 List the three main hospitality-related industries and for each, give two examples of businesses which fall into those categories.

2 Explain briefly two of the functions of the related industries.

3 Give examples of jobs which fall into the three categories of career opportunities.

4 List four personal attributes, explaining why they are important to employers.

5 List three sources of job information, explaining the suitability of each.

6 Explain what the term 'employability skills' means.

7 Why is it important for you to be able to match your own skills with required employability skills and how can this be done?

8 What is the benefit of having a personal development plan?

9 Why is it important when applying for a job that your CV, letter of application and application form are well presented?

10 List five interview skills, explaining why each skill is important to have.

7 Basic Culinary Skills

Introduction

Most people have eaten a meal out either in a cafe, restaurant, hotel or bistro. There has been a huge growth in the number of meals eaten outside the home. It's not uncommon for people to eat out two or three times a week. Consumers are becoming more adventurous in their choices, but also more critical about the quality of what they eat and quickly complain when things go wrong. Customers make judgements about their enjoyment of food and how it might be improved or made more interesting.

This unit is all about food preparation and cooking. It enables some culinary skills to be developed, as well as considering how to buy food and cost basic recipes for a business. The unit ends with a look at how food can be presented and how to critically evaluate dishes to improve quality.

How you will be assessed

Unit 7 is assessed internally, so the Centre delivering the qualification will assess you against the criteria. On completion of this unit you should:

7.1 know about purchasing food and the associated purchasing documents

7.2 understand the costing of dishes

7.3 be able to prepare and cook dishes using different categories
    of food

7.4 be able to present and review dishes.

Assessment grades

The Edexcel Assessment Grid for Unit 7 details the criteria to be
met. In general, to gain a pass (P) you are asked to describe,
calculate, prepare, cook, present and review; to gain a Merit (M)
you are also asked to explain, accurately calculate and show
proficiency; and to gain a Distinction (D) you are also asked to
assess and reflect.

7.1 Know about purchasing food and the associated documents

This section covers:

- purchasing food
- documents used in the purchasing cycle.

Purchasing food

Purchasing is the technical term used in catering for buying. Purchasing food in catering is a very skilful job that requires a great deal of knowledge and experience of food and **commodities** (raw products).

In most catering businesses where food is prepared it is usually very difficult to calculate exactly how many customers are going to be served. Many catering outlets do not require customers to book; they just arrive. There are many reasons that affect the number of customers that will come into a business:

- weather
- time of day
- season of year
- location of business, such as seaside or city centre.

A catering business needs to have in place well thought-out arrangements for buying so that what is needed is always available, either in stock or ready for delivery.

Hospitality businesses such as cafes, restaurants, hotels, contract caterers and hospitals buy food or commodities from suppliers in a number of ways. Food is purchased either daily, weekly or monthly depending on the style, size and location of the business and of course on the type of food that is being bought. As an example, fresh fruit and vegetables may be bought on a daily basis, while frozen foods might be purchased once a week and groceries such as tea and coffee once a month.

Suppliers should:

- be able to supply what is wanted at a price that is acceptable
- know their products
- be able to supply the products when the caterer needs them
- have a good trading reputation
- use correct storage and delivery procedures.

Types of suppliers

There are many types of supplier that can supply food to a catering business. Most catering businesses buy from a range of suppliers depending on:

- what is being bought
- the size of business they run, such as small owner-managed or part of a large national chain with buying contracts
- the amount of food being purchased.

Wholesale

This type of supplier will only supply to recognised businesses and not individuals, as they are not open to the public. They usually specialise in one product such as meat, fish or fruit and vegetables and will only supply in large quantities. The advantages of using a wholesaler are that:

- the items the caterer wants are usually in stock
- the prices charged are very competitive
- there is a wide range of items to choose from
- deliveries can be made direct to the caterer at a specified time.

Retail

Shops in the high street in every city and town are known as retailers; they supply to the general public. A supermarket is an example of a retailer. They buy goods in large quantities that are then repackaged and sold to shoppers in smaller amounts. The advantage of using a retailer is that food items are available in small quantities and this can prevent over-buying. They often have long opening hours and are open when other types of supplier are closed. The disadvantage of buying from a retailer is that they are usually the most expensive in terms of price.

Specialised

These suppliers are often small independent businesses that concentrate on one or only a few product items. They can be very knowledgeable about the products they supply, as well as supplying products that cannot be found anywhere else. Frequently the specialist supplier may actually produce or manufacture the items they supply. Cheese and smoked meats are examples of products that can be purchased from a specialist supplier.

Local

These suppliers are based in the same location or area as the businesses they supply. The attraction of using a local supplier for a catering business is that they can have flexible delivery arrangements, as journey distances are small. They can also specialise in supplying a range of local products that an area can be well known for. Many restaurants and hotels advertise the fact that they serve locally sourced products. This is a good way of increasing business and giving customers something new and different that they may not have tried before.

Over to you

In small groups, think of a retail shop that you use on a regular basis. Write down all the reasons why you use this retailer. Discuss the reasons with the rest of your group.

■ *A specialised supplier*

National

These are suppliers that supply customers over the whole country. They are usually very large companies that supply everything a catering business will need in one weekly delivery, or they may provide one main product such as meat or **dry goods** (groceries). National companies usually have a minimum financial value for each delivery. It is also necessary to set up formal accounts, and possibly have a **contract** (legal agreement), which can create a lot of paperwork, particularly for a small business.

Market list

These are price lists usually produced on a weekly basis from a local or national market that specialises in a particular product. Examples are Smithfield for meat and Covent Garden for fruit, vegetables and flowers; both are in London.

- Buying in a market may not be very convenient, as they tend to open very early in the mornings.

- The buyer needs to have good knowledge of the products they are buying.

- The buyer also has to manage transport arrangements as markets tend not to have delivery services.

- The advantage of going to market is that some good bargains may be had and that the quality can be very high.

Cash and carry

This is a large warehouse where the chef or caterer goes in person to buy the goods and products needed. To use a cash and carry you need to be a registered business, as they do not supply the general public.

- Most towns or areas have their own cash and carry.

- They hold a large range of items, including meat, fruit and vegetables, frozen foods and groceries.

- It is possible to buy everything a catering business needs.

- The items are often available in a variety of package sizes, from small to very large.

- It is usual to pay for purchases at the end of the buying process and transport

■ *A cash and carry can be a large place*

> ## Key points
>
> There are many types of suppliers that can supply a hospitality business, and suppliers are chosen with regard to:
>
> - what is being bought
> - the size of the business
> - the amount of food being purchased.

everything back to the workplace yourself. This can be hard work if lots of things are needed, and also requires a large vehicle.

For many small catering businesses this is a very popular way of buying as it is flexible, it creates less paperwork and it can be done at a quiet time.

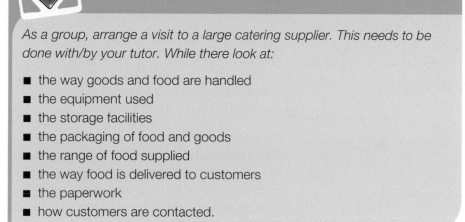

Activity

As a group, arrange a visit to a large catering supplier. This needs to be done with/by your tutor. While there look at:

- the way goods and food are handled
- the equipment used
- the storage facilities
- the packaging of food and goods
- the range of food supplied
- the way food is delivered to customers
- the paperwork
- how customers are contacted.

Documents used in the purchasing cycle

Good control of food and what food is purchased is an important part of a chef's work. Effective management of purchases means that:

- only food that is needed is bought
- wastage or unused food that has to be thrown away is kept to a minimum.

As buying involves spending large amounts of money as well as entering into legal agreements with suppliers, it is important that strict procedures supported by formal paperwork and documentation are used. This applies even in the smallest catering operation such as a snack bar or a seaside bed and breakfast (B&B).

Business documents

- Although standard documents are used in all businesses, there is no standard design. Many companies have their own ideas about size and layout.

- Quite a lot of business paperwork can be filled out on a computer using especially designed software to match the individual business needs. This makes the information and presentation of paperwork much easier to understand as often handwriting is difficult to read and this can cause mistakes to be made.

- Record keeping and payments can also be done electronically.

■ Even though computers are widely used there is still a need for paper records as they are often more convenient to use in a practical work situation like a kitchen.

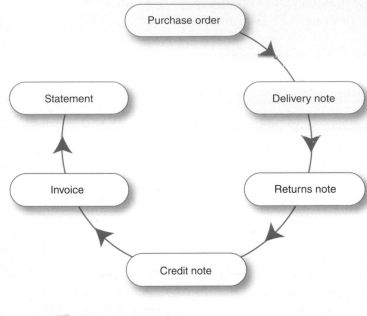

The purchasing cycle

The **purchasing cycle** is a term given to the system used in a catering business to place, receive and pay for orders of food and other goods from outside suppliers.

To illustrate how business documents are used, a dish offered by Seagulls Bistro, Farmhouse Crumble taken from the standard recipes at the end of this unit, is tracked through the system.

Purchase order

Once the quantities needed for the dish have been calculated by the chef at Seagulls, orders will need to be placed with suppliers if items are not held in stock. As the dish is a vegetable crumble, most of the items needed are from the greengrocer or fruit and vegetable supplier, the Fruit Bowl.

A **purchase order** will be completed showing how much of each item is needed, together with the required delivery day. The order will be completed in duplicate (two copies) and either telephoned, sent or given to the supplier.

One copy will be kept by Seagulls Bistro. Orders made by phone must be confirmed in writing using a purchase order, which is sent to the supplier.

Delivery note

When the supplier (in this case the Fruit Bowl) delivers the order of vegetables to Seagulls Bistro it is accompanied by a **delivery note**. This is a note prepared by the supplier which shows what is being delivered and the amounts. This should match exactly what was ordered. Seagulls Bistro will check the actual food items delivered against the delivery note for quantity and quality.

Returns note

Unfortunately the carrots were of such a poor quality that they were refused and had to be sent back to the supplier. A **returns note** was completed showing the item and the quantity that was returned.

Credit note

The supplier will send Seagulls a **credit note** to cover the value of the carrots and they will not be charged for them at the end of the month. Credit notes are the only documents used in purchasing that are printed in red; this is so they stand out.

Over to you

Write out a purchase order to cover the food for a small lunch for 35 people who are having Farmhouse Crumble and French bread. Use the standard recipe number 2 at the end of this unit.

Talking point

Think of other reasons why something that has been purchased might have to be sent back to the supplier.

Invoice

An **invoice** is a bill for goods received. The supplier for the delivery that was required will make out an invoice. Each separate purchase order will have an invoice made out by the supplier showing what was delivered and the price to be charged. This is the amount now owed by Seagulls Bistro. It must keep all the invoices it receives from the supplier and use them to check that it only pays for food it had delivered. This is done at the end of each month.

Statement

A **statement** of account is prepared each month by the supplier. It shows the transactions that have taken place during the month, as well as the amount owed at the end of the month. Any credit notes will also be shown and the amount taken off the final monthly bill. It's a summary of all the invoices and credit notes.

Normal practice in a commercial catering business is to pay at the end of each month for all the goods that have been bought and not every time a delivery takes place. Payment is usually by cheque from a bank account and not in cash. Large companies can also make payments using the electronic banking system (BACS) without the need to use cash or cheques. This is a very quick and secure way of making payments.

In summary

- Purchasing food for a catering business is a skilful job and money can be lost if it is done badly.
- Care needs to be taken when choosing a supplier to ensure that good-quality food is bought.
- A set of formal business documents is used to support the purchasing cycle. These are: purchase order, delivery note, returns note, credit note, invoice and statement.

Practice assessment activity

Levels P1/M1/D1

P Describe the purchasing cycle that Seagulls Bistro should use to effectively purchase food for its business. (P1)

M Demonstrate the use of purchasing documents; this could be in your school/college kitchens. (M1)

D Write how the purchasing cycle and use of documentation can improve the control of food purchases. (D1)

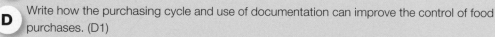

7.2 Understand the costing of dishes

This section covers:

- calculating costs of products
- calculating prices.

Talking point

Do you buy things if they are very cheap or on special offer? If so do you always need them?

Calculating costs of products

Understanding the costs of the products and raw materials that are purchased by a catering business is an essential part of a chef's role. The profitability of a business is dependent upon good buying that includes knowledge of cost. Many items that are bought have prices that fluctuate. This means they can go up or down on a daily or weekly basis, often according to the season of year or unusual weather conditions. These fluctuations may need to be reflected in menu prices charged to customers.

Ingredients and other items

Ingredients are the foods that go into dishes. Chefs use a **dish-costing sheet** to help calculate the costs of each portion or recipe. This information helps to calculate the **selling price** or the **menu price**. Good sources of information for the caterer showing what is available and their cost are trade journals, magazines, suppliers' price lists and catalogues.

Seagulls Bistro – Dish-costing sheet

Recipe No. 1 Cheesy Bake	4 portions	Date of costing September 2007
Ingredients	**Quantity**	**Cost**
Sliced bread (own choice)	400 g	47p
Butter	25 g	8p
Medium eggs	4	72p
Milk	600 ml	40p
Fresh basil	25 g	22p
Cherry tomatoes	375 g	84p
Cheddar cheese	175 g	123p
Parmesan cheese grated	25 g	40p
Seasoning		5p
Chopped parsley		5p
	Total cost of ingredients	£4.46
	Cost of 1 portion	£1.12 rounded up
	Selling price	

Portion control

A **portion** or serving is the amount of food that a customer will be given, such as:

- a slice of apple pie or gateau
- volume of fried chips
- weight of raw steak for grilling.

When calculating the cost of a portion it is necessary to know what the ingredients cost and also the size of a portion or serving.

Activity

- Write a list of ten of the food items you eat most often.
- Work out the portion size of each item.
- Why do you eat this size of portion?

Case studies

Seagulls Bistro makes and serves Cheesy Bake for £4.95 a portion. The chefs make it in dishes that hold ten portions. This means that £49.50 is the sales return from ten portions. However, if only nine portions are obtained because the staff give servings that are too generous, the bistro will lose £4.95 in income.

The scenario in this case study is not an uncommon problem in catering. On the other hand, to give too little of something or too small a portion can upset customers and cause offence. Customers will leave the bistro hungry and feeling that they have not had good value for money. They may not return. Judging how much of something a person can eat comes with experience. Remember not everybody has the same size appetite.

■ *Foods portioned for cooking and serving*

Specialist equipment

This can be used to help ensure that portions are just right for size, volume and quantity. Equipment such as scoops, ladles and spoons that are a known size are used for serving. Containers and dishes can be used for cooking individual portions. Fast-food restaurants and national chain businesses use very sophisticated equipment and packaging to ensure absolute accuracy in portioning as they sell many thousands of portions each day.

■ *Specialised equipment for portioning food*

Recipes

A **recipe** is a set of instructions on how to make a food dish, showing all the ingredients needed with weights and amounts. Recipes should be followed quite closely.

However, flair and imagination play an important part in catering and so variations on recipes are common. From a business view it is necessary to know that costs and profit will be maintained as well as the dish tasting and looking the same every time it is produced. Regular customers may have a favourite dish and will want it always to taste the same.

Standard recipes are used to help manage food production. These state:

- the name and quantity of all ingredients
- the method of production and service instructions
- the expected yield (how many servings) from that quantity of ingredients.

The example below shows a standard recipe taken from this unit. It has been multiplied for 4, 10 and 25 portions. The recipe would also be costed out so that the costs of production were known and the selling price worked out according to the **gross profit** requirements. Regular checks need to be made on costs of ingredients by reviewing invoices and price lists from suppliers. Where necessary the prices charged to customers may need to be increased. A manager or the head chef will do this.

Recipe No. 1 Cheesy Bake – a savoury version of bread and butter pudding served with french bread

4 portions	10 portions	25 portions	Ingredient
400 g	1 kg	2.5 kg	Sliced bread (own choice)
25 g	65 g	165 g	Butter
4	10	25	Medium eggs
600 ml	1.5 litre	3.75 litre	Milk
25 g	65 g	160 g	Fresh basil
375 g	940 g	2.35 kg	Cherry tomatoes
175 g	440 g	1.1 kg	Cheddar cheese
25 g	65 g	165 g	Parmesan cheese, grated
			Seasoning
			Chopped parsley

Costs of meals and functions

Any catering business must be able to calculate what an item being sold has cost. The selling price has to be fixed at a level that:

- will make a profit
- cover all the costs
- be acceptable to customers.

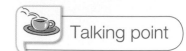

Consideration needs to be given to what is being charged by competitors where a number of similar outlets are in the same location.

Dish costing shows how the cost and eventual selling price for each individual dish is calculated. The **menu** is made up of many dishes set out in the order in which food is eaten, with starters at the beginning and ending with sweets and puddings. Each dish will need to be individually costed and priced in accordance with business policy. With some **set menus** customers can eat a whole meal of several courses for one price. Here expensive dishes need to be balanced with more economic ones. This gives a balance of prices so that customers can afford to eat and a profit still be made.

Functions such as weddings and parties all have special menus. These are designed and costed in advance of customers making enquiries. They are similar to set menus, with customers charged an inclusive price per guest for the meal. The type and time of the function and the number of courses chosen will influence what is to be eaten and the price. Functions are dealt with in detail in *Unit 4: Planning and Running a Hospitality Event*.

Think of a function you have been to. What did you have to eat?

■ *Menus for functions are costed according to customer requirements*

Calculating prices

Profit is the term used for the amount of money a business makes.

Sales is the amount of money a business takes over a period of time.

Gross profit is the amount of money left after the **production costs** are taken away. Gross profit is expressed as a percentage (%) of sales, and is sometimes known as the gross **profit margin**.

Production costs include items such as:

- **food:** the costs of all food purchases
- **labour:** wages, holiday pay, overtime and pensions
- **overheads:** gas, water, electricity, rent, rates, advertising, insurance, telephone and computer network.

Identifying profit margins

Not all dishes make the same level of profit. A business will determine how much profit is needed to pay bills and leave money over at the end of the month. Some items make high levels of profit. Soup is a good example where a tasty and popular dish can be made at quite low cost. Other items can make only a small contribution to profit. Generally a business will have a policy to make a percentage of gross profit overall each month.

Once a menu item such as Cheesy Bake has been costed out, that is the costs of ingredients have been identified, then the profit level needed can be added and the selling price calculated.

Menu selling prices

As seen from the dish-costing sheet, the food cost of four portions of Cheesy Bake is £4.46 and the gross profit required is 60 per cent.

The selling price will be calculated by using the following formula:

food cost multiplied by (x) 100 divided by (÷) 100 minus (−) required food gross profit:

$$\frac{\text{(food cost) £4.46} \times 100 \text{ (required gross profit 60\%)}}{40} = \text{(selling price) £11.15}$$

As the £11.15 is for four portions, we must divide this by four to find the cost of one portion: £11.15 ÷ 4 = £2.79 (rounded up).

Add in the cost of the French bread and VAT (value added tax) and that gives us a menu selling price of £3.95.

This method can be used to work out any selling price.

Food cost percentage

Another term for gross profit is kitchen percentage when applied to a food production situation. The kitchen percentage is another calculation needed to help manage costs. This calculation expresses the food cost as a percentage of the selling price using the following formula:

kitchen percentage = food cost = 40% of the selling price

For Cheesy Bake:

$$\frac{\text{(food cost) £4.46} \times 100}{\text{(selling price) £11.15}} = 40\%$$

Fixing the price of menu items is a very important task.

- If prices are set too high, customers may go elsewhere
- If prices are set too low they may not cover the costs of production.

In summary

- Dish costing is used to help determine the menu prices for dishes.
- Standard recipes are used to help maintain costs and keep quality high.
- Gross profit is the money left after the production costs are taken away; this is sometimes known as kitchen profit.
- Standard costing calculations are used to work out costs and profit levels for food.

Practice assessment activity

Levels P2/M2

P Using costing sheets, cost three dishes and calculate the selling prices. You can use the standard recipes provided in this unit and one other. Scale the recipe to provide enough portions for one person, for 16 people and for 36 people. (P2)

M For the three dishes costed, calculate the selling price for one portion using gross profit margins of 45%, 60% and 80% and use your calculations to justify this price. (M2)

7.3 Be able to prepare and cook dishes using different categories of food

This section covers:

- preparing food items for cooking
- cooking
- food categories
- food items.

Preparing food items for cooking

Cooking is a technical activity that requires careful working methods from staff in the kitchen. In this section you will learn about:

- weighing and measuring
- food preparation techniques
- selecting and using equipment.

Weighing and measuring

Chefs need to understand basic weights and measures so they can follow instructions given in **recipes** to ensure successful outcomes. Food is expensive to buy and chefs need to be accurate in weighing and measuring so that food is not wasted and money lost. Recipes may be written using two sets of measurements – metric and imperial. Temperatures are shown in degrees **Celsius** (°C) or **Fahrenheit** (°F).

It is very important not to mix metric and imperial measures when following recipes: use one or the other.

Common weights, measures and temperatures

Metric	Imperial	
Weight		
kilogram (kg) = 1,000 g	pound (lb) = 16 oz	
gram(me) (g)	ounce (oz)	
Capacity		
litre (l) = 100 cl/1000 ml	gallon = 8 pints	
centilitre (cl) = 100 ml	quart = 2 pints	

Metric	Imperial	
millilitre (ml)	pint = 20 fluid ounces (fl oz)	

Freezing point/boiling point of water

Celsius (°C)	Fahrenheit (°F)	
0°C/100°C	32°F/212°F	

Oven temperature (adjustment needed for fan ovens)

Celsius (°C)	Fahrenheit (°F)	Gas mark
120	250	½ (slow)
140	275	1
150	300	2
170	325	3
180	350	4 (moderate)
190	375	5
200	400	6 (hot)
220	425	7
230	450	8 (very hot)
260	500	9

Food preparation techniques

Before food items can be cooked they often need to undergo some basic preparation. For some foods this can be quite a basic task. For example in salad or sandwich making food items may be only washed and cut. For more complex dishes such as the Farmhouse Vegetable Crumble (Standard Recipe No. 2) it can be more involved as food items need to be grated, peeled, chopped or diced before cooking can take place.

The table shows some of the preparation techniques used in the kitchen. Chefs need to be able to select the correct tools and equipment for the tasks they have to do so that they can be efficient, work in a safe manner and not waste food. As a general rule the larger the job the larger the tool.

Technique	Equipment	Function
Peeling	7.5 cm small cook's knife, vegetable peeler	To remove outer skin or layers from fruit and vegetables such as potatoes or apples
Chopping	Large cook's knife, hand-held chopper, food processor	To cut large food items into smaller pieces for cooking or eating, such as chicken; or as for nuts or parsley when used as an ingredient in a recipe

Technique	Equipment	Function
Dicing	Large cook's knife	To cut raw or cooked food items into cube-style pieces when used in dishes such as fruit salad or soups. The dice can be large or small
Grating	Hand grater, food processor	To reduce the density of foods such as cheese, carrots when used as toppings, for example on pizzas or salad items
Creaming	Wooden spoon, hand or bench food mixer, food processor	To incorporate air into fat and sugar as part of the cooking process, as in sponge cakes
Rubbing	Usually done by hand	To incorporate fat and flour together in baking, as for a vegetable crumble topping
Folding	Metal spoon	To combine ingredients in a gentle way so there is no reduction in volume or lightness, such as in making sponge cakes
Beating	Wooden spoon, hand or bench food mixer, food processor	To incorporate air into fat and sugar as part of the cooking process such as in sponge cakes
Stirring	Wooden spoon, spatula, electric mixer	To blend ingredients – solid, liquid or both
Mixing	Wooden spoon, spatula, metal spoon, electric mixer	To blend ingredients – solid, liquid or both
Seasoning	Salt, pepper mills, garlic crusher, mustard pot	To improve the flavour of foods

Activity

Identify some basic foods that are prepared prior to cooking. You can look in the standard recipes to help you get going. Try to find two foods for each technique. Discuss your findings with your group.

Activity

Use the kitchen at your school or college and identify all the different items of equipment used for food preparation. Has the kitchen all the equipment needed so you can do all the methods identified?.

Preparation of raw foods can be a time-consuming activity for a chef. Foods can be purchased for cooking with most if not all of the preparation already done by the supplier or producer. This has become very popular and a huge range of completely prepared items is now available for use in the catering industry. These are sometimes referred to as **convenience foods**.

Preparation equipment

Equipment used in the preparation of food must be clean, safe and in good working order. A wide range of equipment and utensils is available to use in the kitchen. What is actually needed depends on the range of food being cooked, and this is influenced by the style and size of the menu.

Small-scale equipment

Small-scale equipment includes:

- knives
- potato peeler/apple corer
- lemon zester
- round scoops for cutting fruit
- garlic crusher
- poultry secateurs (strong scissors)
- kitchen scissors.

Knives

Most chefs own their own knives; they are the 'tools of the trade'. They are very expensive to buy and are always looked after very carefully. Knives are made of many different materials including:

- **carbon steel** with wooden handles – these can be difficult to keep clean
- **combination** of stainless steel with plastic handles – this combination makes them easy to keep clean and hygienic
- **stainless steel** including the handles – these are easy to keep clean and well maintained.

Chopping boards

Chopping boards are available in many sizes and colours. Today the trend is for them to be made in strong plastic so that they may be easily washed and sterilised. Some are colour coded to stop cross-contamination – that is germs spreading from one food to another or from cooked food to raw or uncooked food. Each food type has its own colour board. Many chefs prefer to use the traditional wooden ones. These, however, are more difficult to keep clean and free of bacteria.

Large-scale equipment

There are a lot of mechanical devices that can be used in the kitchen to help with food preparation to reduce the time it takes to complete repetitive and boring tasks. The use of mechanical devices also:

- enables staff to be used more effectively
- can contribute to reducing kitchen costs
- produces a better-quality finished product.

Large-scale mechanical equipment includes:

- electric mixers
- liquidisers/blenders
- food processors
- slicers.

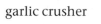

Over to you

Chopping boards are sometimes colour coded for different foods to stop cross-contamination by germs. Investigate and identify the colour codes, and match them with the food.

■ *A wide range of small-scale equipment is used in food preparation*

■ *Large mechanical devices can help reduce preparation time*

This type of equipment can be dangerous if not used properly by trained staff. Some items such as meat slicers also should not be used by anyone under 18 years of age. Make sure you are aware of proper practices and all the safety requirements and legislation, as detailed in *Unit 3: Safety in Hospitality*.

Cooking

What is cooking?

Many foods that we eat are **cooked** by applying heat to them. When heat is applied changes take place in the structure, texture and taste. These changes are affected by:

- the way the heat is applied to the food
- the length of time the heat is applied
- the temperature the food is cooked at.

Why is food cooked?

Some foods cannot be eaten raw so cooking is essential. Food is cooked to:

- develop, improve and/or alter its flavour
- improve its digestibility and therefore allow the nutrients it contains to be more easily absorbed by the human body
- destroy harmful bacteria and micro-organisms which could damage health
- improve the appearance of many food items
- extend the life of some **perishable** items (those that go bad quickly).

■ *Food can be cooked in many ways and for many reasons*

What happens if food is overcooked?

- Overcooking can destroy the nutritional value of food so it will not be as useful to the body as it should be.
- Food becomes unpalatable (unpleasant to eat) or inedible (uneatable) by unfavourably changing the flavour, texture, structure and colour.

Methods of cooking

There is a wide range of cooking methods used in catering today. Some of these were outlined in *Unit 5: Healthy Lifestyles*.

Boiling: This involves submerging food in water and cooking it at 100°C (212°F) – the boiling point of water. Wherever possible the cooking water should be used, for example for making gravy, and not thrown away as it will contain water-soluble nutrients such as vitamins.

Case studies

A brisk pace

The local walking group have phoned to ask if your school/college could provide a lunch for them when they are on their next walk. They have looked at the map and found that they will be walking by at about lunchtime. Your school/college is located near a historic place of interest, which is why a lot of walkers visit the district.

Your tutor has said yes in principle to providing the lunch.

Using your knowledge of catering and cooking, list all the questions you will need to ask the organiser of the group so that you can prepare the lunch for the group.

Grilling: When food items are grilled they are cooked by placing the item either under the heat source, above the heat source or a combination of both, such as in toasting. Food items cooked in this way need to be good quality, tender and in small amounts. Foods that are overcooked when grilled have a tendency to dry out and become unpalatable very quickly.

Barbecuing is a type of grilling where the food is basted (coated) with a sauce or marinade prior to cooking. The smoke created by the barbecue adds flavour to the food.

Deep-frying: Food is cooked by immersing it completely in pre-heated fat or oil. Deep-fried items are frequently dipped in batter or breadcrumbs to protect them from the heat. In this process of cooking some of the nutritional contents of the food are 'sealed in', but the food has a high energy content because of the fat it contains. Foods cooked this way are very popular.

Shallow frying: This is the fast cooking of small, delicate food items in a shallow pan or on a metal griddle plate in a small amount of pre-heated oil or fat. Foods cooked this way need to be of good quality.

Roasting is the cooking of food items in the dry heat of an oven or a spit. Oil or fat is added to keep the foods moist and give them a crisp outer coating. High temperatures are used, which gives foods the characteristic dryness. Sunday roasts of beef, chicken or turkey with roast potatoes are pub favourites. Roasted vegetables are also becoming popular.

Baking: In this method food items are placed in greased pans or on trays and baked in an oven, which is basically a box that heats up to a controlled temperature. The cooked products can look similar to fried foods, but because there is no fat added the energy content of the food is lower and therefore baking may be considered a healthier way of cooking.

Stewing is the slow and prolonged cooking of small pieces of meat, poultry or game in a small amount of liquid, often with added flavourings

Talking point

What is your favourite way to cook something to eat?

Activity

Using some recipes, identify three food items which could be cooked by each of the methods of cookery. You can find recipes in books, magazines and in supermarket information displays.

Think of a meal you had recently, maybe in a restaurant, on holiday or on a special occasion. Why did you enjoy it? What were the points that made it successful?

Discuss your findings with your group.

such as vegetables, in a covered container. The cooking liquid forms part of the finished dish. **Casseroling** is a similar method of cookery. An example of food cooked this way is beef and vegetable stew with savoury dumplings.

Poaching: This method involves cooking food in a liquid that is below 100°C (212°F). Frequently the liquid to be used is brought to the boil, the food added and the product is then held at a simmering temperature – that is 90°C (195°F) until cooked. Alternatively both the liquid and the product can be brought slowly to the required temperature and then held at that temperature. Foods cooked this way are often tender, juicy and full of flavour.

Simmering is similar to boiling but at a slightly lower temperature. The food to be cooked is placed in the boiling liquid and brought to the re-boil. The heat is reduced for a gentle boil to take place; this is known as simmering. Simmering is preferable to boiling as there is less shrinkage and evaporation, and the texture and colour of foods being cooked are not damaged.

Steaming: In this method the food is cooked by the heat given out by steam (water vapour) as it condenses. Steaming can be done in saucepan-like containers or specially made high-pressure steamers that cook foods at very high speeds. The steam may come directly into contact with the food or with the container holding the food. Steaming is a highly favoured method of cooking as much of the nutritional content of the foods is retained and not lost in cooking.

Seasoning

■ *A range of seasonings*

Many foods are seasoned during cooking to improve and bring out their flavour. Traditional seasonings are:

■ salt – table salt, sea salt
■ pepper - ground white and black pepper
■ mustard - English (hot), French (mild)
■ garlic – fresh cloves.

A large range of foods from around the world are eaten today and new seasonings have become common, including:

■ soy sauce, ginger and chilli peppers
■ commercially made seasonings such as Worcestershire and Tabasco sauces.

Marinades are mixtures of oils, vinegars and spices used to soften and flavour foods prior to cooking. Foods are soaked in marinades for a period of time so that they can absorb the flavours. Some foods that are marinaded (or marinated) are fish, meat and chicken, often before grilling.

Foods are seasoned:

- during preparation before cooking takes place, such as putting salt and black pepper on steak before grilling

- while cooking is taking place, such as putting garlic into a soup

- after cooking has finished just before serving, such as sprinkling fried chips with salt.

Care should be taken not to overuse seasoning in cooking as too much can spoil the taste of food and make it unpleasant to eat. It is worth remembering that it is better to have to add more seasoning towards the end of the cooking rather than add too much at the beginning, as it is impossible to remove seasonings once added.

Artificial additives

Some commercial seasonings may contain lots of artificial (man-made and chemical) additives. There are many people who do not wish to eat these chemicals as they can cause health problems. Monosodium glutamate (MSG) is an example that is used to enhance flavours in food and is popular in Chinese cookery.

Tasting

Tasting is an important process in cooking. It takes time and experience to learn the skill of tasting the food being cooked to ensure that:

- the food is fully cooked

- the flavours have been developed and the dish tastes as it should

- the level of seasoning is correct

- the texture and consistency of the food is right. This is especially so with soups and foods that have been cooked in sauces to ensure that they are not too thin or too thick.

Timing

Good timing is essential when cooking, and an accurate clock is a necessary item of equipment for all chefs. All recipes give guidelines for preparation and cooking times. These can be very accurate and must be kept to.

Time plans are useful tools to help identify the tasks and sequence of work and how long individual tasks will take. With experience time plans can be done in your head, but this might take many years of practice. Until then write them down.

Here is a sample time plan for roast chicken, roast potatoes and vegetables.

Activity

Using a local supermarket, identify a range of commercially made seasonings which could be bought to use in a restaurant or bistro.

Sequence	Task	Time	Risks/special requirements
1	Turn oven on to gas mark 7 (electric 220°C)	10.30 a.m.	
2	Wash and peel potatoes and leave in water	10.30 a.m.	
3	Season chicken and place in roasting dish	10.45 a.m.	If frozen chickens are being used, make sure they are fully defrosted before cooking
4	Put potatoes in oven	11 a.m.	
5	Put chicken in oven	11.15 a.m.	
6	Check potatoes	11.30 a.m.	
7	Turn chicken over	11.45 a.m.	Be careful not to splash yourself with hot fat
8	Put pan with water on stove for vegetables	11.55 a.m.	
9	Cook vegetables	12 noon	
10	Check chicken and potatoes	12.05 p.m.	
11	Serve meal	12.10 p.m.	

Some rules for time plans:

- Dishes with long cooking times should be cooked first and started as soon as possible.
- Those with short cooking times may be prepared and kept chilled until required for use.
- Allow for some things to take longer to prepare and cook than expected.
- Dishes with short cooking times should be cooked and finished last.
- Some items are only cooked when they are needed as they become unpalatable very quickly; these include omelettes, fried foods and grilled steaks.
- Some items have no set times for preparation and cooking so can be prepared when time allows and kept ready for use, for example grated cheese as used in Cheesy Bake or chopped parsley used in Farmhouse Crumble.

Activity

Write a time plan for a meal for four people to be served at 12.30 p.m. Use some of the dishes you are going to cook in practical classes.

Equipment used in cooking

Equipment used in cooking is wide and varied. Generally the more that is paid for equipment the better it is in terms of quality. Cheap light pots and pans produced from thin metal will not conduct (spread) the heat evenly, but will develop hotspots which cause food to burn and stick. They will also damage easily – handles fall off and lids don't fit – so have quite a short useable life. Heavy thick-based pots conduct the heat more evenly and produce the best results in cooking.

Traditionally cooking pots and pans were made of copper, as this metal is the best conductor of heat. They are very expensive and difficult to keep clean and serviceable. Today stainless steel and aluminium are used for making cooking pots and pans.

■ *Good-quality pans are more efficient and last longer*

Food categories

Food and ingredients in catering are known as **commodities**. The main categories are:

■ fresh

■ chilled

■ frozen

■ pre-cooked.

Foods that have been chilled or frozen have been through processes that preserve or keep them for use at a later time. Preserved foods are widely used in catering today.

Foods are preserved because most food items that are bought for use in a catering business are perishable, that is they have a very short life before they start to lose quality or become unusable and unfit to eat.

The temperature at which food is stored influences how quickly it starts to spoil (go off). Food spoilage is caused by micro-organisms and bacteria that are naturally present in the air and on food items. Micro-organisms spoil the colour, texture, flavour and nutritional value of foods. There is more information on this in *Unit 3: Safety in Hospitality*.

Fresh

Fresh foods are just that – 'fresh'. They have not been through any preservation methods and will not keep for a very long time before the quality starts to reduce. Some simple preparation such as washing and packaging may have been carried out by the suppliers and producers.

■ *Fresh foods are a healthy choice*

Many fresh foods are grown and produced in the area where they are eaten.

Eating fresh foods in season is becoming increasingly popular with some customers as it reflects a trend for wanting less packaging, fewer preservatives in food, shorter distances between the producer and the customer ('food miles') and therefore less pollution through transport.

■ Examples of fresh foods are fruit, vegetables, bread, cakes and potatoes.

■ Fresh foods are usually in season. This means they have just been picked or harvested as they have come to the end of the growing period. At this time the quality is very good.

■ The nutritional value of fresh foods can be very high.

■ Fresh foods are usually stored at room temperature or placed in a cool room out of direct sunlight or extreme cold.

■ Fresh foods are normally bought on a daily basis, as it is not possible to keep them for long periods.

■ As many fresh foods have not been prepared in any way they can be the cheapest way of buying the food item for the caterer.

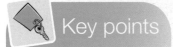

Key points

■ Fresh foods may not last for very long so should be used soon after purchasing.

■ Chilled food must be stored between 1°C and 8°C (34°F and 46°F).

■ Frozen foods should be stored at −18°C (0°F) or below.

Chilled

Foods are chilled to slow down the rate of spoilage. Chilled foods are delivered, stored and kept at temperatures just above freezing. They are stored between 1°C and 8°C (36°F–45°F) in specially designed cabinets or refrigerators.

Some chilled foods are simply fresh foods stored at a lower temperature to help maintain quality and hygiene. Some chilled foods have been totally prepared and just require cooking or simple reheating. They are usually safe to eat and keep their quality for up to four days (96 hours) if correctly stored. The damage caused by micro-organisms is slowed down but not completely stopped. Therefore it is necessary to throw foods away that have not been eaten within the four-day time scale, as there may be a build-up of harmful bacteria. However, manufacturers may print guidelines on the packaging of some chilled foods. These would include use by dates, correct handling, storage and serving advice giving the foods a slightly longer life than four days. These manufacturers' guidelines must be followed.

■ A wide range of high-quality chilled foods is available for today's caterer.

Over to you

What kind of food do you eat? Fresh, frozen, chilled or pre-prepared? Why is this?

■ *Chilled foods must be stored correctly and usually eaten within four days*

- Examples of chilled foods are meat, fish, fruit juices, yoghurt, cheese, cream and a wide range of ready-made meals such as Chinese and Indian foods and pizzas.

- Chilled foods are very convenient to use.

- Chilled foods can be expensive to buy when compared with fresh foods as the supplier has done much of the preparation.

- The costs of packaging can be high.

Frozen

Foods are frozen to stop the growth of micro-organisms. The normal storage temperature of frozen foods is minus 18 degrees Celsius (−18°C/0°F) or below. No bacteria can grow at this temperature. The freezing of food does not kill any bacteria that may be present and therefore careful handling is still necessary. When frozen food is thawed the bacteria will begin to grow again, so the food must be eaten or used within a short time or thrown away.

Frozen food may be stored for some months, the lower the temperature the longer the storage time, although there may be some loss of quality. Almost all foods either cooked or raw may be frozen.

■ Frozen foods need to be kept frozen until use

- There is a very wide range of frozen food to buy, which is usually available all through the year – there are no seasons.

- Examples of frozen foods are meat, fish, vegetables, fruit, breads, cakes, pastries and puddings, as well as complete meals.

- The quality can be very good.

- The nutritional value of some frozen foods such as vegetables is as good if not better than their fresh equivalent.

- Frozen foods can be expensive to buy, as preparation and packaging costs are included in the price but there is no preparation wastage.

Pre-cooked foods

These are foods that have been cooked by the producer or supplier, are ready to serve and eat and often require no further preparation by the caterer. Pre-cooked foods are available in either multi or single portions depending on what is being bought. These foods need careful handling and storing, as they can be a source of bacterial food poisoning due to the fact that they are not cooked again once purchased.

■ *A wide range of pre-cooked foods is available*

■ Examples of pre-cooked foods are delicatessen meats such as salamis, roast beef, meat pies, pasties, samosas, whole roast chickens, poached fish such as salmon, pates and salads.

■ These foods can be expensive to buy as all the preparation and cooking has already been done.

Food items

Meat is the edible flesh and organs of animals and birds. Meat is rich in protein – body-building food.

■ Meat is the general term for beef and veal from cows, lamb and mutton from sheep and pork from pigs, which are domestic animals especially reared for eating.

■ Poultry is the term used to describe meat from domesticated birds reared for eating, such as chickens and turkeys.

■ Game describes meat from wild animals and birds that are eaten, such as venison from deer, and birds such as pheasant.

■ Offal is the term used to describe the edible internal organs of animals, such as liver and kidney.

Meat alternatives are a vegetable alternative to meat and also contain body-building proteins. They are suitable for those who do not wish to eat meat or who just want to reduce the amount of meat in their diet.

■ Soya beans are used to produce a bean curd called tofu, which is either bland or lightly smoked, and textured vegetable protein (TVP). This is the name given to soya mince chunks. It is used in the same way as minced beef or lamb.

■ Nuts, which contain high amounts of protein, can be used instead of meat in vegetarian dishes.

■ Legumes are peas, beans and lentils and are known as pulses. They are high in protein and dietary fibre and are widely used in Asian and vegetarian cookery.

Fish are an excellent source of protein. Fish eaten today come from a number of sources:

■ saltwater fish from the sea, for example cod, haddock and tuna

■ freshwater fish such as trout and bream from rivers and lakes

■ *Fish comes in lots of varieties*

- farmed fish grown in large tanks of salt or fresh water, such as salmon, trout and bass

- Shellfish are saltwater creatures that are either harvested from natural resources in tidal mudflats or estuaries or from shellfish farms. Examples are lobsters, crabs, prawns, oysters, mussels and scallops.

Farmed fish are a good alternative to wild fish as some species have been overfished and are in danger of extinction. There are now lots of newer varieties of fish to try, which helps conserve the stocks of endangered fish.

Fruit is the fleshy seed container of a plant. Fruits are an essential part of a good diet and are classified into five main groups:

- soft fruits – strawberries and raspberries

- stone fruits – plums and peaches

- hard fruits – apples and pears

- citrus fruits – lemons and oranges

- tropical fruits – bananas and pineapples.

Vegetables are plants grown to be eaten. Vegetables are very rich in vitamins and minerals and so are important parts of the daily diet. Vegetables are classified by the part of the plant they come from, for example:

■ Fruit doesn't need to be boring

- roots – carrots and turnips

- tubers – potatoes

- bulbs – onions and garlic

- stems – celery and asparagus

- leaves – cabbage and spinach

- flowers – cauliflower and broccoli

- pods and seeds – peas and green beans

- vegetable fruits – cucumber, tomato, aubergine (eggplant) and squash.

Dairy produce is the general term for milk and the products that are produced from it, such as cream, butter, cheese and yoghurt. Milk generally comes from cows but goats' milk is growing in popularity as a number of people are developing allergies to cows' milk and its products.

Eggs are also regarded as dairy produce from a catering perspective. Hens' eggs are the most commonly used but eggs from ducks, geese and quails are also available.

Dry goods is a collective term used in catering for all the food items that may be regarded as groceries in the home. The food items are dry in terms of their preserved state, as much of the moisture has been removed during the preservation or manufacturing process. Dry goods are stored in cool, dry conditions such as a larder or storeroom.

Activity

As a class, arrange to buy eight different vegetables that members of the group may not have eaten before. Try one from each example. Prepare the vegetables for tasting. They can usually be eaten raw so may not need cooking. Make notes of the names, where they come from and comment on how they taste.

Examples of dry goods are: tea, coffee, flour, sugar, pasta, rice, biscuits and breakfast cereals. Baking goods such as sultanas, raisins and currants and are known as dried fruit.

Tinned and bottled goods: These were methods of preserving foods before the invention of refrigeration and the deep freeze. They are still used today and a very wide range of foods is available in either tinned or bottled form, especially from overseas. Foods preserved this way have a long **shelf life**, that is, they can be stored for a long time after buying.

Some foods preserve very well in this way, for example tinned tuna fish, salmon, tropical fruit and exotic ingredients for Indian or Chinese dishes such as coconut milk and water chestnuts. Bottled items can include pickles, sauces, vinegars and other condiments for cooking, fruits such as blackcurrants and plums and a range of speciality foods, including soups.

Some foods such as tinned carrots do not preserve well using these methods as the heating process damages the texture and reduces the vitamin content.

Activity

As a class, arrange to buy eight different exotic fruits that members of the group may not have eaten before. Prepare the fruits for tasting. Make notes of the names, where they come from and comment on how they taste.

In summary

- There is a huge range of foods from around the world to eat today, and for some customers a good choice is a top priority.
- Chefs need to be aware of current trends in food commodities and eating styles when buying food.
- Commodities are bought in either a fresh, chilled or frozen state.
- Foods are classified into different categories for ease of recognition.

Practice assessment activity

Levels P3/P4/M3/D2

This assessment gives you an opportunity to plan, cook and evaluate a food dish. Evidence for these criteria can be a photograph of the dish, notes of how it was made and equipment used.

P Make six dishes of your own choice, present them ready to eat and review the dishes you have cooked. (P3/P4)

M Show proficiency on three occasions when producing dishes that are appetising and make effective use of the ingredients. (M3)

D Reflect on how you prepared the dish and make recommendations for future improvement. Obtain written feedback on the taste, texture and appearance of the dishes from four consumers. (D2)

7.4 Be able to present and review dishes

This section covers:

■ presentation of dishes

■ reviewing the cooking process and cooking outcomes.

Presentation of dishes

Good presentation of food is an important part of the meal or eating experience. Customers 'eat with their eyes'. Where food looks unattractive, customers will quickly turn off and begin to look for faults in the catering.

Presentation of food is an art. This is where the chef or caterer shows individuality, flair and imagination and displays creative talent.

Some rules for good presentation:

■ Food must look clean and fresh.

■ Dishes and equipment used to serve food must complement the food and be the right size and shape.

■ Hot food must be served hot, that is above 63°C (145°F).

■ Cold food must be served cold – below 8°C (46°F).

■ *Good presentation is important*

Serving equipment

Plates
Food can be very attractively presented on plates by the kitchen staff. Complex **garnishes** (see below) and layouts can be made as the food is placed directly in front of customers without the need to transfer it from serving dishes.

Plates come in interesting shapes, designs, sizes, patterns and colours. The caterer has a huge range to choose from. Plates range from plain white to the most complex handmade bone china using gold-leaf designs. Highly colourful plates can distract from the food that is being served rather than complement it, and plain white china is considered a very good background for most foods. The plate that is used should reflect the style and quality of the food as well as the character of the establishment.

Serving dishes
The choice of serving dishes plays an important part in the customer's appreciation and satisfaction of a meal. The quality, shape and size are all factors to take into account when choosing what to use. Some dishes

Activity

Obtain some catalogues or brochures of china and equipment from suppliers. Identify some suitable china to use in Seagulls Bistro. Why did you make your choices? The Internet can be a good source for information.

■ *Ovenproof dishes can save time*

■ *Poorly presented food is not very appealing*

■ *Garnishes improve the appearance of dishes*

come with lids to help keep food hot. This is useful when customers sit some way from the kitchen, such as on an outside terrace or patio.

Ovenproof dishes enable food to be cooked in the container in which it is served and even eaten. Not only does this save washing up but also foods are kept hot and good portion control is achieved as the kitchen staff can determine the portion – one dish is a portion. The use of these individual dishes also enables quick service to be achieved, as food does not need to be portioned by serving staff.

Placing food attractively

The appeal of cooked food can be lost when it is not attractively placed on plates and serving containers. The shape, size and quantity of food will determine how food is arranged. Plates must be the right size to hold the amount of food that is being placed on them within the rim. Otherwise dishes will look cramped and carelessly prepared, with wet foods spilling off onto tablecloths and clothing.

Garnishes

Garnishes are made of fresh fruit and vegetables and are used to make the finished dish appear more appetising. They must be edible and should contribute to the food or dish in terms of form, colour and texture. They should complement the food and lift the presentation but not distract from it.

Some examples of garnishes:

■ a lemon wedge served with fish

■ oranges, lemons and limes sliced with the skin scored to make a cartwheel effect

■ slices of scored cucumber; cucumber skin cut into strips

■ gherkins and olives cut into attractive shapes

■ parsley in small 'picks' or finely chopped

■ radishes cut into roses, celery and spring onion twirls

The range and variety is endless.

Review

Planning

Cooking is a highly organised activity. Good forward planning is the key to success. When starting to cook a meal you will need to think about:

- the number of people that are being catered for
- the budget available
- the dishes to be cooked
- how the food is going to be purchased
- who is going to do the cooking
- whether there is enough correct equipment to cook and serve the food
- the time the meal is needed.

Timing

Being able to plan the times of your practical work is important, as the cooking of food needs to be sequenced with the time that it is required for eating. It takes practice to get timing right, but it is always better to have dishes ready slightly before they are needed rather than too late. Extra time can always be given to presentation if things are early.

Working method

Being able to plan your work will help you to be efficient, effective and economic with your time. Those working in kitchens need to work safely as well as efficiently. Kitchens are dangerous places where accidents can happen with misuse of tools and equipment.

Some tips for efficient working.

- Work surfaces should be clear of unnecessary equipment.
- Store food away correctly and always off the floor.
- Wash equipment and tools and put away immediately after use.
- Be aware of others working around you.
- Understand emergency procedures.

■ *No accidents here*

Quality of menu items

There are a number of factors used to judge the quality of a dish.

Appearance: Does the dish look clean, fresh, appetising and appealing or tired and stale. Has the dish been prepared with care or just thrown together.

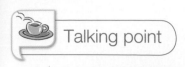

Think of a meal you have eaten that you did not enjoy. Why was this so? Discuss your reasons with your group.

Colour: Overcooking damages the colour of food; food looks washed out or even burnt. Undercooked items look bland and unappetising and can be unsafe to eat. Gauging the colour of food is part of the skill of a chef.

Texture: Overcooking food affects its texture; some, like meat, become tough; others such as pasta and vegetables become sloppy and slimy. Undercooking also affects the texture of food, leaving many too hard to eat and unpalatable. Generally the more a food is cooked or kept hot the more moisture is lost and dried-up foods have little appeal.

Following recipes carefully, using a time plan and giving thought to presentation will avoid many of the poor quality factors identified.

Feedback

It is important when cooking food for other people to eat that their views on how it looks, tastes and eats is taken into account. This is called customer feedback and it features very highly in successful companies. Give customers what they want, not what you think they want is a good rule for success.

Customers can help with quality control by identifying how a dish or meal can be improved. They have a perspective that the chef cannot have and can provide helpful criticism such as:

■ *Customer feedback can be useful*

- too much food; we couldn't eat it all
- not enough to eat; we are still hungry
- the food was cold
- there was too much seasoning.

Feedback can be obtained in several ways. In catering those cooking and serving are often face to face with their customers, and just simply asking them if they are enjoying the food gives instant feedback. More formal and structured information can be obtained by using printed questionnaires and formal interviews using especially trained staff, possibly from an outside specialist organisation.

Key points

- Listen to customers and watch what they leave on their plates.
- Customer feedback can help with quality control.

In summary

- Good presentation is an important part of the meal experience. Food can lose its appeal when not attractively placed on plates or serving dishes.
- Select plates and serving dishes to complement foods being served.
- Garnishes are used to make the product more appetising and are made of fresh fruit and vegetables.
- Good planning is the key to success in cooking a meal.
- When reviewing the quality of prepared and cooked food look at its appearance, colour and texture.

Test your knowledge

1 List the main reasons for choosing a supplier.

2 Why is food dangerous to eat when it starts to go off?

3 Name the business documents used in the purchasing cycle.

4 List six items of equipment that can help with portion control.

5 List the techniques used in the kitchen for food preparation.

6 What happens when food is overcooked?

7 Name the methods of cookery.

8 What is the reason for using seasonings in cooking?

9 Describe the four categories of food.

10 List some rules for good presentation of food.

Standard recipes

Here are some recipes for use when studying this unit. They will be used to illustrate the costing of dishes, weighing and measuring food, identifying some basic terms in catering relating to preparing and cooking of dishes.

Weights and measures have been given in metric and imperial units. Choose one set of units and stick to it – do not mix the two. Ingredients have been listed in the order in which they are used in making the dish.

Recipe No. 1 Cheesy Bake – a savoury version of bread and butter pudding

		4 portions
Metric	**Imperial**	**Ingredient**
400 g	14 oz	Sliced bread (own choice)
25 g	1 oz	Butter
4	4	Medium eggs
600 ml	20 fl oz	Milk
25 g	1 oz	Fresh basil
375 g	13 oz	Cherry tomatoes
175 g	6 oz	Cheddar cheese
25 g	1 oz	Parmesan cheese, grated
		Seasoning

Service instructions

Serve on a hot main course plate with the food placed in the centre of the plate. Sprinkle with chopped parsley. Served with crusty French bread.

Method

1   Preheat the oven to 180°C (gas mark 4)
2   Cut each slice of bread in half to make triangles and spread with butter
3   Whisk together the milk and eggs, season with salt and pepper and stir in the basil
4   Wash the tomatoes
5   Pour a little of the egg mixture into the bottom of a 1.5 litre (2¾ pint) ovenproof dish. Arrange a layer of bread on top (butter side up) and sprinkle over half of the cheddar cheese; scatter some of the tomatoes over the cheese and then pour over more egg mixture
6   Repeat the layers of bread and cheese, and then pour over the last of the egg mixture. Top with the remaining tomatoes and sprinkle the top with the Parmesan cheese
7   Place the dish in a deep roasting tin, then pour water into the tin until it comes halfway up the sides of the dish. Place in the oven for 40–45 minutes, or until the top is crisp and golden brown, and the egg mixture has set
8   Serve hot with a green salad

Note: The tomatoes may be cut in half.

Recipe No. 2 Farmhouse Crumble – a vegetarian savoury crumble

Metric	Imperial	4 portions
		Ingredient
		Crumble topping
150 g	6 oz	Wholemeal flour
100 g	4 oz	Butter
100 g	4 oz	Grated cheddar cheese
50 g	2 oz	Chopped mixed nuts
		Filling
600 g	1½ lb	Mixed vegetables such as swede, turnips, parsnips, potatoes, carrots
100 g	4 oz	Finely chopped onion
50 g	2 oz	Butter
25 g	1 oz	Wholemeal flour
200 g	8 oz	Tomatoes
250 ml	½ pt	Vegetable stock
125 ml	¼ pt	Milk
		Chopped parsley
		Seasoning

Method

1 Preheat the oven to 190°C (gas mark 5)
2 Make the crumble topping by sieving the flour and rubbing in the butter
3 Add the grated cheese and nuts
4 Wash, peel and rewash the vegetables and dice into small cubes
5 Cook the onion without colour in the butter in a large saucepan
6 Add the rest of the vegetables and continue to cook without colour for a further 10 minutes
7 Stir in the flour; add the other ingredients including the liquid which must be added carefully, stirring well between each addition
8 Bring to the boil and reduce the heat; cover with a lid and simmer for about 15 minutes until the vegetables are just cooked
9 Transfer to an ovenproof dish and sprinkle the crumble topping over the vegetables
10 Bake in the oven for 30 minutes or until golden brown
11 Serve with crusty bread and Worcestershire sauce

Note: Olive oil can be used instead of butter.

8 Serving Food and Drink

Introduction

Today when people go out to eat they don't just go for the food and drink they go for a whole package – 'the meal experience'. This can be in an exotic Thai restaurant serving authentic food, a luxury city centre hotel, a gastropub serving traditional meals or a simple high street cafe. The enjoyment and fun of going out to eat includes the atmosphere and style that is created by the catering business.

Although the food and drink is an important part of the occasion, the standard and quality of the service and the attitude of staff providing that service can make or break the occasion for the customer. Satisfying the customer is what serving food and drink is all about.

This unit will help you understand the personal skills and qualities that those working in food and drink service need to develop. You will also learn how to get ready for customers, prepare a food service area effectively and serve meals efficiently.

You will gain practical skills in serving food and drink and practise customer care skills. To complete the unit you will learn how to review the success of a food and drink service occasion.

How you will be assessed

Unit 8 is assessed internally, so the Centre delivering the qualification will assess you against the criteria. On completion of the unit you should:

8.1 understand professional, safe and hygienic practices in food and drink service

8.2 be able to prepare for food and drink service effectively

8.3 be able to provide food and drink service including customer care

8.4 be able to apply review techniques to assess the success of food and drink service occasions.

This unit has a practical element to it. You will be serving food and drink on a number of different occasions. You should keep an evaluation log to support this practical work, and at the end of each practical lesson identify what you have learned.

Assessment grades

The Edexcel Assessment Grid details the criteria to be met. In general, to gain a Pass (P) you are asked to describe, prepare for service, provide food and drink service and describe; to gain a Merit (M) you are also asked to explain, compare and apply; and to gain a Distinction (D) you are also asked to evaluate and analyse.

8.1 Understand professional, safe and hygienic practices in food and drink service

This section covers:

- personal presentation
- professional attitude
- safety and hygiene.

Personal presentation

You need to know how to correctly present yourself for work in a food and drink service situation. As you have learned in *Unit 2: Customer Relations in Hospitality*, good personal presentation and cleanliness is essential. Job roles in food and drink service involve working with the public and you need to impress customers coming to use the business, as well as be a good colleague to your fellow workers.

Personal hygiene and freshness

You must:

- have fresh breath – clean your teeth regularly and use a mouthwash. Frequent visits to the dentist will ensure your teeth are in order and look good when you smile.

- keep your hands perfectly clean and your fingernails short

- not wear nail varnish as it can flake off and contaminate food being served

- wear only a hint of perfume or aftershave as too much can mean that the food you are serving can taste to the customer of what you're wearing.

Personal appearance

You need to be clean and smart on every occasion. Your clothes must also be clean, smell fresh and be free from spills or stains from food and drink. At work many people wear a uniform supplied by their employer. It's usually smart and well tailored, designed to match the style of the business and easy to care for. You may also find that the employer cleans the uniform for you. Whatever you have to wear it must be well laundered, pressed and of a size that fits you properly.

Over to you

Think of some occasions when you were close to people who were not good to be near. What did you think? What did you do?

■ *"Actually, I'm not feeling hungry any more!"*

Hair needs to be clean and preferably cut short. There is a tendency for hair to drop out into food and drinks so it should always be well groomed. Long hair needs to be tied back and pinned up so that it cannot flop into items being served and onto customers. Beards and moustaches must be well cut and short, but the preference is to be clean-shaven when working with food. Designer stubble may be trendy in some professions, but not in catering.

■ *Looking good is important when serving customers*

■ *I don't remember ordering this*

Talking point

In pairs, discuss how personal appearance can be improved. Give your ideas back to your group.

Key points

- A well-groomed appearance is appreciated by all.

- Clothing needs to be well fitting and spotlessly clean.

- Hairstyles are best kept short and tidy.

- It's best to wear very little jewellery, perfume and aftershave.

- Shoes need to support and protect feet.

Over to you

Can you think of occasions when you saw catering staff not being as clean as they should be?

Jewellery for both men and women must be kept to an absolute minimum. It can get in the way and may also be dangerous. Jewellery can be valuable so is best left at home. Body piercing has grown in popularity but is not appreciated by everyone. Many employers have rules regarding this, and they may not allow staff to wear piercings when working with food and customers.

Footwear, like clothes, needs to be clean, smart and safe. It's best to wear shoes that support your ankles and cover your feet for protection in case of spillages. Flip-flops, open-backed shoes, sandals and high heels can be dangerous as they may cause you to slip over or twist your ankle.

Good posture

Posture is about body position – how you hold and move your body. When working in a food service outlet good posture is needed to prevent possible health problems such as a bad back or strains on knees. This can be simply done by learning to stand evenly on two feet with legs slightly apart and arms placed at your sides when not walking.

If you look good you will feel confident and be able to do your job well.

Professional attitude

Good service and proper customer focus is down to developing the right attitude towards the role of serving. This attitude is being professional, treating the customer and their requests with respect. You don't have to be servile (overly willing to serve) to provide efficient service, but good skills will impress both the customer and the boss. In turn they will respect you.

Hospitality is a service industry and to do well you need to like helping others. There can be occasions when customers are difficult to manage. It is never good practice to argue with them as this can only make the situation worse. Always seek someone in higher authority when a complaint is made or difficulties are encountered. For more on dealing with complaints see *Unit 2: Customer Relations in Hospitality*.

Hygienic practices

Good hygienic practices are essential when working in a food and beverage service situation. It can be very off-putting when eating or drinking for customers when staff are displaying their personal bad habits. Remember when you are working with the public you are on show; it's a bit like being on the stage.

- You must wash your hands thoroughly before starting work.

- Cover any cuts with a waterproof dressing; these are usually blue in catering.

- You must not smoke in food and drink service areas.

- Do not cough or sneeze over food; this spreads germs.

- Avoid unhygienic habits – do not lick your fingers, pick your nose, ears or teeth, scratch your hair, spots or bottom. All these habits transfer bacteria onto your hands and then to the food and drinks you are serving.

Attentiveness

When you work in food and drink service you need to be aware of what is going on around you. You need to look for things to do rather than waiting to be told and you need to anticipate the needs of customers before being asked. A positive attitude to your work is essential. Serving staff can upset customers if they spend all their time talking to each other and not looking after their customers. You need to be efficient, friendly and focused.

Body language

You have learned about body language in *Unit 2: Customer Relations in Hospitality*. You know when someone you are talking to is bored and not listening or does not want to be near you. So does the customer. Always:

- welcome customers with a smile
- have good eye contact when talking to them
- look interested in the customers and in what you are doing

> ### Talking point
>
> Think of situations where you were given really excellent service or help. What made it so good? Discuss your findings with your group.

- *I wonder if my team won?*

Attention to detail

A good eye for detail and care in the way you do your work will prevent mistakes and avoid complaints from your supervisor and customers. Cleanliness and tidiness of the food service outlet, table lay-up and service area preparation are all examples of tasks where accuracy and attention to detail are needed.

Communication skills

As you have learned in *Unit 2: Customer Relations in Hospitality*, the ability to communicate well in a positive, confident manner is a skill that those working with the public need to develop.

Listening

This means listening carefully to what is being said to you and showing that you understand. When taking orders for food and drink it's a good idea to repeat the request to confirm you have understood correctly.

Speaking

Speak clearly and precisely, using good grammar to ensure that whoever you are speaking to can hear and understand you.

Dealing with messages and orders

It is important to pass on messages and orders accurately and promptly. Mistakes and delays with food and drink orders:

- irritate and annoy the customers
- create a lot of unnecessary work for colleagues
- loses money for the business.

Teamwork

As you learned in *Unit 1: Exploring the Hospitality Industry*, almost all jobs in hospitality involve working with others as part of a group, often of all ages and backgrounds. Good people skills and being reliable are essential in catering.

Case studies

Getting settled in

Seagulls Bistro is very popular. Its new menu is attracting so many customers that two new members of staff, Gill and George, have had to be taken on. Gill is a trainee chef in her first full-time job and has yet to start any training. George, who has not worked in catering before, is to work in food service but might do some bar work as well.

The manager has asked you to help your two

new colleagues settle in to the bistro's work routine, particularly explaining the company's dress code.

Make a list of all the things you will need to tell them. How are you going to approach this task? Is there anything which you might have to be sensitive about so as not to cause offence?

Using codes of practice

Codes of practice are normally prepared for a business by senior management. They are a set of rules to ensure:

- the safety of staff members
- that staff know what's expected from them
- the business runs smoothly
- that standards are understood and maintained
- the public image of the business is protected and enhanced
- that customers get value and enjoyment from using the business.

Seagulls Bistro code of practice

1 It's a company requirement that all staff wear their uniform when on duty.
2 Your uniform must be clean, tidy and well pressed.
3 Jackets and aprons must be changed for a clean one when they are soiled with spots of food or drinks.
4 No substitute garments are allowed.
5 Name and role badge must be correctly attached and visible for customers.
6 Fingernails must be kept clean and short, and coloured nail polish avoided.
7 The wearing of perfume and cologne must be kept to a minimum as strong smells can adversely affect the taste of food being served.
8 The wearing of jewellery is restricted to a wedding ring as items can fall off and get lost in food.
9 Long hair must be tied up to prevent it falling into food and drinks being served.
10 Shoes must be clean, well polished and flat-heeled, covering the foot for protection – a requirement under health and safety.

Talking point

Think of some of the advantages of working in teams.

Safety and hygiene

Working safely and maintaining correct hygienic practices are not only essential but also required by **legislation**. This legislation applies to all businesses, those who work in them and those who visit premises. This is such an important issue that a separate whole unit – *Unit 3: Safety in Hospitality* – is devoted to this subject.

Here are some tips to help you work safely when serving food and drink. Follow these and you will avoid harming others and yourself.

General safety

Restaurants, cafes and bars can be dangerous places not only for the staff but also for the customers. The Health and Safety at Work Act (HASAWA) 1974 requires employees and employers to ensure a healthy, safe and secure environment for the public and employees. You should always be observant and report anything that could be a safety problem.

We will now look at health and safety issues particularly relevant to food and drink service.

Opening and closing doors

In a restaurant, bistro, bar and service area there are usually doors that lead to the kitchens or cellars. Accidents occur when people rush, throw open or kick doors open. Colleagues who are holding trays full of food and equipment may have accidents because they are unable to see what is going on.

Tips to reduce or avoid accidents.

■ *Swing doors can cause accidents if care is not taken*

- There is usually one door for going into the kitchen and another separate door for coming out; rules for using these must be followed.

- There may only be one door into the kitchen. In this case a large glass panel in it will enable people to see what is happening.

- Cellars where drinks are delivered to and stored might have doors in the floor, so appropriate safety guards need to be used when they are open.

Carrying trays

Always use a tray when carrying equipment – it helps reduce work and is much safer than holding lots of equipment in your hands.

- Trays can be very heavy when overloaded with crockery and glasses, which can cause muscle strain.

■ *A properly loaded tray will help prevent accidents*

- Always place items evenly over the tray's surface

- Don't pile things up too high – they might drop off.

- Always pick a large tray up with two hands.

Small round trays called **salvers** are used to clear glasses and small items such as cutlery. These can be held in one hand by placing the fingers under the centre of the salver. This leaves one hand free for doors and steadying. Sometimes a napkin or serviette is placed on top to stop things slipping about and to mop up spilt liquids.

Dealing with spillages and breakages

Unfortunately spillages and breakages occur even when care is being taken. These need to be dealt with immediately as they may injure customers and other colleagues who could slip or trip on them.

Dealing with spillages

■ Liquid spillages need to be mopped up using the appropriate equipment and surfaces left dry.

■ Floor spillages can be wet for some time and special signs warning of a wet surface need to be used (see page 93).

■ Spillages on tables and over customers can be difficult to clean up. Where it's serious a manager needs to be called.

Dealing with breakages

■ You have a duty of care to ensure safe disposal of broken items.

■ Broken glass is the most difficult item to clear up due to the risk of being cut.

■ Never clear broken glass or crockery up with bare hands; always use a dustpan and brush or any special equipment kept for the purpose.

■ Broken glass and crockery must be safely disposed of, usually in special bins. This will prevent accidents occurring at the time of rubbish removal.

There is also a risk of small pieces of glass or china falling into food and drinks near to the point of an accident. If there is any risk that customers' food and drinks have been contaminated then the food and drink must be changed, at no charge.

■ *It is important to follow correct procedures*

Over to you

Practise using a tray, loading it with unbreakable objects of different weights and see how the tray balances. Put a paper napkin on before loading and see whether it makes a difference to items slipping.

Safe handling of food and drink

You have learned in *Unit 3: Safety in Hospitality* how customers are at risk of becoming ill if the food and drink they consume is not handled safely or is dirty. As more and more meals are eaten away from the home incidents of food poisoning have increased.

There are codes of practice and rules and regulations regarding the safe handling of food and drink. You need to be familiar with these and comply with the requirements when you are at work. Unit 3 covers in detail the essential aspects of safety that apply to the hospitality industry.

Safe storage of items

■ Items such as trolleys, tables and chairs must be stored so that they do not cause a hazard to customers or staff.

Talking point

Can you think of examples of when a spillage might happen?

- Stack tables and chairs in manageable piles, not too high, and ensure the piles are not likely to tip over.

- Unused equipment should not be kept where customers can go.

- Flexes on electrical equipment such as vacuum cleaners must be carefully wound up so no trailing cables are left lying around.

■ *An accident waiting to happen?*

Crockery

- Crockery is heavy and difficult to move.

- It is best stored on shelves or in cupboards which have been especially designed to take the weight and offer some security.

- Don't make piles too high; they can topple over and break.

- Store heavy items near to the ground to reduce lifting, but not so near that items become dirty.

- Always store crockery in a clean area.

- Moveable trolleys are available that are designed for moving crockery.

Cutlery

- Cutlery (knives, forks and spoons) should be stored in especially designed containers or drawers in **sideboards**. A diagram of a sideboard is shown further on in this unit (see page 262). This will stop damage and make it easier to move the heavy cutlery about.

- Where containers are used, fork prongs and knife blades should be pointed downwards to reduce the risk of accidents, as they can be sharp.

- Storage equipment for cutlery should be cleaned regularly as cutlery goes into people's mouths and therefore must be scrupulously clean.

Glasses

Glasses can be easily broken or chipped, which means they cannot be used. Glasses should be stored:

- upside down to stop dust getting into them
- near to where they are needed
- on clean surfaces free from drink spillages
- each type and size of glass together
- on specially designed racks or shelves above the bar counter at head height.

Glasses can be arranged in very attractive displays when they are being stored, which adds to the customer appeal of a bar or restaurant.

■ Good storage of glasses can look attractive

Clean work areas

Food and drink work areas must always be clean and tidy; they are often on view to customers. It's also not very pleasant to work in dirty, messy surroundings.

- Don't let packaging and wrappings build up – throw rubbish out regularly.

- Empty drinks bottles and cans should be placed in suitable containers for returning to suppliers or disposal, which can include recycling.

- Used glasses and crockery should be taken to wash-up areas and not left where they were used.

- Cleaning cloths and swabs should be kept out of sight and not left on service areas unless they are being used.

■ Not very pleasant for staff or customers

Hygienic working practices

This section has shown you the importance of personal hygiene necessary for those working in the hospitality industry. Not only must those working with food and drink be clean, but they must also learn to work using clean practices. These practices will help to prevent food poisoning and the spread of disease.

Over to you

Can you think of other things that make a work area look unpleasant and not very good to work in?

In summary

- Good personal hygiene and freshness is essential as serving food and drink involves working near to customers and colleagues.
- Hospitality is a service industry that requires those working in it to develop a professional attitude towards the customer that is not servile but efficient, friendly and focused.
- A food and beverage outlet can be a dangerous place both for its staff and its customers. To reduce accidents and the risk of personal injury those working in hospitality must learn how to correctly use and manage service equipment as well as work surroundings.

Practice assessment activity

Levels P1/M1

P Describe the factors that create a professional, safe and hygienic approach when providing food and drink service. (P1)

M Explain the importance of delivering professional, safe and hygienic food and drink services. (M1)

8.2 Be able to prepare for food and drink service effectively

This section covers:

- food and drink outlets
- setting up service areas
- service equipment
- service items.

Food and drink outlets

As you learned in *Unit 1: Exploring the Hospitality Industry*, there is a huge variety of different outlets for the public to choose from when they go out to eat or have a drink. Where they choose to go depends on a number of factors:

- how much they are able or willing to spend
- the occasion – is it for a quick bite to eat or a family celebration?
- how much time they have.

Talking point

Can you think of other reasons to choose somewhere to eat? Discuss them with your group.

Restaurants

Restaurants provide food and drink, generally at high prices, and give high levels of service in very comfortable surroundings. There are many styles of restaurants, some owned by celebrity chefs, others offering styles of food from all round the world such as Chinese, Indian and Thai.

Current trends in restaurant eating include:

- vegetarian and vegan dishes on menus
- the use of organic and locally sourced products
- the use of commodities that are without chemical additives.

■ *Eating out can be a special occasion*

Cafes

These are usually small, inexpensive refreshment places located in almost every village, town or city. They serve light meals and snacks, with fried breakfasts being very popular. Drinks served are hot and cold beverages, and non-alcoholic items such as fruit juices and canned drinks. Food can be of a high quality and the service very friendly, as the people who are providing the food and service usually own the cafe.

■ *Cafes can offer friendly service and good-quality food*

■ *Cafe-bars can offer a continental atmosphere*

Cafe-bars

These are more upmarket than cafes, serving a wider range of foods, which can include items such as Spanish tapas or snacks, and Greek mezes. Wine and other alcoholic drinks are served, as well as coffees, teas and other beverages. Often these outlets provide outside and pavement areas where people can sit. These areas can be very attractive when good-quality furniture, umbrellas and plants are used.

Coffee shops

As the name suggests these are outlets that primarily serve coffee, which can come in quite a range – from espresso to cappuccino to latte (see page 277). There is usually a selection of other hot drinks and perhaps mineral waters. Food can be limited to cakes, pastries and biscuits, but some outlets also serve sandwiches, wraps, baguettes and toasted items.

Fast food

With a great variety of styles and quality of foods to choose from and open often 24 hours a day, these outlets are found in every shopping centre, airport, railway station and motorway service station in every town and city in the UK. Fish and chips, hamburgers, pizzas, fried chicken, jacket potatoes, ice cream, doughnuts, pancakes and Mexican tacos are all examples of fast foods. Fast food has popularised eating out for the public, reflecting today's more informal lifestyle.

Public houses

The traditional pub is a trademark of the UK. Historically only serving beer during limited opening times, pubs now are often open all day. They serve drinks of all descriptions, including many non-alcoholic ones, as well as a wide range of foods from bar snacks to full family meals. Accompanied by adults, children are now allowed into most pubs, and there are often play areas both inside and in the garden.

The gastropub is a modern innovation where high-quality food is provided by skilled staff for customers looking for interesting and innovative food. The surroundings are rather more relaxed than the formal atmosphere of a restaurant. Menus are more extensive than a pub's. The trend for a more relaxed style of eating has meant that gastropubs have rapidly grown in popularity.

Setting up service areas

Cleaning

In any hospitality business the customer's first impressions on entering the outlet are of great importance. Food and drink outlets have to be visually as well as hygienically clean. They must also smell fresh, free from stale odours of old food and drinks. There is nothing more unpleasant than going to eat a meal in an outlet that is visually dirty, with sticky tables and chairs and soiled carpets stained with spilt drinks.

Although cleaners may be employed it's the responsibility of service staff to keep work areas, furniture and specialist equipment clean and presentable. Tasks will include:

- dusting and arranging furniture
- vacuuming furniture, carpets and other floor coverings
- polishing counter tops and tables
- cleaning specialist equipment used for serving and food displays.

Tips for cleaning a food and drink service area:

- always clean the room before laying tables
- open windows to freshen up the room
- clean, dust and vacuum the highest things first
- dust before using the vacuum cleaner
- always use clean cloths, brushes, dusters, mops and buckets; it's difficult to clean using dirty equipment
- don't store cleaning equipment where the customer can see it
- the floor is the last thing to be cleaned
- empty the vacuum cleaner so it's ready for next time.

Organise and lay tables

The style of organising and laying up tables depends on the type of outlet. Tables can be round, square or rectangular. Round tables take up more space than square and rectangular ones but are friendlier to sit at.

Many outlets use tables that are fixed to the floor. For service they just need wiping over with a clean cloth and sanitiser. Condiments, napkins and menus are checked and refilled/replaced where necessary if they are kept on tables.

In more formal outlets where customers might have to book, tables can be arranged in the room according to the number of customers they expect to serve. The exact layout can change every day.

Once tables are in position cloths or coverings are put on. Before they are laid with equipment tables should be checked to ensure they don't wobble. A small piece of card or wine cork placed under a leg should stop any wobble.

■ *Table layout can be simple or elaborate and stylish*

- Equipment needs to be inspected for cleanliness before it is placed on the table.

- A large plate can be used as a guide for spacing cutlery. This is placed in front of where each customer is going to sit and then the required cutlery placed round it.

- Glasses and **cruets** (salt and pepper pots) should be put on next with any table arrangement such as flowers last of all.

- It's a good idea to check everything is in place before customers arrive. A supervisor or restaurant manager usually does this.

Prepare sideboard

This is where all the equipment that is needed for serving customers is kept. Often a team of people will work from one sideboard. Sideboards are placed around the service area at convenient points for staff to use. Some are fitted with electrical points so that lights and food hotplates can be used.

Sideboards need to be cleaned and stocked with cutlery, crockery and service trays, table coverings and condiments every service time. There is usually a required order in which the equipment is stored for ease of access by the team. The design of the sideboard will influence where items go.

Service trays	Cutlery	Condiments
Crockery		Table coverings

■ *A sideboard showing location of equipment*

- Sideboards need stocking with equipment and laying out each day or service time.

- A check needs to be made for cleanliness to ensure that there is no build-up of dirt or waste food from the previous service time.

- Trays and crockery for customers' use needs preparing and placing in the appropriate location.

- There should be enough service equipment to enable all dishes to have separate tools to avoid messy presentation.

Some sideboards have electrically heated food heaters, plate warmers and equipment areas. These need to be turned on in time for them to reach the required temperatures. They must also be turned off at the end of each service time. It's quite easy to forget to do this.

Reporting problems

- Report to your supervisor any problems you come across while getting ready for service.

- Problems with equipment and furniture need attending to promptly.

- Problems may mean customers get poor service, which can result in complaints or an accident happening. For example, a chair may have a loose leg or an electrical item a faulty flex or plug.

Service equipment

Over to you

What factors in food service areas would put the customers off?

Service units

Service units are specially designed equipment for displaying food and drink for sale. They can be very attractive to look at and often are designed to match the style of the outlet. Customers can quickly see what is available and make a choice. Customers can help themselves to the food being displayed or are assisted by staff. Service units are a very good way of selling food when presentation is attractive. When they are badly managed presentation and hygiene can be poor and have the effect of turning customers off.

Heated units

Heated service units are designed for particular styles of food service such as a carvery service for roast meats, or where a wide selection of hot food is offered.

- They keep hot foods hot, at a temperature of 63°C or above. This temperature is a legal requirement to stop bacterial growth.

- They are used in outlets such as pubs, fast-food chains, shopping malls and contract catering.

■ *Heated service units are used in many food outlets*

■ *Refrigerated service units are found in well-equipped cafés*

Refrigerated units

These are chilled units designed to keep food below 8°C, which is a legal requirement to help prevent bacterial growth.

■ Refrigerated service units are essential for food displays of salads, sandwiches, baguettes and desserts.

■ In pubs and cafe-bars they are used to display and keep wine, bottled beers and lagers, fruit drinks and designer waters chilled ready for service.

Trays

Trays are made in a number of shapes and sizes and from materials that ensure they are strong and easily cleaned.

■ Trays should always be clean – any that are chipped and scratched should not be used as they may harbour germs.

■ Round trays are usually used for drink service and taking dishes of food to tables.

■ Square and oblong trays are used for clearing dirty crockery and glasses away to service points and wash-up areas. They are also used to bring food from the kitchen to the food service point or dumb waiter.

■ Oblong trays are available at self-service counters for customers' use

■ Food trays should be stored on or to the side of dumb waiters and self-service counters.

■ Drinks trays, sometimes known as salvers, need to be kept behind or on the bar counter. Linen napkins or paper serviettes can be placed on them to help soak up any liquid spills.

Table coverings

The type of outlet will decide the style of table covering to be used.

Tablecloths

Tablecloths can be made from linen, cotton, polyester or a mixture such as polycotton. These cloths will need to be laundered either on or off the premises. A good stock will need to be kept in a dry, dark, secure place.

When laying a cloth don't handle it too much as this causes creases, which spoils the appearance as well as leaving dirty marks.

■ Tablecloths should be large enough to cover the surface of the table and hang down each side by at least 30 cm (12 in).

■ Some of the table leg should be covered for good presentation.

■ White is the preferred colour as this gives a good background to equipment, food and table decorations.

■ Light pastel colours are also used and these are often placed over white cloths.

Key points

■ Hot food must be kept hot at a temperature of 63°C or above.

■ Cold food must be kept cold at below 8°C.

- Highly patterned cloths can detract from the visual appearance of the food and the decor of the restaurant.

Disposables

Disposable tablecloths are available in a wide variety of styles, colours and qualities. Disposables range from simple paper cloths that can only be used once, to high-quality cloths which can substitute for linen. They can initially be expensive to buy but there are no laundry costs. Storage should be in a dry area to prevent items from becoming damp and discoloured.

Placemats

Placemats can be used to provide colour and interest to a table or counter layout. They can be used instead of tablecloths or placed over tablecloths. Placemats are available in a wide range of styles, some with printed designs of the restaurant, local scenes or the company logo. They can also be used for advertising. Some restaurants print their menus on disposable placemats which are changed for every new customer. Placemats can be made from paper, plastic, china, glass and slate, as well as washable melamine.

Menus

As you have learned, a menu is a list showing customers what is available to eat and how much it costs. Menus should be displayed near the entrance to an outlet so that customers can see what is available and the costs before they go in. This is a requirement in law.

- *Menus can be simple or elaborate depending on the type of outlet*

Menus can also be used to tell customers about other facilities or opportunities that are available to them, such as special deals. Menus are used as a marketing tool for the outlet and therefore should be attractively presented.

There are many styles of menus ranging from a simple sheet of paper or a blackboard, to elaborate printed menus with leather covers. On some menus each dish is individually priced: this is an **à la carte** menu. On others a complete meal may be taken for one price and this is called a **table d'hôte** menu. These are French terms but widely used in the hospitality industry.

Dishes are laid out in the order in which they are eaten, starting with starters and ending with desserts, beverages and drinks. For a sample menu layout see section 8.3.

Activity

When you next go out to eat or are just passing a catering outlet, ask if you can have a copy of their menu. (In another activity you might have already obtained a copy of a menu that you could use.) Many outlets will keep old ones to give out; they make good souvenirs and help advertise the outlet.

- Look at the menu to see how it is laid out.
- See what is being served.
- Look at the prices.
- What else is on the menu besides food and drinks?
- Show the menu you have obtained to your group.
- Identify the good points.
- How could things be improved?

Service items

Crockery

This is another term for china used at the table. Crockery is available in many styles, shapes and sizes and costs. The crockery should blend in with other items on the table and is often bought in a style, colour and pattern to match the outlet's decorations and character.

The better the quality of the china the longer it will last so crockery that is hardwearing and durable needs to be bought. This will not easily chip and will be able to be washed in a mechanical dishwasher without damage. It is important to use a dishwasher in commercial food service, as crockery needs to be completely free of germs and scraps of food. Chipped and cracked china must not be used, as it will harbour bacteria and germs, possibly spreading food poisoning from one customer to the next.

There are a number of classifications of crockery:

- hotel earthenware – the cheapest and least durable

- stoneware – more durable than earthenware

Crockery you might see in a bistro

- porcelain – identified by a semi-translucent body, this has a high resistance to chipping and cracking

- bone china – very hardwearing and the most expensive to buy but the most elegant to use, especially in an exclusive restaurant or hotel.

When laying a table check:

- that there are no chips or cracks in the crockery

- that there are no smears from dishwashing

- the menu to see what food is to be served. This will enable the correct crockery to be made ready for service.

Cutlery

Cutlery is the general term for the equipment used for eating: knives, forks and spoons. There are many styles, shapes and sizes but the simpler the design and style the better. Most cutlery is made of stainless steel, which is easy to maintain. Luxury restaurants may use silver plate that requires a great deal of cleaning and maintenance but looks very smart. Fussy designs hold scraps of food that are difficult to wash off. Cutlery must be dishwasher proof and easy to maintain.

■ *Cutlery comes in many styles, shapes and sizes*

When laying a table for a meal, ensure that:

- the cutlery is really clean and free from smear marks

- damaged cutlery is not used

- you have laid the correct cutlery for what is going to be served.

Glasses

Glasses need to be spotlessly clean and free of chips and cracks. A chipped glass can cut a customer's lips and cause a nasty injury. Glasses are chosen for their shape, size and feel. They complement the drink being served and make a table layout look elegant.

- Generally each different drink has a specially designed glass to be used for it, for example a lager glass, wine glass or water glass.

- Dirty glasses can spread germs so they need to be cleaned in a glass washer and left to dry.

- Glasses should not be dried with a cloth to prevent germs on the cloth spreading to the glasses and smears spoiling the appearance of the glass.

Service utensils

These are larger items of cutlery that are used to serve food. They are stored on the dumb waiter or service counter. They must be checked for

Key points

- Crockery needs to be hardwearing and durable.

- Cutlery must be dishwasher proof and easy to maintain.

- Glasses need to be spotless and free from chips and cracks.

cleanliness to ensure that there are no scraps of food or smear marks left on them.

Activity

Working individually:

1 *Position and cloth a table suitable for three customers to have a formal three-course meal including bread rolls.*
2 *Lay a table for a formal meal for three people where they will be eating soup, chicken or fish followed by a dessert.*
3 *Position all the other necessary equipment on the table, such as glasses, butter plate, table number, napkins and flowers.*
4 *Get your teacher to check that the table is ready for service.*

Condiments and sauces

Condiments and sauces are seasonings that are used to bring out the flavour of foods. A wide range is usually available for customers to select from. They should be readily available and kept on the customer's table or near the service point. Good hygiene is essential and tops of bottles and containers must be very clean.

Sugars – Demerara or brown sugar and white caster or granulated sugar are used for sweetening drinks.

Sweeteners such as saccharin or Candarel are an alternative to sugar and are used by customers who wish to eat less sugar.

Cruets are containers used for salt and pepper. Mustard can also be included – English (hot) and French (mild).

Sauces – A wide range is available and what is offered depends on the foods being served. Examples are tomato ketchup, HP (brown) sauce, Worcestershire sauce, mint and horseradish.

How condiments are served depends on the outlet's style and policy.

- They can be offered in pre-wrapped individual portions that are convenient, hygienic and easy to control from a cost perspective. These are used in motorway service stations and fast-food outlets.

- Cafes and guesthouses may serve condiments and sauces by just placing the bottles and containers they are bought in on the guest's table or on the sideboard. Where this is done care needs to be taken to ensure that the tops of bottles and containers are clean.

- Sugar left out in an open bowl goes hard as it absorbs moisture from the air, and also attracts pests such as wasps. Airtight containers should be used and the sugar put away after service finishes.

- Sometimes sauces and mustards are placed in small glass bowls and served with a teaspoon. A plate needs to be placed underneath for the dirty spoon. This is quite a costly way of serving condiments as much of it is wasted because what is left cannot be put back in the containers.

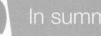

In summary

- The hospitality industry offers a huge range of outlets: restaurants, cafes, cafe-bars, coffee shops, fast-food restaurants and pubs.
- A dumb waiter or service counter must be prepared for service and contain all the equipment that the service team will need to serve meals.
- A food and drink service area needs to be prepared for service by cleaning the room, laying the tables with all the required table coverings, crockery, cutlery and glasses, all of which must be spotlessly clean.
- A menu is a list of what is available to eat.

Practice assessment activity

Level P2

P As part of the team preparing for the service of a meal:

- Prepare a written checklist that identifies step by step what equipment is needed to correctly lay a table for a three-course meal for three or four customers.

- Using your checklist, lay up your own table for three or four customers with all the linen, crockery, cutlery, glasses and other items needed for customers to eat the meal. Use the menu to help you confirm that you have laid everything needed.

- Prepare a sideboard for service, ensuring that all the service equipment is clean and placed in the appropriate place.

- Clean the area surrounding your table and sideboard.

- Ask your teacher/lecturer/supervisor to check your work. (P2)

8.3 Be able to provide food and drink service including customer care

This section covers:

■ customer care

■ style of service

■ food

■ drinks

■ clearing work areas.

Customer care

We have learned that customer care is an important area of hospitality. Our customers need to be treated considerately to ensure they come back. A meal not served cannot be held until the next day; the opportunity for a sale has been lost.

Greeting and welcoming customers

Customers need to be made welcome and to feel at ease. Even in the simplest outlet customers need to be greeted and seated at an appropriate table or counter.

Over to you

Practise greeting and welcoming each other as you would customers of a restaurant.

■ It's good manners to greet customers with a 'good morning', 'afternoon' or 'evening' depending on the time of day.

■ Customers are normally greeted at the entrance or door of the outlet.

■ Wherever possible address customers by their names; but only use first names if you know the customers very well.

Identifying customers' needs

After welcoming customers it's necessary to find out what they would like. Where bookings are made this is the time to acknowledge the booking. This can be done simply by asking 'Can I help you?' or 'Do you have a booking?'

Providing information

Key points

■ Customers need to be made welcome and to feel at ease.

■ Wherever possible address customers by name.

■ Food and drink service staff are salespeople.

Customers need to be given information about what is available to eat or drink. This is the time to tell them about special promotions or offers that need to be sold, as well as giving them copies of the menu. Sometimes they need to be told where the toilets are and where they can leave their coats. It's important to remember that food and drink service staff are also salespeople. This is the time to sell.

Taking orders

Quite often customers know what they want; if so they are probably regulars. It may just be a simple matter of checking and then serving the food to them. Some customers need advising and talking through what they might have, explaining the menu. It's therefore necessary to understand fully what's on the menu or, if behind a bar, what's in stock. How the customer's orders are taken down will depend on establishment procedures.

The main ways of taking customers' orders are by:

- using a **duplicate check pad** – two copies are made: the top copy is sent to the kitchen and the bottom one is kept by serving staff.

- using a **triplicate check pad** – three copies are made: the top copy goes to the kitchen, the second is kept by service staff and the third copy goes to the cashier to complete the bill.

- **electronic keypad** – this is a hand-held computer terminal that has a code for each menu item. The order is printed out in the kitchen or bar.

Tips for taking a food order.

- Take order pads and a pen to the table.

- Ask the customers if they are ready to order.

- Face the customer and look at them – it's a good idea to smile.

- Do not lean over the customer or on tables and chairs.

- Answer any questions that arise; always offer to find out the answer if you don't know it.

- Give suggestions if needed.

- Make sure you understand the order before you leave the table by repeating the order back to the customer.

- Thank the customer for their order.

⑤

4 x tom basil soup
1 x risotto
2 x steak

20

■ *A restaurant order check*

Activity

Role play

1 *Work in small groups using two or three menus from different hospitality businesses.*

2 *Using the menus, practise writing down orders for food. Some of the group can act as customers and others as restaurant staff. Change roles. Restaurant order pads should be used.*

3 *Get colleagues from another group to check the orders for mistakes.*

4 *Identify mistakes and why they were made.*

Communicating with colleagues

In a service industry where the customer is in contact with those serving them effective communication is a major factor in ensuring customer satisfaction. How the team you work in and your other colleagues communicate with each other will impact on the standard of service customers receive and how your colleagues respond to you.

Tell colleagues what is required

You need to be effective in how you write customers' food and drink orders to ensure no mistakes are made. The orders should be clear and easy to read as kitchens are busy places.

Seek information

At some stage you will need to seek information from a more experienced colleague or a more senior member of staff. This may be written as in a memo or spoken as when you use the phone.

Being over-familiar

You must not chitchat, use bad language or argue with your colleagues if it is likely that customers could hear what is being said. Being at work is not like being at home or out with your friends. A certain degree of formality with customers and colleagues is essential.

Activity

You have just taken a food order for lunch for six people. Two of the customers have said that the last time they ate lunch at this outlet the food was so cold they did not enjoy the meal.

- Think about how you might communicate this to the chef without causing any upset and ensure the meal is hot this time.

Activity

Write out an accurate food order for a party of three people who are having a three-course lunch and beverages. They will each have a different starter but the same main course, vegetables and potatoes. This will be followed by three different sweets, finishing with coffee. Use an à la carte menu that you have obtained.

Passing and receiving orders

- There is usually a formal procedure to take food orders to the chefs.
- Written orders are taken to the kitchen.
- In some outlets only more experienced or senior staff take orders from customers and junior colleagues take the order to the kitchen or service point as well as fetching and carrying the food and equipment.
- Orders can be passed direct to the kitchen by the waiting staff through electronic keypads (see above).

New orders

When taking a new order to the kitchen it is normal to shout 'check on'. This alerts the kitchen team that another order needs preparing. The head chef then instructs the kitchen team to prepare what is required.

The food is needed

When the customers are ready to eat or enough time has passed for the food to be cooked, it is usual to go to the kitchen to enquire if the food is ready for that table number.

Where electronic keypads are used chefs will be familiar with the system employed to place orders 'on', but food will still need to be called away or requested using the keypad.

Teamwork

Working in the hospitality industry is all about working in teams. Without contributing to a team effort a food service outlet would not be prepared on time or the customers served to the standard expected. Teamwork is covered in more detail in *Unit 1: Exploring the Hospitality Industry* and *Unit 6: Developing Employability Skills for Hospitality and Related Industries*.

Timing

An important part of the role of serving customers is being aware of time. How long have the customers had to wait for:

■ a table

■ a menu

■ the order to be taken

■ their drinks to arrive

■ the food to arrive

■ their bill?

Special needs and requests

Many customers have special dietary needs, which have been looked at in *Unit 5: Healthy Lifestyles*. These may be due to:

■ a health problem such as requiring gluten-free or diabetic products

■ cultural or religious reasons

■ dislike of a food item.

Many customers also have special requests. Customers might:

■ wish to have an alcohol-free drink because they are the driver in a party

■ need a highchair for a baby

■ need help getting to their table because they have a disability

■ have ordered a birthday cake which needs to be served.

Service staff need to be able to guide and advise customers when queries arise. A good knowledge of the outlet's food and drink is essential.

Over to you

Can you think of any other special requests a customer may have?

Activity

You could arrange a visit to a food and drink outlet to investigate the type of special requirements customers have. Make a list of all the things you find out.

Style of service

Staff need to be very skilled in serving techniques as careless serving will spoil the presentation and enjoyment of the food. Food and beverages may be served in a number of styles, and the style adopted by the outlet depends on a number of factors:

- the type of outlet
- how much time the customer has available
- the type of food being served
- the cost of the food or meal
- the type of menu.

■ *Plated food served with style*

■ *Counter service is found in many outlets*

Plate service

This is where food is presented on plates. Sometimes food is simply plated in the kitchen for ease of serving and then placed in front of the customers, as in a guesthouse. Another example is when the chefs require elaborate presentation of dishes that would be spoilt by serving with a spoon and fork, such as in a very upmarket restaurant.

Silver service

This is the most skilful, elaborate and costly type of service to provide. For **silver service** food is served with a spoon and fork onto customers' plates from service dishes. A meal served in this style requires a lot of time, equipment and staff as the customer has everything brought to them. Luxury hotels and restaurants serve food in this way.

Counter service

For this style of service customers queue in front of a counter and make a selection from foods that are already prepared or choose food to be cooked to order by staff. Sometimes the cooked foods, such as grilled steaks, are brought to the customer's table by staff. This avoids long queues and ensures that the food served is hot and fresh. Trays, crockery and drinks are all collected by customers at the same time as food. Payment is to a cash point where condiments, cutlery and serviettes can also be collected.

Self-service

Self-service is where customers help themselves from counters or buffets to food that is either plated into single portions or held in multi-portion containers.

Vending is also a type of self-service where fully-automated machines dispense a wide range of snack food, drinks and confectionery. Vending is used where staffing would be uneconomic or not necessary, such as railway stations, minibars in hotel bedrooms and drinks stations in office blocks. See *Unit 1: Exploring the Hospitality Industry* for more on vending machines.

Buffet

A **buffet** offers a wide selection of foods presented on a table or a purpose-built counter. Customers either help themselves or can be assisted by staff from behind the buffet. This style of service is often used for functions and breakfast in hotels. Buffet service allows for a large number of people to be served in a short space of time by relatively few numbers of staff.

- Staff need to be skilled in food presentation, as dishes and equipment need to be attractively displayed.

- Food service skills are needed as often customers like food served to them while they make their choices.

- Efficient clearing away of used crockery, cutlery and glasses is needed as turnover of customers can be quite brisk, especially at breakfast.

Talking point

Think back to a number of occasions you have had a meal out. What style of service did you receive? Match the styles of service with the occasion.

Food

Although most food outlets specialise in a particular style of food, they all tell customers what they can have to eat by using a menu, as detailed in section 8.2. The range and number of courses depends on the size and style of the outlet as well as what the customer is going to pay. There is a standard order and layout for menus, as shown below. See also page 10 for an example of a restaurant menu.

Starters

Sometimes these are known as appetisers. Starters are small tasty dishes to start a meal and stimulate the appetite, hence their name. They should be colourful and well presented.

Here are some examples of dishes in each course; you may have already tried some of these.

Dish	Served with
Potato wedges	Chilli dip
Tomato soup with fresh basil	Garlic croutons and crème fraiche
Caesar salad	Fresh Parmesan cheese shavings
Mixed melon platter	Raspberry coulis
Coarse game terrine – red onion chutney	Toasted brioche
Chicken satay	Peanut sauce
Deep-fried whitebait	Cayenne pepper, lemon wedge

Main courses

Dish	Served with
Penne with creamed spinach and goats' cheese	Crunchy garlic bread
Grilled Greek sea bass	Lime butter
Beer batter-fried fillets of pollock	Tartare sauce and lemon wedges
Roast foreribs of English beef	Horseradish sauce
Coq au vin	
Thai green chicken curry	Fragrant rice
Cumberland sausages and mustard mash	English mustard
Slow-cooked lamb shank	Redcurrant jelly or mint sauce
Grilled sirloin steak and garnish	English or French mustard
Roast vegetable cheese and cranberry bake	Parmesan cheese

Side orders

Dish	
Steak chips	Mixed salad
Baked jacket potato	Green beans
Mustard mash	Fresh vegetables of the day – chef's choice
Fragrant rice	Braised Savoy cabbage and bacon

Desserts

Dish	Served with
Apple and blackberry pie	Cornish clotted cream
Strawberry and raspberry pavlova	
Marmalade bread and butter pudding	Custard sauce
Vanilla panna cotta	Caramelised orange slices
Tropical fresh fruit salad	Mango sorbet
Profiteroles	Hot chocolate sauce
English cheeses and biscuits	Celery sticks

Drinks

Hot drinks are known in hospitality as **beverages**. Coffee, tea and chocolate are three popular hot beverages. They can be served as part of a meal, for example at breakfast, as a morning or afternoon drink or at the end of a meal such as lunch or dinner. A wide choice is available to customers who can be served at a bar or counter or more formally sitting at a restaurant table.

Coffee

Coffee can be made from either an instant form or from ground coffee beans. The instant variety can be made directly in a mug or jug. Ground coffee comes in vacuum packs to keep it fresh and can be made in a variety of specialist equipment such as Cona machines and cafetières, which are glass jugs available for one or more people.

■ *Drinks machines can make a range of beverages*

Coffee machines can make a large range of speciality coffees, usually from fresh coffee beans which are ground when the customer orders a drink. This is the freshest way of making coffee. Many customers have their personal favourites which may include:

■ latte

■ mocha

■ espresso

■ cappuccino.

Serving coffee in well-designed mugs or cups increases the customer's enjoyment, and small tasty biscuits can be served alongside.

Serving coffee after a meal

Each customer needs a coffee cup, saucer, under plate and spoon, known as a coffee set. This is placed in front of the customer. Coffee can be poured from a large jug such as from a Cona machine, served in individual

Activity

Visit a local coffee shop and list all the hot drinks they serve. Identify the difference between the types of coffee they serve.

pots from a tray or made in a cafetière and left on the table for customers to help themselves. This is a good way of serving coffee.

Tips for serving coffee

■ make sure cups and mugs are very clean

■ make sure the coffee is hot

■ make sure the coffee is not too weak or strong

■ serve with hot milk or cream

■ serve brown or demerara sugar with coffee.

Tea

■ *A selection of teas*

Teas can be purchased in a variety of ways and the style of the outlet will influence the method of service.

Tea bags are easy and convenient to use as the amount needed is already measured out. There is a wide range of good-quality teas available in this style. It is possible to purchase special containers for using in an outlet that can be left on a counter for customers to choose from.

Bulk leaf tea takes a little more time to prepare and serve but is enjoyed by those who like tea.

String and tag is a one-cup tea bag with an identification tag which can be left outside the pot or cup for ease of service.

Tips for serving tea

■ make sure equipment is very clean

■ tea must be made with boiling water

■ make sure the correct amount of tea is used

■ serve with cold milk

■ serve with white or caster sugar.

Herbal and **fruit teas** also come in bags and are popular for those who want a healthy alternative.

■ Herbal teas are peppermint, camomile and rosehip.

■ Fruit teas are raspberry, blackcurrant and apple.

Hot chocolate

Drinking chocolate is made from fresh chocolate granules or a powdered chocolate drink mixed with either hot water or milk. Hot chocolate can be made

■ *A coffee or tea break*

directly into a mug for serving. Commercial chocolate drinks usually have sugar already added, so extra sugar is not needed. Always serve a spoon with this drink as it separates out and needs frequent stirring by the customer. It can be served with whipped cream on top.

Alcoholic drinks

Wine

Wine is an alcoholic drink made from grapes and can be drunk on its own or to complement food. There are a number of types of wine:

Red: served with red meats, pasta and strong-flavoured foods such as game and cheese

Rosé: light pink in colour, served with light/white meats, pasta and drunk on its own

Dry white: served with fish and shellfish

Sweet white: served with desserts

Sparkling: served with desserts and at celebrations (Champagne).

Wines need to be served at the correct temperature to get the maximum enjoyment from them:

- red wines at room temperature
- white wines and rosé slightly chilled
- sparkling wines cold.

Non-alcoholic drinks

Clean, fresh tap water should always be available. It's a good idea to place a jug of iced tap water on each table just prior to service. Customers should not have to ask for water. Slices of lemon are sometimes added, but this may not be to everybody's taste.

Bottled water

As people have become more health conscious, bottled water has gained in popularity as an alternative to alcohol. It is available in a number of varieties from the UK and abroad.

Sparkling (carbonated) water contains carbon dioxide to make it effervescent or fizzy.

Natural spring waters are obtained from springs in the ground and can be still (not fizzy), carbonated or naturally sparkling.

Mineral waters have a natural mineral content which many people consider to be good for promoting health.

Bottled waters should be served with ice and, if requested, a slice of lemon or lime. Some customers ask for bottled water because they prefer its taste to that of tap water, and also because it is considered a more natural product as there might be a lot of chemicals in some tap water.

Other non-alcoholic drinks

There is a need to provide a good range of non-alcoholic drinks as it's sensible for drivers not to drink alcohol. These could include freshly squeezed orange juice, local apple juice, real lemonade and ginger beer.

Clearing work areas

It is important that work areas are always clean and clear of dirty and spare equipment. It can be dangerous to have equipment lying around and trip hazards may be caused. Remember catering work areas are busy places. *Unit 3: Safety in Hospitality* covers this in more detail.

Customer areas

- These must always be kept free of dirty and used equipment.
- When clearing from a sideboard or moving glasses always use a tray or salver – it's much safer.
- Crockery when being cleared should not be stacked too high on trays; it can fall off and it's very heavy to carry.
- Work quietly – it's very disturbing for customers when staff are clumsy or noisily moving around with crockery and glasses.
- Using a linen napkin on a tray or salver helps to deaden any noise and prevents equipment from slipping about.
- Remember that customers can see everything.

Service areas

- Turn off any electrical equipment.
- Clear any food counters and return all food to the kitchen.
- Turn off the power supply at the main switches.
- Clean all serving equipment and replace it for the next service time.
- Replenish stocks of plates, bowls, cups and saucers and serving dishes.
- Ensure that all equipment and floors are free of debris and waste food.
- Empty waste bins and clean or sanitise them.
- Wash and sanitise any cleaning cloths and/or equipment to prevent cross-contamination.

Key points

- It's a good idea to use a checklist when clearing down work areas to ensure nothing is left out.
- A good range of plain, well-designed glasses complement the service of wines.

In summary

Correctly preparing for service in a food and beverage area is extremely important. When this is done well it:

■ provides a very welcoming atmosphere for customers
■ reduces the possibility of customer complaints
■ ensures customers are served quickly and efficiently
■ makes staff feel confident as all the equipment, food and drinks they need to do their work properly is to hand.

Practice assessment activity

Levels P2/P3/M2/D1

While you may practise customer care skills in a role-play situation, the practice of food and drink service skills should be undertaken in different real settings. To enable you to do this a college restaurant or work placement could be used.

P Prepare for food and drink service by carrying out appropriate procedures. (P2)

P Provide food and drink service on at least three occasions, using suitable customer care skills. (P3)

M Compare the types of customer care skills necessary when delivering four different types of food and drink service. (M2)

D Evaluate your ability to deliver professional, safe and hygienic food and drink service using effective customer care skills. (D1)

8.4 Be able to apply review techniques to assess the success of food and drink service occasions

This section covers:

■ review techniques

■ assess success.

Review techniques

Food and drink outlets need to review on a regular basis how well they are doing. All businesses need to undertake reviews if they are to be customer focused – that is providing the customer with what they want, not what you think they want. There could be a big difference. This is particularly so in a service industry.

Getting the opinions of your customers should be an everyday occurrence, not just when something goes wrong or you receive a complaint. Hospitality outlets survey their customers for feedback to establish if they are:

■ meeting their customers' expectations and needs

■ providing good-quality products and services

■ giving value for money.

Feedback is also used to:

■ get help in identifying any customer needs that are not being met appropriately

■ identify members of staff who have given exceptional service as part of any company incentive scheme, such as a monthly bonus or employee of the month award

■ assess their success or to make recommendations for improvement to senior managers or owners where poor quality issues are identified

■ help identify possible new products.

This topic was covered in detail in section 2 of *Unit 3: Customer Relations in Hospitality*.

Collecting information

As you have learned in *Unit 3: Customer Relations in Hospitality,* various survey techniques are used to collect information from customers. Make sure that all staff are aware of the need to protect customers' details from misuse under the Data Protection Act 1998.

Postal survey

This is a survey conducted by post and therefore a database of customers is needed. This type of survey allows customers time to think about their answers and they may give more honest answers than with face-to-face type surveys. This method, however, might not produce many responses.

Comments cards

Comment cards (see page 54) can be left on tables or at a reception area for the customer to fill in. There is usually an option for them to include their name or address on the card if they want a reply to the comments or be entered for any prize draw or incentive such as discounts given to encourage a response. The card may have tick boxes with space at the end for a comment.

Talking point

Questionnaires

These are likely to have more in-depth questions than comment cards and also invite the customer to make comments. The customer or sometimes a member of staff can complete these. One disadvantage is that customers may not like to give a negative comment if staff are completing the questionnaires with them, so a true picture may not be given.

Why do food and drink outlets ask their customers to give their views on the food, drink and service they have received?

Activity

- Obtain two or three comment cards or customer questionnaires from food and drink outlets.
- Review them for style and design.
- What kind of language do they use?
- What questions do they ask?
- How much space is there for customers to respond?
- What information about the guest(s) do they ask for?
- Why do you think the outlet wants this information?
- Are there any incentives for the customers to complete the questionnaires?

Assess success

It's important to use the right approach and use clear, friendly language when asking customers to make comments and judgements on service they have received. When surveying customers certain information needs to be collected.

Customer profile

This is where customers give personal information about themselves and their visit to the hospitality outlet. Some examples could be:

- date of visit

- age range: under 18, 18–25, 26–40, 41–55, 56–65, 66 and over
- gender: male or female
- meal type: breakfast, lunch, afternoon tea or dinner
- economic grouping: working, part-time working, semi-retired or retired
- name and address.

Customer perceptions

This is where customers answer questions and give a quality rating about the product and service they received. Some examples could be:

- How did you find out about us: recommendation, saw an advertisement, just passing or have visited before?
- How do you rate the food: excellent, very good, good, poor, very poor?
- How do you rate the choice of food you were given: excellent, very good, good, poor, very poor?
- How do you rate the service you have received: excellent, very good, good, poor, very poor?
- How do you rate the attitude of staff: excellent, very good, good, poor, very poor?
- Did you receive value for money? Yes/No.
- Would you come back again? Yes/No.
- Would you recommend us to other people? Yes/No.
- Are there any other services you think we should provide?
- Any other comments you wish to make.

In summary

- All businesses need to review how well they are doing if they are to be customer focused – that is providing the customer with what they want, not what you think they want.
- Various techniques can be used, such as postal survey, comment cards and questionnaires, to gain customer feedback on the quality of food and service.
- Getting the opinions of your customers should be an everyday occurrence not just when something goes wrong or a complaint is made.

Practice assessment activity

Levels P4/M3/D2

This assessment activity can be linked to your practical food and drink service sessions where the customers can review the food, drinks and service they have received.

P Describe the review techniques that can be used to assess the success of food and drink service. (P4)

M Apply two review techniques to assess the success of food and drink service. (M3)

D Analyse the responses received from the review techniques and make recommendations for improvements to food and drink service. (D2)

Test your knowledge

1   List the important points that must be observed for personal freshness and presentation when working in a food and drink outlet.

2   When communicating with work colleagues what must you consider?

3   How should spillages and breakages be dealt with in a food service outlet?

4   List the main accompaniments that should be stocked ready for service on a sideboard.

5   What are the legal temperatures that hot and cold food must be stored at?

6   What information must a menu have on it?

7   List the points for cleaning a food and drink service area.

8   List the information that must be obtained from customers when taking a food order.

9   What are the five main types of food service?

10 What are the benefits of getting the opinions of customers?

9 Accommodation and the Front Office

Introduction

Accommodation and the front office are central to the operation of many hospitality businesses, and are commonly known as 'housekeeping' and 'reception'. The impressions guests receive from these areas can impact hugely on guest satisfaction and ultimately on the success of an organisation.

Accommodation does not just relate to hotels, but also covers the wider area of self-catering apartments, halls of residence and residential care homes, as well as non-residential centres such as conference venues. It revolves around the provision of sleeping accommodation and the related activities of cleaning and servicing rooms.

Unit 9 first considers the roles and responsibilities of those people working in accommodation services. It then looks at how the housekeeping and front office department are linked and how important it is that these two departments should work together. Finally the unit examines the skills needed to work in these departments.

How you will be assessed

Unit 9 is assessed internally, so the Centre delivering the qualification will assess you against the criteria. On completion of the unit you should:

9.1 understand the purpose of accommodation services

9.2 understand the purpose of the front office

9.3 know how accommodation and front office departments link together

9.4 be able to demonstrate skills involved in accommodation services and the front office.

Assessment grades

The Edexcel Assessment Grid for Unit 9 details the criteria to be met. In general, to gain a Pass (P) you are asked to describe, identify and demonstrate; to gain a Merit (M) you are also asked to compare, explain or design; and to gain a Distinction (D) you are also asked to analyse and evaluate.

9.1 Understand the purpose of accommodation services

This section covers:

- purpose
- accommodation services
- job roles
- responsibilities
- green issues.

Purpose

This section covers the job roles and responsibilities of accommodation services, but first you need to recognise the purpose of the departments so that you can begin to understand how important they are to the successful running of any hotel.

Accommodation services may be defined as the provision of a clean, comfortable and safe environment. Guests get their first impression of an outlet when they enter the foyer or entrance hall, mainly from the appearance that it presents. This first impression is most likely to be gained before the guest has had any food or drink; in fact, the guest may not use the food and beverage facilities at all. Therefore it is vital that the outlet provides clean, comfortable and safe surroundings. The service offered by the accommodation services or housekeeping department can be found in **residential** and **non-residential** outlets.

Housekeeping

The accommodation services department is often referred to as the **housekeeping** department, particularly in residential establishments.

Residential
Residential accommodation services are provided in all those places that provide away-from-home sleeping and/or living accommodation. This includes:

- hotels
- hostels
- hospitals
- holiday camps.

In any residential establishment the accommodation services department must ensure that the accommodation is clean, comfortable and safe.

Over to you

Make a list of all the places where someone might stay away from home. Discuss how the needs of customers in these establishments may differ.

Non-residential

Non-residential accommodation services are provided in a variety of places, including leisure centres and conference venues.

First impressions are no less important here and, as with residential outlets, they must provide accommodation which is clean, comfortable and safe.

Meeting guests' needs

As we have already noted in *Unit 2: Customer Relations in Hospitality*, it is vital that all hospitality outlets are aware of the needs of their guests and that they strive to meet these needs. This is no less true of accommodation services. The main aims of accommodation services depend not only on the number of bedrooms, but also on what the establishment believes the customer wants.

The objectives of the accommodation department include:

- providing a clean and comfortable environment
- maintaining health, safety and security
- meeting budget forecasts
- providing efficient and effective services.

Services offered will depend on the nature of the outlet. The service offered in a hospital or a nursing home will be based around the need to operate a thorough and regular cleaning programme that doesn't disturb anyone or attract attention. The service offered in a hotel will be based around the need to provide a quick and thorough service to a consistently high standard.

Accommodation services

Below is an explanation of the services provided in a selection of outlets, including:

- hotels
- self-catering apartments
- halls of residence.

Hotels

There are many different types of hotel, as you have learned in *Unit 1: Exploring the Hospitality Industry*. They will differ in shape, age, size and type, factors which dictate the work of accommodation services. For example, in a first-class luxury hotel the range of services offered by the department may include ironing, laundry, providing bigger rooms and setting standards. All hotels need to be clean and offer a discreet service that does not disturb the guest.

Key points

- Accommodation services can be found in residential and non-residential establishments.
- In both cases the accommodation provided must be clean, comfortable and safe.

Self-catering apartments

Customers staying in self-catering apartments often rent them for a week or more. They may be working away from home or on holiday. The level of service offered in the apartments can vary. However, generally they will be serviced before the customer arrives and once they leave. If the customer is staying for two weeks or more their apartment may be serviced once a week.

Halls of residence

Halls of residence provide accommodation to students who are attending university away from their home. The facilities offered vary from one hall of residence to another. In some the students have their own bathroom, and in others they share a bathroom. Some halls of residence are self-catering, with cooking and laundering facilities provided. The students will be largely responsible for their own cleaning, but cleaners will be employed to clean public areas such as corridors and landings. A warden or bursar will be in charge of the halls of residence, making sure that the students take care of the premises.

Job roles

Just as the service offered differs from one type of establishment to another, the organisation of staff also varies enormously. Here is a look at a selection of staff that might work in accommodation services.

Manager, housekeeper

The way in which the management of the accommodation services is structured will be influenced by factors such as size, type and location. However it is the manager or housekeeper's responsibility to run the department efficiently and to meet the budget. An eye for detail is essential if you are a housekeeping manager.

As well as maintaining standards and controlling the budget, managers will usually also be responsible for:

- staff training
- staff welfare and discipline
- allocation of duties
- ensuring maintenance requirements are dealt with
- key control
- guest laundry
- lost property.

The manager of accommodation services might be known by a variety of titles, and this too may depend upon the type of establishment. Examples are:

- hotel – executive housekeeper, housekeeper
- hostel – bursar, halls' manager, housekeeper
- hospital – domestic services manager.

As the size of the outlet increases, so the manager needs more supervisory and **operational** staff, with an assistant as a deputy or assistant housekeeper. In large outlets the manager may be so busy that they have little time to check the work of the **room attendants** on a regular basis. If this is the case then the deputy, assistant or floor supervisor will take on this role.

In a hotel a manager may have some or all of the following staff work for them.

Floor supervisor

The floor supervisor will be responsible for checking the cleanliness and hygiene of allocated bedrooms, corridors and public areas, ensuring that they are cleaned and serviced to the required standards. They will supervise a team of room attendants, providing support and assistance. They may also have responsibilities for training staff.

Room attendant

The room attendant's role is to ensure that rooms allocated to them on a daily basis are cleaned and presented to the standard required by the hotel and expected by the customers. The number of rooms they clean will vary between hotels, but servicing between 10 and 15 rooms in an 8-hour shift is usual.

■ *A housekeeper makes regular checks on standards*

A room attendant's duties include:

- changing bed linen and towels
- making beds
- vacuuming floors
- treating stains, for example carpet stains or damage to polished wood
- restocking guest supplies such as shampoo and soap
- checking the general condition of the room and notifying their line manager of any malfunction or damage.

Over to you

Look for vacancies for these jobs on the Internet to find out how the roles differ from one establishment to another.

Cleaner

The cleaners will usually clean the public areas of a hotel. They will often start work very early in the morning so that they do not get in the way of customers who may be eating breakfast, checking out or arriving for meetings. Like all other staff in the department they will be expected to clean and maintain the area they are responsible for to a given standard.

Linen porter

The linen porter's role is to provide clean, well-laundered linen (sheets, towels and so on) to the room attendants and restaurant staff. In hotels that use an outside laundry for their linen, the linen porter will be responsible for:

- receiving linen and housekeeping deliveries
- counting and checking linen
- keeping linen records in good order
- storing linen away and keeping the housekeeping linen room in good condition and order.

It is worth noting here that, although the accommodation services team may not have much contact with the guests, they will still be expected to offer them high levels of customer service.

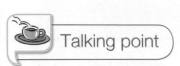

Talking point

In small groups, discuss what cleaning will be carried out on a daily, weekly or monthly basis.

Responsibilities

Cleaning and cleaning schedules

Most staff employed in the housekeeping department are involved in practical cleaning and room servicing. Whether they are a room attendant or a cleaner they will usually follow a cleaning schedule or routine. This means that they will have a set order of doing their work. This will prevent them from missing anything out, making sure they are thorough and consistent.

Some cleaning is carried out every day, but more thorough cleaning might be carried out on a weekly or even monthly basis.

A very special clean is necessary periodically. Periodic cleaning is often referred to as 'spring cleaning' or annual cleaning. This is often carried out at convenient times depending on **occupancy** (how many rooms are let). It might include washing walls or ceilings or deep-cleaning carpets.

Servicing of bedrooms and bathrooms

As you have learned, accommodation services will need to complete their work to given standards, which may vary from one establishment to another. However, whatever that standard might be, it is fair to say that when a customer checks into their bedroom they will expect it to look like it has not been used before. They will not want to feel as though somebody else has slept in the bed or used the bathroom. The cleaning schedule or 'order of cleaning' will help the room attendant to achieve this for the customer.

In section 4 you will learn about the routine or order of cleaning for a bedroom and a bathroom so that you are able to demonstrate that you can service these areas yourself.

■ *Cleaners have a set routine so nothing is left out*

Pest control

Although standards of cleanliness are generally excellent in hotels and residential establishments, higher room temperatures and a lack of natural ventilation provide ideal conditions for certain pests. Failure to remove dirt, dust and food debris can encourage pests to stay in a building and breed.

■ *A couple of unwelcome guests*

The most common pests to be found are:

■ insects – moths, larvae, cockroaches, flies and spiders

■ rodents – rats and mice.

Apart from the threat to standards of hygiene, the presence of pests can be very upsetting to guests and give a poor impression of the establishment.

Waste disposal

The hygienic disposal of waste materials is very important. It will help to:

■ control pests such as rats and mice

■ prevent the spread of germs and infection

■ limit the risks of fire.

Waste should be kept in tightly covered bins or plastic sacks. Bins should be emptied frequently and kept clean. Special care should be taken with the disposal of cigarette waste and broken items such as glasses or crockery.

Green issues

Laundry

As you have learned, bed linen and towels in guests' rooms are changed frequently. This is expensive and not very environmentally friendly. Managers are increasingly looking at ways to cut down on the amount of laundry they do. The frequency of linen changes can be altered so that hotel guests' linen is only changed every two or three days instead of every day.

Many hotels have introduced a towel reuse programme where guests are asked to leave their towels hanging on the towel rail if they wish to use them again or drop them in the bath or leave them on the floor if they want them replaced.

Reducing the amount of linen and towels laundered:

■ saves water, energy and laundry chemicals

■ reduces the amount of waste water generated by the laundry.

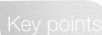

- Hotels are increasingly trying to find ways to conserve energy.
- They do this by trying to change bed linen and wash towels less often.
- Staff and guests are encouraged to switch lights off.

Energy conservation

Another way of being more environmentally friendly is by saving energy.

- Housekeeping staff should make sure the television and all lights are turned off before leaving a prepared guestroom.
- In some hotels guests are asked, via notes in the room, to turn lights off and adjust heating or air conditioning when they are not in the room.
- In other hotels the keycard being placed in an electronic box activates the electricity. This means that the guest can't leave anything switched on when they're not in the room.

Pollution and waste disposal

Housekeeping staff should be trained in the safe and proper handling, use and disposal of housekeeping chemicals. Dispensing systems can be used to dilute (weaken) and safely transfer chemicals from bulk containers to the refillable pump bottles used by housekeepers. Harsh cleaning chemicals are being replaced with milder and safer alternatives.

See *Unit 3: Safety in Hospitality* for more detail about the health and safety issues relating to chemicals and their use.

In summary

- Accommodation services can be found in a wide variety of residential and non-residential establishments, including hotels, halls of residence, hospitals, conference centres and leisure centres.
- The main purpose of accommodation services is to provide a clean, comfortable and safe environment for customers.
- The roles and responsibilities of staff vary enormously from one establishment to another, but all staff are responsible for maintaining standards.
- The manager of accommodation services must ensure the department operates economically and efficiently. An eye for detail is essential.
- It is becoming increasingly important for the department to operate in an environmentally friendly way.

Practice assessment activity

Levels P1/M1/M2

Visit two organisations that provide accommodation services. Find out what staff roles there are in the department and the responsibilities of staff in these roles.

 P Produce a report describing and comparing the roles and responsibilities of the staff in each organisation. (P1/M1)

M Design a cleaning routine for cleaning a hotel bedroom. (M2)

9.2 Understand the purpose of the front office

This section covers:

■ purpose of the front office

■ front office

■ job roles

■ responsibilities.

Purpose of the front office

In this section you will cover the job roles and responsibilities of the **front office** department. Firstly you need to recognise the purpose of front office so you can understand how important the department is to the successful running of any hotel.

Front office is sometimes referred to as reception, but you will learn when you read this unit that it is much more.

 Talking point

In small groups, list all the encounters that a guest may have with front office from the time they start to choose a hotel to stay in until the time they leave the hotel.

Did you include some of the following encounters in your list?

■ telephone the hotel to find out about prices and facilities
■ make a reservation
■ arrange special requirements such as a restaurant booking, flowers in the room or disabled facilities
■ pay a deposit or pre-pay for the room
■ check in/out
■ make a restaurant booking
■ enquire about the hotel or the local area
■ check/pay their bill.

As you can see, the front office department has a great deal of guest contact and it plays a vital role in providing the services that guests expect during a hotel stay. In fact it is often called the 'nerve centre' of the hotel.

■ *Front office staff must make a good first impression*

Front office staff are expected to present an appropriate image for the organisation and deal competently with guests and any problems they come across.

The purpose of front office is to:

■ provide guests with a good first impression of the hotel

■ encourage guests to make a booking when they make an initial enquiry about the hotel

■ communicate guests' needs to other departments of the hotel effectively

■ encourage guests to spend their money in other areas of the hotel, such as the restaurant

■ play a part in ensuring the guests are happy with their stay.

Welcome and first impressions

The welcome that guests receive will determine their first impression of the hotel. When a guest checks in, their initial and most important impression of the hotel is from the receptionist at the front desk. The greeting given to the guest needs to be cheerful, clear and sincere.

Also important is the appearance of the front office area. If the reception area is untidy and looks chaotic it creates a bad impression of the hotel. It

Key points

■ The front office is often thought of as the nerve centre of the hotel.

■ The welcome guests receive will determine their first impression of a hotel.

■ Guests must be greeted warmly and sincerely.

may also cast doubt on the efficiency of the rest of the hotel, for example the kitchen.

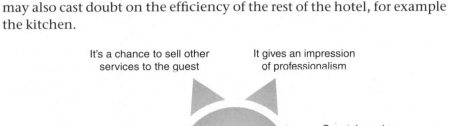

It's a chance to sell other services to the guest

It gives an impression of professionalism

There may be a mistake on the booking

Guests' needs are more likely to be met

Guests will feel more at ease with the front office staff

Guests will feel that you care

They may have special needs that they haven't mentioned

■ *The importance of greeting*

Talking point

In small groups, discuss why it is important that guests are greeted warmly and their needs identified and checked when they arrive at a hotel.

Did your group suggest any of the ideas in the diagram?

The guest cycle

The flow of business during a guest's stay at a hotel can be represented by a four-stage **guest cycle**.

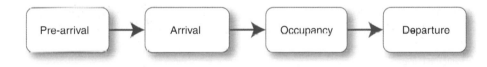

Pre-arrival → Arrival → Occupancy → Departure

1 Pre-arrival

During this stage the guest chooses which hotel to stay in. This choice can be influenced by a variety of factors, including:

■ previous experience of the hotel

■ recommendation

■ location

■ ownership

■ star rating

■ competition.

The guest's choice may also be influenced by the ease of making the booking and the attitude and selling skills of the reservation staff.

All hotels need some kind of advance booking system to record bookings. Some hotels will have a central reservations office where staff take reservations for all of the hotels in the company. In many hotels there is a separate reservations department. Increasingly customers make their reservations online. There must also be a system of communicating details of bookings to other departments of the hotel.

2 Arrival

The arrival stage of the guest cycle is known as **check-in** and includes registration and rooming. The receptionists will carry out this function at the front desk. It is their responsibility to check the guest's needs and to ensure that these are communicated to the rest of the hotel. It is an opportunity to promote and to sell other hotel services and to make sure that the guest has everything they need.

It is at this stage that the guest's account is opened, and it is now usual to ask for some kind of payment.

3 Occupancy

Throughout the occupancy stage the front office represents the hotel to the guest. A major objective of the front office is to satisfy guests' needs in a way that will encourage a repeat visit. As the front office is often seen as the communication centre of the hotel, it must be able to provide the guest with information about:

■ the rest of the hotel:

■ other parts of the business

■ the surrounding area.

Once the guest has checked in to the hotel, charges can be applied to their account, for example for drinks in the bar. This is known as **posting** and it is done throughout the customer's stay.

4 Departure

The fourth stage of the guest cycle is departure (**check-out**). How you handle customers at this stage is as important as how you handle them on their arrival. A bad experience at this time could completely spoil a pleasant stay and discourage customers from returning to your establishment.

At this stage the receptionist:

■ determines whether the guest was satisfied with their stay

■ encourages the guest to return to the hotel

■ presents the guest's account for settling.

Front office

Since hotels vary so much, the organisation of the front office will vary from one hotel to another. Many hotels earn the bulk of their income and profits from the sale of rooms, so it is essential that the reception department is organised and staffed to maximise sales.

As a rule, the larger the hotel, the more likely it is to have specialist roles. In this case front desk might be divided into:

- reception
- switchboard
- advance reservations
- night audit
- guest services.

In smaller hotels reception may carry out all of these functions.

Uniform service in a small hotel may consist of hall porters (working in the day) and night porters; but in a large five-star hotel the range of staff may also include a **concierge** (see Job roles, below).

In some hotels all of the above functions will be broken down into two areas called **front desk** and **back office**.

Over to you

Contact a range of hotels in your local area and find out how many staff work in the front office and how the department is organised to provide a service to guests 24 hours a day.

Front desk

Front desk consists of reception, guest services and porters. The work done here covers those activities undertaken at the arrival, occupancy and departure stages of the guest cycle. Responsibilities here include:

- check-in
- registration
- guest accounting
- check-out
- guest services
- some administration
- customer care
- answering the telephone.

Back office

Back office consists of reservations and some administration. The work done here covers those activities undertaken at the pre-arrival and departure stages of the guest cycle. Responsibilities here include:

- taking reservations
- dealing with booking amendments and cancellations
- communicating with other departments
- night audit.

These responsibilities will be looked at more closely later in this chapter.

Job roles

Manager

The manager of the front office may be known by various titles, including:

- revenue manager
- front office manager
- rooms division manager
- front of house manager.

In addition, the size of the management team will vary according to the size and style of hotel. The manager or management team will have the following similar responsibilities to the manager of accommodation services.

Receptionist

To ensure that 24-hour coverage is provided where it is needed staff are divided into three shifts: morning; afternoon; night reception (this service may not be provided in hotels with fewer than 50 bedrooms). Receptionists:

- check in guests
- answer queries
- take reservations over the counter
- post charges to guests' accounts
- liaise (communicate) with other departments of the hotel
- check guests out and balance their takings. They may prepare the takings for banking but this can be carried out by the accounts department.

Shift leader

Where a hotel is large enough to have a team of receptionists working at a time, the hotel will often employ a shift leader to make sure the shift runs smoothly. Their duties will include:

- supervising the daily operation of reception
- assisting the manager in their absence with regard to the everyday operation of reception to the standards required
- taking the lead in the event of an emergency
- controlling and monitoring the issue of departmental keys and **floats** (money in cash tills)
- taking responsibility for the training of new team members.

Telephonist

A large hotel will have a telephonist who operates the switchboard. They may also:

- answer enquiries
- help callers to find who they need to speak to
- take messages
- page (summon) someone in the hotel.

Reservation staff

As we have previously seen, many hotels will have a separate reservations department. They tend to work between 8 a.m. and 6 p.m. They are really salespeople for the hotel and are responsible for maximising revenue (income) for the department.

■ *Telephonists do not just answer the phones*

Concierge

The **concierge** is usually in charge of the team of hall porters, door staff and pages. The concierge supplies guests with:

- directions to local attractions or other places
- tickets to the theatre, opera or concerts and sports events
- restaurant reservations
- car hire
- airline and train tickets
- other special requests.

Hall porter

Based in reception or at the porter's desk, the hall porter will:

- carry guests' luggage
- call taxis
- take charge of left property
- answer queries
- take messages for guests
- sort the mail.

They may also assist the concierge, and help housekeeping, restaurant or banqueting staff set up rooms, or move larger items of furniture. In some hotels, the porters help park guests' cars.

Most hotels will have a night porter who may be responsible for:

- serving snacks and early breakfasts
- delivering newspapers

Activity

Using the Internet, explore job vacancies for the job roles described above. For each role note the qualities and skills that are required.

- wake-up calls to guests
- dealing with departures.

Responsibilities

Reservations

The reservations office plays a crucial role in filling the hotel's bedrooms at the best prices. When taking a reservation the staff should follow this process:

- check that there is a room available
- take the necessary guest details and allocate a room type
- give the guest a room rate and explain what is included in the rate
- explain the cancellation policy
- relate hotel and location information to the guest
- ask the guest to guarantee payment for the booking by giving a credit card number or a company letter
- make sure the booking is recorded accurately.

Check-in and registration

When guests arrive at the hotel they must check in and register. Registration is a legal requirement and guests must provide their full name and nationality to the receptionist. At the check-in stage the receptionist:

- greets guest(s)
- registers guest(s)
- takes a credit card imprint or payment
- allocates room and issues key or keycard as appropriate
- takes restaurant booking if applicable
- arranges newspapers, early morning call
- checks guest's needs have been met
- directs or has the guest(s) escorted to their room.

Keycards serve as room keys and as a form of identification for the guest. Keycards and registration forms, which the guest must complete and sign when they check in, are prepared in advance to speed up the check-in process.

Guest accounting

As we saw earlier in this section, the receptionist is responsible for posting charges onto the guest's bill. In small hotels the receptionist may post all the guest's charges, including drinks in the bar, meals in the restaurant and room service. In larger hotels each department will be responsible for posting their own charges to the guest's account and receptionists will only post the accommodation charge.

Over to you

Visit a local hotel to find out the system they use for taking reservations.

- How do they record reservations?
- How are most of their reservations made?
- How do they communicate arrival details to other departments in the hotel?

Whatever system of posting charges is used, the receptionist will need to ensure that guests have not exceeded their credit limit and that all charges have been posted. At the end of each shift the receptionist will need to count their takings to make sure they have the correct amount of money.

Check-out

As the guest leaves there are a number of tasks that have to be completed. The receptionist should ensure that:

- the bill is ready for the guest
- there is plenty of change in the till
- there is a supply of pens for the guest to use.

The check-out process should include the following steps:

- check and present the guest's account
- accept appropriate payment
- check that the guest enjoyed their stay
- collect the key from the guest
- bid the guest farewell and wish them a safe journey.

Once the guest has left the hotel the receptionist must ensure that the account has been closed.

Guest services

Some four- and five-star hotels employ staff called guest service representatives or managers. These staff have a very similar role to the concierge. Where there are no staff employed in this role, front office has a very big responsibility to make sure the guests feel welcome, relaxed and even pampered. This includes:

- ensuring guests are aware of all the services the hotel offers and they know how to book these services
- dealing with complaints and answering queries
- making sure special requests (such as flowers in the room on arrival) are carried out.

Administration

There are a number of administrative tasks that need to be carried out in the front office. These may include:

- checking reservation documentation for accuracy
- distributing reports to other departments
- preparing money for banking
- checking that guests' bills are accurate.

Over to you

Visit a local hotel and ask them how they maintain guests' accounts and ensure that all charges are posted.

Key points

- Registration is a legal requirement and guests must provide their full name and nationality.

- Hotel reservation staff are also salespeople responsible for maximising income for the department.

- Receptionists must ensure that all charges have been posted and that guests have not spent more than their credit limit.

■ *Guests should feel pampered, not just welcome*

Customer care

All front office staff play an important role in making sure that guests are happy with the service they are being offered. You will have read about how customer service can be provided to guests in *Unit 2: Customer Relations in Hospitality*. Front office staff should:

■ display good personal skills

■ have good verbal and non-verbal communication

■ make sure they always welcome guests with a smile.

Answering the telephone

Whether answering the telephone is the job of a switchboard operator or the receptionist, as you have learned in Unit 2, it must always be answered in a professional manner.

Security

Unit 3: Safety in Hospitality dealt with the security problems faced by hotels. There are many ways in which front office staff can contribute to the security of a hotel. These include:

■ issue and control of keys

■ dealing with lost and found property

■ provision of a safety deposit service so that guests can store their valuables

■ careful handling of cash

■ protection of guests' information from improper use

■ reporting suspicious incidents or suspicious people to the relevant person.

Virtually all hotels will have recognised policies to deal with the security of guests. This has become increasingly important in light of recent terrorist attacks. As front-line members of the hotel team, it is vital that front office staff are vigilant and aware of the security risks they may come across.

In summary

- Front office is the nerve centre of a hotel because it is the communication centre and main point of contact for the guests.
- The organisation of the department will depend on factors such as size, style of business and services offered.
- The front office department is made up of front desk (reception, switchboard, reservations) and uniform services (concierge, hall porter).
- Staff have responsibility for taking reservations, checking guests in and out, maintaining guests' accounts, answering the telephone and providing a high level of customer service.

Practice assessment activity

Levels P1/M3

Working in groups, visit the front office of two hotels and find the following information.

P Identify the staff employed in the front office department. (P1)

P Briefly explain the roles and responsibilities of these staff. (P1)

M Describe the activities undertaken by staff at each stage of the guest cycle. (M3)

Present your findings to the other groups.

9.3 Know how accommodation and front office departments link together

This section covers:

- meeting customer needs
- communication
- documentation
- standards
- statistics
- security.

As you have learned, both the front office and the accommodation department are concerned with rooms – front office with selling them and accommodation with preparing and servicing them. For this to be done effectively there must be a continuous exchange of information between the two departments and each must understand the work of the other.

In *Unit 2: Customer Relations in Hospitality* you learned the important role that effective communication between staff has in making sure that customer needs are met. In this section you will learn more of how the accommodation and front office departments must communicate with each other.

Meeting customer needs

The accommodation and the front office departments continuously work towards the satisfaction of the customers. Each department is dependent on the other for information and/or services if they are to meet the customers' needs.

The accommodation department relies on the front office to let them know:

- how many guests are arriving and departing each day
- when VIPs (very important people) are expected
- when special requests have been made by guests.

Front office relies on accommodation to let them know:

- when rooms have been serviced and are ready for re-letting.

Activity

List the information that must be communicated between the front office and accommodation departments in order to meet customer needs.

Did you include the following?

From front office to housekeeping:

- arrivals
- departures
- guests in house
- forecasts
- guests' special requirements

- group arrivals
- room status
- early departures
- late arrivals.

From housekeeping to front office:

- when rooms are serviced
- room discrepancies (guests in wrong rooms)

- damage to rooms
- lost property.

Room types and facilities

When a reservation is taken the customer will be asked what type of room they need. Types of room vary from hotel to hotel and may include:

- **Single** – contains a single bed and is for one customer only
- **Twin** – contains two separate beds for two customers
- **Double** – for two customers but with one bed
- **Family** – usually suitable for a family of four. This may contain bunk beds or a sofa that opens into a double bed.
- **Executive** and **superior** rooms – designed to provide a more luxurious environment than standard rooms. They are usually more spacious, with a sitting area in addition to the bed to provide extra comfort.
- **Suites** and **mini suites** – offer a more substantial form of accommodation. They normally consist of one double bedroom (possibly two), plus a sitting area with lounge-style furniture, that is a sofa and armchairs.

Some hotels have rooms adapted specifically for guests with disabilities or special needs. These are examples of the types of adaptations that may be available:

- wheel-in showers
- raised toilet seats
- manual or electric bath hoists
- manual or electric bed hoists
- alarm systems in rooms
- vibrating alarms.

The accommodation team should be told when customers with disabilities are booked so they can ensure the room is adequately prepared for them.

Over to you

From visits or brochures, discuss the types of rooms found in local hotels or bed and breakfast accommodation.

■ *Many hotels now have rooms adapted for guests with disabilities*

Over to you

Pay a visit to a local hotel to see what kind of special requests they get and the system they have in place to make sure the guest gets their request.

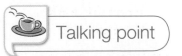

Talking point

In groups of three or four discuss how a computerised reservation system can enhance communication.

Special requests

Some 'special requests' will be dealt with by the front office, but others need to be referred to the accommodation department. A guest's special request could be for foam pillows instead of feather, flowers in the room on arrival, a ground floor room or a room with a view.

Another request may be for an extra bed in the room, usually for a child. The accommodation department will put the extra bed into the room once told by the front office that it is needed. Front office must not let more extra beds than the hotel has.

Communication

A lot of information needs to be communicated between the front office and accommodation departments. To make sure this happens there should be efficient and easy to use methods of storing and communicating information.

Reservation systems

The reservation system plays a very important part in helping to ensure that communication between front office and accommodation is accurate. It holds all the information that both departments need to ensure that the needs of customers are met.

Manual systems

Most hotels now record bookings via a computer but smaller hotels may still use a manual system, although this is becoming quite rare. A manual system uses a 'bedroom book', as shown below, and is only suitable for hotels with up to about 20 rooms. The bedroom book has a page per day and a line per room. Customers' names have to be entered each day that they are staying. Details of each booking are recorded on a reservation form.

Computerised systems

Computerised systems are a much more efficient way of dealing with reservations in hotels that have more than about 20 rooms. There are many systems available and they can speed up the booking process considerably.

- Room availability can be established at the touch of a button.
- They will act as a reservation form.
- They will recognise if the customer has stayed before as soon as you key in the name of the customer.
- They can provide an enormous amount of information used to analyse the hotel's business and plan for the future.

DATE: ....

Room Number	Room type (single/double/twin)	Name	Number of persons	Remarks	Date of departure
16	Double	Brown	2	Breakfast in room	Monday 14th January
23	Single	Peskavic	1	Vegetarian	Sunday 20th January

■ *Bedroom books may be used in small hotels for taking bookings*

Forecasting

A forecast is a general prediction (estimate) of occupancy that is produced by the front office to help other departments to plan. A forecast is produced by:

■ looking at the previous year's occupancy

■ checking the level of advance bookings

■ assessing any changes in the market, such as a new hotel or visitor attraction opening in the area.

The forecast will allow the accommodation services manager to complete staff rotas, plan cleaning schedules and make sure there is sufficient linen, cleaning materials and guest supplies.

Reports

Each department of the hotel will use a number of reports to enable them to operate efficiently. Using computerised systems, departmental staff will download and update the reports they need. Front office staff will need to prepare and distribute reports for a manual system.

Key points

■ Most hotels now use computer systems for taking bookings.

■ Some smaller hotels with fewer than 20 rooms still use a manual reservation system, writing bookings in a bedroom book.

■ Forecasts are used to estimate how many bookings will be taken.

Each report will serve a specific purpose. Here is a list of those most commonly used by the accommodation department.

- arrivals list
- guest list
- departure list
- special requests
- room status report/occupancy report.

Documentation

Arrivals list

The arrivals list shows all guests due to arrive, their length of stay and any special requirements they may have. In some hotels the rooms will have been pre-allocated and the arrivals list will show the room number of the arrivals. In other hotels rooms are allocated by the front desk when each guest arrives.

Departures list

The departures list shows all guests due to leave the hotel that day. It is usually prepared in room number order and it will contain a special note if the guest is leaving later than the usual departure time. This is to prevent housekeeping disturbing the guest.

Room status report

A room status (or occupancy) report tells the housekeeper the status of each room. It is produced on a daily basis and used by the accommodation team each morning to prepare a list for each room attendant, with details of the rooms they need to clean that day. It gives the following information about each room, whether it is:

- a stay – this means it is let and the guest will stay at least for the following night
- a departure – this means the guest is leaving that day
- vacant and ready for re-letting
- unavailable owing to redecoration or repair work.

Once the rooms have been serviced the accommodation service department must update the room status so that the front office knows which rooms are ready to let to new guests.

DATE: ....

4pm release

Guest name	Room type	Number of persons	Date of departure	Rate	Room Number	Remarks

Guaranteed

Guest name	Room type	Number of persons	Date of departure	Rate	Room Number	Remarks

■ *An example of an arrivals list*

Standards

One of the responsibilities of the accommodation manager is to ensure that standards are set and maintained. It is important to ensure that all the staff carry out their cleaning and service tasks in a consistent manner. The key to consistency is to have performance standards. These state:

■ what job must be done

■ how the job must be done.

Sample performance standards:

Hand basin

1 Clear sinks of all toiletries and other items
2 Remove hair from plugholes
3 Spray all surfaces with cleaning solution including splashbacks, taps and inner and outer surfaces of the basin
4 Use a damp cloth to clean all surfaces, ensuring that all marks are removed
5 Run tap and rinse off all surfaces with clean water
6 Dry and polish all surfaces.

When performance standards are set, employees will be trained to the standard and will perform their tasks in the most efficient and effective manner, ensuring quality.

Checks and checklists

Once performance standards have been set there must be a system for checking that they are being met. In accommodation services this is done using checklists. These will be completed by the manager, the supervisor or the floor housekeeper (see section 9.1, pages 290–291).

Use of the checklists will:

- keep the staff alert and make sure that they are not tempted to slack
- identify if training is needed
- highlight areas that have not been thoroughly cleaned
- highlight maintenance needs.

Statistics

Statistics are a very useful method of identifying how a business is doing. The presentation of information in a standardised form makes it easier for managers to see if a business is doing as well as expected. Most businesses will compare actual performance against forecasted performance, and how they are doing this year against how they did the same time last year. There is little point in setting budgets if no one is going to check that they are being met.

Statistics can be used to make decisions about how to operate the business. If the manager of a resort hotel knows that July is the busiest month they will make sure that customers are being charged the full rate. Here are the most common statistics used by front office and accommodation.

Occupancy

The most commonly used statistic in a hotel is occupancy – the number of rooms sold out of the number available. Levels of occupancy are of great interest to the hotel manager. To calculate room occupancy, express the rooms sold as a percentage of the rooms available.

For example, if the White Hart hotel has 100 rooms and sells 85 of them, the room occupancy is 85 per cent.

$$\frac{85 \text{ rooms sold}}{100 \text{ rooms available}} \times 100 = 85\%$$

It will be looked at on a daily, weekly, monthly and yearly basis and allows comparisons to be made. For example, if in July (31 days) the hotel sells a total of 2,325 rooms, the occupancy will be 75%:

$$\frac{2325}{3100} \times 100 = 75\%$$

If the previous July the hotel had sold 1,860 rooms the occupancy would have been 60 per cent:

$$\frac{1860}{3100} \times 100 = 60\%$$

The manager could then compare levels of occupancy for the two years and compare them with any forecasts.

Average room rate

The average rate shows how much a room is being sold for across the hotel.

For example, if the room revenue at the White Hart hotel is £6,500 and it has sold 85 rooms, the average room rate is £76.47.

$$\frac{\text{room revenue} = 6500}{\text{rooms sold} = 85} = £76.47$$

Figures are normally expressed excluding VAT (value added tax). Like the occupancy rate, the average room rate will be worked out on a daily, weekly, monthly and yearly basis.

Security

We have learned from *Unit 3: Safety in Hospitality* and section 9.2 that security is a major issue. Everybody likes to work in a secure environment, and maintaining effective security is the concern of everyone working within an establishment. It is essential that guests feel secure and with the rise in terrorist attacks it is becoming increasingly important that there are systems in place to make sure that guests are as safe as possible. Staff can only maintain security if they know the risks and how to deal with them. It is therefore essential that they are trained in this area.

Control of keys

There are usually three types of keys used in a hotel:

- the **master**, which opens all doors
- the sub-master, which opens a selection of doors (this might be a whole floor or a set of rooms)

- individual room keys.

It is very important that there are systems in place for issuing and collecting these keys as the loss of a key could have serious consequences.

Master and sub-master keys are often issued by the front office. To make sure that the keys can be tracked down, staff are usually asked to sign them in and out in a key book. To make sure the keys are only issued to those authorised to use them, the front office should have a list of who can take each key out with the key book.

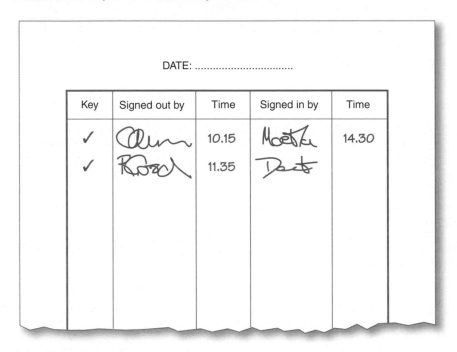

DATE: ....

Key	Signed out by	Time	Signed in by	Time
✓		10.15		14.30
✓		11.35		

- An extract from a hotel key book

Lost property

All lost property should be:

- reported to the supervisor
- recorded in a book
- held in a secure place
- returned to the owner if possible.

Data protection

You learned about the Data Protection Act 1998 in *Unit 2: Customer Relations in Hospitality*, but it is worth mentioning it again here because front office staff have a particular responsibility for the protection of customers' data. Front office staff must be made aware of their responsibilities under the Data Protection Act and the front office must be a secure area.

Over to you

List the things that the front office department does where attention to security is essential. Now discuss how front office can ensure that its department is secure.

In summary

- Efficient and accurate methods of communication are essential between the front office and accommodation services if guests' needs are to be met.
- A series of reports are generated by the front office and given to accommodation services to ensure that communication is effective. These include the arrivals and departures list, the forecast and the room status report.
- Much of the information for these reports can be extracted from the reservations system. This can be manual or computerised.
- Statistics such as room occupancy and average room rate will help the front office and accommodation departments to plan.
- There are many security risks in the front office and accommodation services and it is essential that staff are trained to deal with these risks.

Practice assessment activity

Levels P2/D1

P Visit a local hotel to find out how information is circulated between the front office and accommodation services and what it is used for. (P2)

P Use the information you have gathered to describe how the front office and accommodation services link together. (P2)

D Analyse how the flow of information between the guests, the front office and accommodation can affect the guests' experience and the success of the organisation. (D1)

9.4 Be able to demonstrate skills involved in accommodation services and the front office

This section covers:

■ accommodation skills

■ front office skills.

Accommodation skills

Accommodation services have become recognised as an area of work which, if carried out effectively, can have an enormous influence on the customers' opinions of the organisation and on overall profitability. It is therefore important that staff have the required level of skill to work within the department.

Bedmaking

One of the most strenuous jobs of the accommodation department is bedmaking – particularly if the bed has blankets and a bedspread rather than a duvet.

It may involve stripping the bed and changing the linen or just making the bed. This will depend upon the status of the room.

■ If the room is a 'departure' the bed linen will always be changed.

■ If the room is a 'stay' the room attendant may only need to remake the bed.

How often the bed linen is changed depends upon the style of hotel. In a luxury hotel it may be changed every day, but in a hostel or hall of residence it might only be changed once a week.

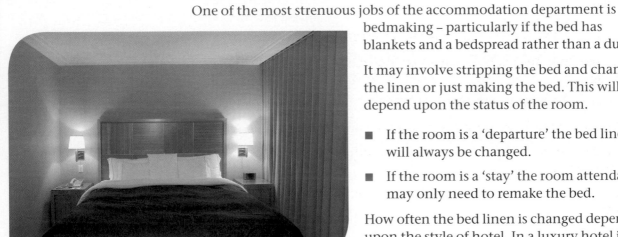
■ *Bedmaking is a skilful and tough job*

There will often be a set procedure for making the bed, including a particular way to tuck in the sheets and blankets. The bed should look as if it has never been slept in before.

Use of cleaning materials and equipment

There are many factors to consider when selecting and using cleaning materials and cleaning equipment. Some of these were covered in *Unit 3: Safety in Hospitality*. These factors are concerned with:

- health and safety
- cost
- the upkeep of the area being cleaned
- the effectiveness of the product.

Cleaning equipment may include:

- mop systems for wet and dry use
- colour-coded cloths
- duster
- bucket
- sponge/abrasive pad
- vacuum cleaner.

Cleaning materials may include:

- multi-surface cleaner
- toilet cleaner
- glass cleaner
- air freshener
- polish.

You should follow this procedure when servicing accommodation.

- Choose the correct equipment and materials for the area you are about to clean.
- Check the equipment is safe to use.
- Make sure you are wearing the appropriate uniform.
- Use the equipment and materials in line with the manufacturers' instructions.
- Store the equipment and materials safely and securely once they have been used.

Relevant legislation

As you learned in *Unit 3: Safety in Hospitality*, the safety of staff is always absolutely paramount. Although housekeeping and cleaning are not high-risk jobs, there are some risks.

It is the responsibility of the employer to ensure that all staff are trained to recognise, understand and deal with these risks. But staff then have an equal responsibility to ensure that they take note of this training and carry out their work as they have been shown – with due regard to health and safety legislation.

As you have learned in *Unit 3: Safety in Hospitality*, the legislation includes:

Activity

Make a list of the health and safety risks in the accommodation services department. Discuss what can be done to minimise these risks.

- The Health and Safety at Work Act (HASAWA) 1974
- Control of Substances Hazardous to Health Regulations 2002 (COSHH)
- Manual Handling Operations Regulations 1992
- Personal Protective Equipment (PPE) at Work Regulations 1992
- Reporting of Injuries, Diseases and Dangerous Occurrences Regulations 1995 (RIDDOR).

To ensure that you work in a safe way and comply with legislation you must:

- maintain a high level of personal hygiene and appearance
- report any hazards that you notice in the workplace
- follow the health and safety procedures of your organisation.

Cleaning and using checklists

As you learned at the beginning of this unit, room attendants and cleaners will often follow a set procedure when cleaning and servicing rooms, public areas and corridors. This is to make sure that they do everything that they should and that nothing is missed out. In most hotels there will be a set routine for cleaning bedrooms and bathrooms.

A cleaning schedule for a hotel bathroom might be:

1 Ventilate room
2 Strip bed and remove dirty linen
3 Empty ashtrays, waste paper basket
4 Clean and restock hospitality tray
5 Remove crockery and all rubbish and litter
6 Remake bed
7 Dust or damp wipe furniture
8 Spot-clean walls, especially areas around light fittings and doors
9 Vacuum carpet
10 Replace stationery and hotel literature as necessary
11 Close window
12 Check any defects and report
13 Check work.

You have already learned something about the use of checklists in cleaning schedules. If there is anything in the room that does not meet the required standard a note is made on the checklist; the problem is then corrected by the appropriate person.

Dealing with waste

You have learned something of this earlier in the unit. Basically, waste can be hazardous or non-hazardous.

The hygienic and safe disposal of waste is very important, and these procedures should be followed:

- Wear appropriate clothing, which may include gloves.
- Put the waste into the correct containers. It is becoming more and more common for businesses to recycle.
- Disinfect the waste containers.
- Wash your hands.

Dealing with contractors

Many organisations use contractors to carry out certain cleaning and servicing tasks such as:

- window cleaning
- carpet cleaning
- pest control
- deep cleaning
- servicing of equipment (such as vacuum cleaners)
- dry cleaning
- laundry.

It is important to build a good working relationship with these contractors and to communicate with them effectively so that they fully understand the needs of your customers and your organisation.

Front office skills

You will have learned from other units about the many skills needed to work in hospitality, but some of the following may be specific to front office services.

Meeting and greeting

Meeting and greeting customers is one of the most important duties that you will have to perform for your organisation, as this is where first impressions are made.

The procedure for meeting and greeting may vary from one outlet to another, but there are some simple rules that you can follow to make sure you meet the needs of the customer and the organisation.

- Greet customers promptly, with eye contact and a warm smile.
- Ask how you can help them.
- Listen carefully to what the customer is saying.
- Help the customer if you can; if not, direct them to the appropriate people, products or services clearly, making sure they have understood what you have said.

Over to you

In groups of two or three, carry out the following role plays in class.

1 *Check in a family of four with two small children, luggage and so on.*

2 *Assist a customer arriving for a conference.*

It might be useful to find out how the front office staff in a local hotel would deal with each of these situations before you attempt the role plays.

Complaints handling

Unfortunately customers will sometimes feel the need to complain. Because they view the front office staff as their point of contact, they will address their complaint to them.

When dealing with complaints you should follow the procedure explained in *Unit 2: Customer Relations in Hospitality* (page 162).

Some complaints are very easy to deal with. For example, if the guest does not have enough towels you can contact the accommodation department and ask them to provide more. In other cases the complaint may be too serious for you to deal with and you may have to contact your supervisor to help you.

Dealing with enquiries

Bearing in mind the enormous variety of enquiries that the front desk may have to deal with, it is very important that staff have a good working knowledge of their place of work and the surrounding area. Enquiries may be made:

Talking point

List all the reasons why you think a guest might make an enquiry.

- by telephone
- in writing
- in person.

In *Unit 2: Customer Relations in Hospitality* you learned how to use these methods of communication effectively, and you should refer to this information when practising these skills for your assessment for this unit.

By telephone

When answering telephone calls, front office staff are the first point of contact that the customer has with the establishment. The impression that they give is therefore very important.

In writing

Enquiries in writing are usually a request for information about the hotel and may come in the form of a letter, a fax or an email. Many hotels have adopted standard letters for answering enquiries.

In person

As you learned in Unit 2, when we communicate in person we do so verbally and non-verbally. Verbal communication comes from what we say and non-verbal communication comes from our body language.

It is very important to be aware of both of these aspects of communication when dealing with customers. In some cases the customer may just want to chat. It is important that you make time for customers who wish to communicate in this way, but you must remember to display a professional attitude at all times.

Local knowledge and information

As part of their role of dealing with enquiries, all members of a front office team are expected to have a good knowledge of the local area and also of the hotel's products and services. It is important that you are able to talk to customers to find out their exact requirements so that you can recommend suitable products and services to them.

Very often because services and products offered by the organisation and in the local area are so complex and change constantly, it may not be possible to learn all the product knowledge. In this case you will need reference material such as street maps close at hand to give correct, up-to-date information.

Selling skills

Selling is an acquired skill and a key task for front office staff. It means actively promoting the services and facilities of the hotel rather than simply responding to the customers' queries and requests. Front office should be aware of what makes the hotel special. This could be a number of things, such as:

- the restaurant has a Michelin star
- there is a spa
- the hotel is very close to a visitor attraction.

Appealing words should be used to describe products and services whenever possible. These will help explain the benefits of staying at the hotel to the guest and help them to visualise your products.

Receive payments

It is important that customers' bills are kept up to date. This is particularly challenging in hotels, which operate 24 hours a day. There must be a system of posting charges to the customers' bills throughout the day so that customers can pay their bills at a moment's notice.

The usual time for a customer to pay their bill is when they are about to leave. As this is your last chance to make an impression on the guest it is important that this process is carried out efficiently and professionally.

Customers may pay their bills using a variety of methods. These include:

- cash
- cheque

Key points

- Greet guests promptly and warmly when they arrive.
- Customers view the front desk as the first point of contact if they have an enquiry or a complaint.
- Enquiries may be made in person, in writing or by telephone.
- Use the verbal and non-verbal communication skills you have learned.
- Show a professional attitude at all times.

Over to you

Collect a brochure from a local hotel or look up their website on the Internet. In pairs, role play selling the positive features of the hotel to a customer who is planning to bring her husband for a long weekend as a surprise to celebrate their 25th wedding anniversary.

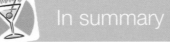
■ *Settling the bill on departure*

- debit card
- credit card
- travel agent voucher
- account to company – a business guest's bill paid by their employer.

Each organisation will have its own procedure for dealing with payments, but it is likely to go something like this:

- greet the customer in a warm and friendly manner
- present the bill to the guest for checking
- explain the charges as required
- ask the customer how they will be paying
- follow the organisation's procedure for that payment method
- check the customer is happy with the service they have received at your organisation
- thank the guest for their custom
- bid them goodbye.

Currency exchange

Many hotels offer services such as exchanging foreign currency and traveller's cheques, or allow the guest to settle their account with foreign currency.

In some hotels changing foreign currency is made easy because the front office computer will have a program which can automatically calculate exchange rates. However, in other hotels it is more complex and the receptionist will need to work out the exchange rate using a calculator.

Whatever system is used, there will be a set procedure for dealing with foreign exchange, which all relevant staff will be shown.

Activity

Research how to deal with the following methods of payment:

- debit card
- credit card
- cheque
- cash.

In summary

- There are a number of skills that are required to work in accommodation services and the front office.
- Skills needed for the front office include: meeting and greeting; handling complaints; dealing with enquiries; receiving payments; selling; local knowledge and information; currency exchange.
- Skills needed for accommodation services include: cleaning; bedmaking; using checklists; use of cleaning materials and equipment; health and safety legislation; dealing with waste; dealing with contractors.

Practice assessment activity

Levels P3/P4/D2

In groups of three, work on the following scenarios:

- Taking a reservation for a business client who would like to book a single room for two nights on a bed and breakfast rate.

- Checking in a family with two small children aged four and six who are staying at your hotel for a weekend in the school summer holidays.

- A customer who is complaining that he does not like his room because it is noisy and hot. There are no other vacant rooms in the hotel.

- A customer who would like to know about a local attraction in your area.

Take it in turns to be the customer, the employee and the observer.

P Role play the scenarios using the skills and techniques learned in this unit. (P3/P4)

D Discuss the importance of the front office on the guest experience and the success of the organisation. (D2)

Test your knowledge

1   Explain the main purpose of accommodation services.

2   List six types of establishment where accommodation services might be provided.

3   Explain three ways in which the accommodation services department can ensure it is environmentally friendly.

4   Identify the four stages of the guest cycle.

5   Describe four ways in which the front office department contributes to the success of an organisation.

6   List five potential security risks in front office.

7   While you are on duty in reception the following situations occur:
    - four guests leave earlier than planned
    - one guest moves rooms
    - two guests extend their stay
    - the secretary of a VIP client calls to say he will be arriving in one hour
    - a day let room is sold again for this evening
    - a cot is requested for a guest arriving that night.

    Explain how you would deal with each of these situations.

8   Explain the use of a checklist in accommodation services.

9   Identify two pieces of legislation that impact on the work of room attendants.

10 Describe the procedure for meeting and greeting a customer.

Glossary

À la carte Menu with each dish individually priced

Anaphylactic shock Condition caused by extreme allergic reaction

Bacterial danger zone Temperatures favoured by bacteria for growth: 4°C–70°C

Beverages Term used in hospitality for hot drinks: tea, coffee etc.

Body language Gestures, poses, movements and facial expressions used to communicate without speaking

Body mass index (BMI) Scale used to work out acceptable weights

Brigade A restaurant kitchen team

Buffet Style of service where customers help themselves to food from a table or purpose-built counter

Calorie Unit of energy in foods

Check-in/check-out Procedure on arrival/departure at a hotel

'Check on' Shout used to alert kitchen staff that an order needs preparing

Check pad Pad used to take customer orders in food outlets

Cleaning schedule Set routine used for cleaning services

Closed question Question requiring a one-word answer

Commis chef Trainee or junior chef

Commodity Raw food product before preparation or cooking

Concierge Hotel worker in charge of porters, door staff and pages

Condiments Seasonings used to bring out flavour of foods

Contract Legal document of agreement

Convenience foods Foods already prepared and/or cooked

Cook Apply heat to food to change its structure, texture and taste

Counter service Food service style where customers queue at a counter and select their food

Craft staff Staff with specialist skills or training such as chefs

Credit note Note given to cover the value of faulty goods/services that the customer will not be charged for

Crockery Tableware/plates on which food is served

Cruet Small container for salt, pepper, vinegar etc.

Customer satisfaction A measure of how products and services meet or exceed customer expectations

Cutlery Knives, forks and spoons used for eating

Delivery note Note prepared by supplier to show what is being delivered and the amounts

Desirable skills Skills an employer would like you to have, but which are not essential to a job

Dish-costing sheet Used by chefs to calculate costs of food portions or recipes

Electronic keypad Hand-held computer terminal with a code for each menu item, used to take food orders in restaurants

Employability skills Skills that an employer is looking for

Essential skills Skills that you *must* have to do a particular job

Extrinsic motivation Carrying out of an action to gain an external reward such as a pay rise (see **intrinsic** motivation)

Feedback Information/criticism/rating given in response to a service or task performed

Float Amount of money in a cash till at the start of business, used for giving change

Food poisoning Illnesses caused by eating or drinking bad food or water

Front desk/front of house Hotel department consisting of reception, guest services and porters

Front office Hotel reception

Function Hospitality event arranged for a special occasion such as a party or wedding

Gross profit (margin) Money left after production costs are taken away, expressed as a percentage of sales

Guest cycle Pre-arrival, arrival, occupancy and departure at a hotel

HACCP Hazard Analysis Critical Control Points – a type of risk assessment for food

Hazard A danger or risk

Housekeeping Accommodation services department

Ingredient Food that goes into recipes and food dishes

Intrinsic motivation Carrying out of an action because of a personal desire to achieve (see **extrinsic** motivation)

Invoice A bill for goods received

Legislation Laws, rules and regulations which must be followed

Mailshot Promotional material sent out to attract customers

Master key Key that opens all doors in a building (e.g. hotel)

Menu List showing available dishes and prices in food outlet

Non-verbal (communication) Communication without speaking – body language, signs or gestures

NVQ National Vocational Qualification

Obese Very fat or overweight

Observation Close watching or monitoring

Occupancy How many rooms are let in a hotel

Open question Question requiring more than one-word answer, used to get someone talking (see closed question)

Operative/operational staff Staff who carry out day-to-day tasks

Overheads Payments for services such as gas, water, electricity, rent, telephone etc.

Perishable Food that goes bad quickly

Portion The amount of food a customer will be given; a serving

Posting Putting charges on to a guest's account during a hotel stay

Press release Information given out by organisations to newspapers/magazines to pass on details about products

Procedure Set method for carrying out a task

Production costs How much a product or service costs a business

Profit The amount of money a business makes after costs are deducted

Purchase The term used in catering for 'buy'

Purchase order Order to supplier showing how much of each item is needed and the required delivery date

Purchasing cycle The system used in catering to place, receive and pay for orders of food and other goods from outside suppliers

Recipe Set of instructions on how to make a food dish, including: ingredients needed, weights, amounts and preparation and cooking method

Risk The chance or possibility that a **hazard** will cause harm

Risk assessment Careful check for **risks** and deciding on measures to avoid them

Room attendant Hotel staff who cleans and prepares guests' rooms

Rota Work schedule or routine

Sales The amount of money a business takes over a period of time.

Salver   Small round tray used to clear glasses or cutlery

Schedule   Routine, rota or order of doing tasks, such as cleaning

Self-service   Food service where customers help themselves from counters or buffets

Selling price   The price customers are charged for goods/services; the menu price in a restaurant

Service units   Specially designed equipment for displaying food and drink

Shelf life   How long food can be stored after buying

Silver service   High-quality serving method where food is served with a spoon and fork on to customers' plates from service dishes

Statement of account   Prepared each month by a supplier, showing items bought and sold and money owed

Table d'hôte   Complete restaurant meal available for a fixed price

Takings   Amount of money made by a business through sales

Turnover   1 Rate/number of staff leaving and joining an organisation; 2 Amount of money a business makes in a given time

Vending   Type of self-service where machines dispense products

VRQ   Vocationally Related Qualification (VRQ)

Legislation

Control of Substances Hazardous to Health Regulations 2002 (COSHH)

Data Protection Act 1998

Fire Safety Regulations, Regulatory Reform (Fire Safety) Order 2005

Food Safety Act 1990

Health and Safety (First-Aid) Regulations 1981

Health and Safety at Work Act (HASAWA) 1974

Manual Handling Operations Regulations 1992

Personal Protective Equipment (PPE) at Work Regulations 1992

Reporting of Injuries, Diseases and Dangerous Occurrences Regulations 1995 (RIDDOR)

Index

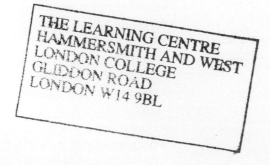